From:- Mum. Christmas 71.

THE TWO-EDGED SWORD

"The word of God is living and effective and sharper than any two-edged sword. It penetrates to the division of soul and spirit, of joints and marrow, and discerns the thoughts and intentions of the heart."

— Hebrews 4:12

THE TWO-EDGED SWORD

AN INTERPRETATION OF THE OLD TESTAMENT

JOHN L. McKENZIE, S.J.

GEOFFREY CHAPMAN
LONDON DUBLIN MELBOURNE 1967

Geoffrey Chapman Ltd,
18 High Street, Wimbledon, London S.W.19

Geoffrey Chapman (Ireland) Ltd,
5–7 Main Street, Blackrock, Co. Dublin, Ireland

Geoffrey Chapman Pty. Ltd,
459 Little Collins Street, Melbourne

Printed September 1960
Reprinted January 1963
Reprinted March 1965
Reprinted January 1967

IMPRIMI POTEST:
GULIEMUS J. SCHMIDT, S.J.
Praepositus Provincialis
Provinciae Chicagiensis, S.J.

NIHIL OBSTAT:
JOSEPH G. KEMPF, PH.D.
Censor librorum

IMPRIMATUR:
✠ PAUL C. SCHULTE, D.D.
Archbishop of Indianapolis
December 9, 1955

TO MY MOTHER

PRINTED IN GREAT BRITAIN BY
FLETCHER AND SON LTD, NORWICH

PREFACE

THE past ten to fifteen years have witnessed a remarkable resurgence of interest in the Old Testament among both Catholics and Protestants. This interest has borne fruit not only in scholarly research and in new translations, but also in a wider presentation of the Old Testament to the general public in college courses, lectures, periodicals, books, and pamphlets. People have begun to ask questions about the place of the Old Testament in Catholic belief and Catholic life to which they do not find a full and satisfactory answer in their books and lectures. There must be few teachers of the subject who have not been asked by their friends why they do not write a book which would present the religious and spiritual values of the Old Testament in terms intelligible to the general reader. This book, probably, would never have been any more than such a casual conversation piece were it not for the courage of Mr. William Bruce. When, in the course of some correspondence on another subject, he indicated that his company would be glad to receive such a manuscript, the author was afraid he could not live with his conscience if he did not accept the challenge.

The book is addressed to the general public: to anyone who thinks himself interested enough in the Old Testament to read a book about it which is not too deep or too heavy or too advanced or too big. Consequently, the book has a few features which need some explanation, if not some indulgence. My professional colleagues will read the book, as they read all such popular presentations; but they will not be surprised if they find nothing here which they could not have done themselves, and done better. My excuse for doing it is that no one else has done it. Were the book written for them, it should have the bibliography and references which are demanded in scholarly work; but the general reader is discouraged by the ponderous apparatus of learning, and I have omitted all footnotes.

As a Catholic priest and a teacher in a Catholic seminary, I write for my fellow Catholics in the first place. But I do not wish to exclude readers who are not members of the Catholic Church. There are no polemics in the work – not because I abstain from them on principle, but because they do not help to disclose those values of the Bible with which the book is concerned. But the reader, whatever his own religious belief, is entitled to know that I accept entirely the teaching of the Catholic Church, and that what I say here is as "Catholic" as I can make it, in the ordinary sense of the term. Readers, whether Catholic or not, may be surprised to learn how much freedom of opinion the Church wishes her members to enjoy. One need not surrender one's intellectual liberty to write as a Catholic, although false ideas about this are current.

It would be presumption to think that this book is "a full and satisfactory answer" to the questions about the religious and spiritual values of the Old Testament. In the course of the book we meet some of the modern attempts at a "spiritual interpretation" of the Old Testament, and we see that they are not successful. Where others have failed, one must be very modest about one's hope of success. Yet the task must be undertaken, and the duty lies first of all on those whose training and experience are in this field. One must hope that there will be some constructive work even in one's failure. What is needed is a complete synthesis of the religious and spiritual values of the Old Testament; much as I should have liked to do this, I found that the task was beyond me. This book can be no more than a beginning of a "spiritual interpretation." But it can be a beginning; the ideas which are discussed here are, in my judgment, of vital significance, and they have been little or not at all exploited in contemporary Catholic writing in English on the Old Testament.

It is no exaggeration to say that there has been, within the past fifty years, a revolution in the study of the Old Testament. This revolution is a consequence of the discovery and interpretation of the languages, history, art, and literature of the civilization of the ancient Near East, in which the Old Testament was lived and written. It has been my intention to present not the "new learning" itself, on which excellent books have been written, but the religious beliefs of the Old Testament as they have been illuminated by the new learning. With a popular audience in view, it seemed best to omit technical arguments and to pass over erudite controversies. The expert will easily see that I have ruthlessly oversimplified some complicated questions and presented my conclusions without all the evidence upon which they rest. I should have been happy to find a way to avoid this and still reach the general reader; as it is, the material is as solidly founded as my own studies and the criticisms of several scholars who read the manuscript can make it.

There is a large admixture of the personal and the subjective in the book; I think there must be. The dead level of perfect objectivity is not always a good ideal, nor always possible. If we are to look for the spiritual significance of the Old Testament, we cannot but look within ourselves. For such a treatment touches the Bible as it has personal interest and personal appeal; unless one experienced this appeal in oneself, one could scarcely communicate it to others. But the reader has a right to know that he is reading a personal interpretation. When I say that I write a "Catholic" book, I do not mean that it is wholly and entirely a statement of Catholic doctrine; I mean that the Church has, as far as I know, said nothing which is contrary to what I say, that my personal interpretation is not out of harmony with her teaching. Except where I say so, I do not pretend to voice the teaching of the Church or the commonly accepted conclusions of scholars. An individual writer cannot speak with authority; he has no competence other than that which is presumed to come from his own reading, writing, and teaching. It is hardly necessary to add that I have never doubted that the Old Testament is a book of the highest spiritual value, second only to the New Testament into which it flowers; indeed, this conviction has grown deeper over the years of my professional work. If I do not communicate this conviction to those who read this book, it is owing to my personal failure to express my mind, not to the weakness of my conviction, and still less to anything in the sacred books about which I write.

Two points of detail must be mentioned. The numbering of the Psalms, from 9 to 147, differs by one in the Douay and Knox Bibles from the numbering used in the King James and other Protestant Bibles. This difference goes back to the Greek and Latin Bibles for the first group and to the Hebrew Bible for the other group. This unnecessary confusion is beyond remedy; with the Confraternity Old Testament, we follow a common practice of giving two numbers for the Psalms, the first indicating its number in the Douay Bible, the second its number in the King James Bible, thus: Psalm 73 (74).

The second point deals with proper names, both personal and local. In many proper names the form used in the Douay, Knox, and Confraternity Bibles, which comes from the Greek Bible through the Latin, differs from the form used in the King James Bible, which is closer to the Hebrew. It is unfortunate that the editors of the Confraternity Old Testament have refused to recognize the fact that the names used in the King James Bible are in possession in the English-speaking world, even among Catholics. I employ the forms used in the King James Bible, as a growing number of Catholic writers do, both here and abroad.

There remains only the agreeable task of acknowledging assistance. I express my thanks to the following members of my own religious community: the Rev. William P. LeSaint, the Rev. William L. Moran, the Rev. Richard J. O'Brien, and some others who must remain anonymous for reading the manuscript and suggesting numerous improvements; to the Rev. P. Joseph Cahill and Brother Eugene J. Nevins for cheerfully undertaking the drudgery of typing the final copy. My thanks are due also to Mr. Aloysius Croft and Mr. Howard Smith of the Bruce Publishing Company; never was an author's path to publication made smoother and easier. I owe a special tribute to Miss Anne Ford of Brookline, Mass., for her wise counsel on preparing the book for publication. I am indebted to more friends than I can mention by name for encouragement given me in the three years which have elapsed since I wrote the first line; there were moments when, had it not been for this kindly encouragement, I might have decided the effort was not worth sustaining. I must acknowledge the assistance given by the theological students of West Baden College since 1942. They have patiently permitted me to work out my ideas about the Old Testament in my classes; and since they are very quick to detect sham and to point out obscurity, their questions and objections are more responsible than I can tell for whatever form my ideas have taken in this book. My acknowledgment to my first and greatest teacher appears in the dedication.

JOHN L. MCKENZIE, S.J.

West Baden College
July 31, 1956
The Four Hundredth Anniversary of the
Death of St. Ignatius Loyola

PUBLISHER'S NOTE

La Lecture Chrétienne de la Bible: Dom Celestin Charlier (Édition de Maredsous) is now available in English under the title *The Christian Approach to the Bible*, Sands 1958. See bibliographical note on page 313.

[illegible] work continuing, I must acknowledge the assistance given by [illegible] Coll[illegible]. They have [illegible] permitted me to work [illegible]

[illegible]

[illegible]

CONTENTS

THE TWO-EDGED SWORD

I

THE SACRED BOOKS

THE Bible is "the Book"; this is what its name means, and this is what it has been for centuries to Jews and Christians. There is something that sets it apart from other books, whatever they may be; it is sacred – sacred in its origins, sacred in its contents, sacred in the reverence which it demands from those who approach it. In the Jewish synagogue, the text of the Torah is carried reverently from its container to the lectern in a little procession; in Protestant churches, the object which first strikes the eyes is the Book, seated in front center as upon a throne; in Catholic churches, the book is carried solemnly by the subdeacon to the place where the deacon will read the Gospel, and before the deacon reads from the book he honors it by incense. The Bible is so treated because it is the traditional belief of these churches that it is the written word of God; many of the modern members of these churches may have modified this traditional belief, but they have retained the hallowed usages of older days – a liturgical profession of faith in the words of St. Paul: "The whole of Scripture is divinely inspired."

These external solemnities are impressive, as they are meant to be; more impressive is the witness of the past, the blood and the toil which have been dedicated to faith in the sacredness of the Bible. Roman Christians faced the beasts and the flames rather than deliver the sacred books to their enemies; Jewish fugitives have carried their sacred scrolls with them all over the world, clinging to their Bible even when they were stripped of all their worldly goods. That we can read the Bible at all we owe to unnumbered scribes of centuries past, who patiently copied out the sacred text in unheated and poorly lighted rooms. Over one hundred editions of the Bible appeared in the fifty years which followed the invention of printing. Those who believe that the Bible is sacred have taken the Bible with them wherever they have gone in the world; it has been written in every language that man has learned to write. No book has been so widely possessed nor so widely read, and no book has sired so many other books; enter the library of any great center of learning, and try to comprehend, in one glance, the contents of the shelves on the Bible. One is appalled; it is a very mountain of learning and of labor. Surely the insatiable human genius has applied itself to nothing else with the same pertinacity. Is not the farmer's wife who reads her Testament by the kerosene lamp driven by the same urge which keeps the famous philologist at the exacting tasks of scholarship? "You search the Scriptures," Jesus said, "because you think you will find eternal life in them."

We are concerned here with only a part of this sacred book, the larger and the older part: the Old Testament. We cannot tell when the Old Testament was first acknowledged by its readers as sacred. In the Gospels, we find Jesus and His followers, the Pharisees, the Sadducees, the common people all agreed that it is a sacred book: the court of final appeal which answers every question and ends every dispute, for no one will question the truth or the authority of the word of God. We find it two or three centuries earlier venerated as a sacred book by the Jews of Palestine and of the great Greek city of Alexandria in Egypt; but earlier than this we cannot trace surely anywhere in Jewish history the conscious possession of sacred books. About four hundred years before the Gospels, when Ezra and his scribes read the Law to the citizens of Jerusalem, who sat patiently shivering in the chill autumn rain, he read them the Law which the Lord had given through His servant Moses; the Law was the law of the Lord, but the book was the book of Moses.

We call the Bible a book; but, when we look at this sacred book, we see that it is really a collection of books: a collection so varied in content and in time and place of origin that we wonder how it was ever assembled. The Old Testament is the collection of the sacred books of the Hebrews. The ancient Hebrew people were members of the great Semitic group of peoples which inhabited most of the Near East from the Mediterranean to the mountains which divide western Asia from central Asia and India. The Hebrew people lived in the country which we now call Palestine (where a new modern state has recently taken the ancient title of Israel), a coastal strip on the eastern Mediterranean between Syria and Egypt. The Hebrews, according to their own traditions, entered this territory twelve or thirteen hundred years before Christ, and there they maintained themselves as an independent political unit until the beginning of the sixth century B.C. They continued to dwell there as a subject people of the great empires of the Persians, the Greeks, and the Romans, until the Romans, angered by their intractable and rebellious conduct, laid the land waste and scattered them through the world in the first century of our era, about forty years after the death of Jesus Christ. Not, indeed, that the Hebrews had not entered the great world earlier; for we find them moving into Egypt, Mesopotamia, and as far west as Rome by the beginning of our era. But until the legions of Titus leveled Jerusalem to the ground, Palestine was the homeland of the Hebrew people.

The sacred books come from almost every century of this long period; the oldest written parts antedate 1000 B.C., the latest books were written a century or less before the birth of Jesus. There is no book of importance whose literary origins are less well known than those of the Old Testament; it is largely anonymous. A few famous household names – Moses, David, Solomon, the prophets – bulk largely in the Bible and in popular recollection; but the larger portion of the book is of uncertain authorship and imprecise date. "It is a waste of time," said Gregory the Great, "to inquire about the author of the book of Job, since the Holy Spirit wrote it." We, unfortunately, are the children of a more sophisticated age, which will not tolerate Gregory's casual damnation of all literary criticism. When we write of the Bible, we must take some account of what can be discovered about the authorship of the sacred books and the time and place of their composition. But we do not know the writers of the Old Testament as we know Shakespeare, Dante, Virgil; and we cannot foresee that we shall ever know them much better than we do now.

The contents of this collection of books are even more diversified than its origins. We open the Old Testament, and we plunge into an unassimilated mass of stories, speeches, poems, songs, wise sayings. This material is ineptly grouped under book titles which tell us little or nothing about the contents of the separate books, and divided into chapters and verses, handy for reference, which fail to define the character of the literature so divided – if, indeed, they do not mislead us. Out of this collection there has arisen a traditional threefold division into history, prophecy, wisdom; but modern learning has found many subdivisions under these three headings. It is not necessary, however, to study modern biblical science to see that a definition of "wisdom" which includes Proverbs and the Song of Solomon must be wide, or to see that one plays with words if one calls Genesis 2–3 and the story of David and Absalom in 2 Samuel 9–20 by the same name of "history."

What we call the "historical books" of the Old Testament contain the traditions of the ancient Hebrews about themselves; some traditions are nearer to the events, some are more remote, but they are all "stories." What we mean by "story" we shall explain in Chapter IV; it is an extremely important idea. Prophecy has this common element in all its forms, that it is the word which a man speaks in the name of the Lord. "Wisdom" is the fruit of the collective experience of the wise, handed on from father to son, proposing the practical way to manage one's life and affairs so as to assure prosperity and avoid disaster; we can take this as a preliminary description, for we shall have to return to this type of literature. Within this threefold classification there is no room for hymns and prayers, such as we have in the Psalms, nor for the Song of Solomon, which stands by itself, nor really for Job and Ecclesiastes, who go far beyond the teaching of the sages, nor for Jonah, which is a moralizing romance. But we must have some easy classification of the books of the Old Testament, and the traditional threefold division, properly understood, will serve as well as any other.

These are the sacred books, accepted by Jews and Christians. Catholics, Protestants, and Jews have never reached an agreement on the exact number of books which are contained in this collection. From the very beginning of Christianity the followers of Jesus adopted the Bible of the Jews of Alexandria; the learned men of Alexandria – and it was a great center of learning – had added to the sacred books some compositions which were not found in the collection of Palestine. After the schism of Jews and Christians, Jews would never accept the Old Testament of the Christians, and many learned men of the early Church believed that the Jewish collection was the true word of God, and that such books as Judith, Tobias, Ecclesiasticus, the Wisdom of Solomon, the Maccabees should not be reckoned as sacred. An opinion which was maintained by men like Athanasius, Jerome, Hilary of Poitiers, Cyril of Jerusalem, Gregory the Great could not easily be called disrespectable. Yet the Church was not with them. When the Reformers of the sixteenth century, misled by the spurious learning of the Renaissance, wished to return to the "pure" Old Testament of the Jews, the Council of Trent, with all solemnity, declared for the tradition of the primitive Church, not for the spurious learning either of the Renaissance or of the biblical schools of the fourth century.

The divergence, however, is relatively slight, if one may make such comparisons; that is, the essential character of the collection is not altered by the presence or the absence of the disputed books. The disputed books, as a group, do not attain either the religious or the literary heights which are attained elsewhere in the Old Testament. This does not, in Catholic belief, lessen their sacredness. The Wisdom of Solomon is as much the word of God as the book of Job, although it is not nearly so profound or well written; Job has meant much more in the history of belief than the Wisdom of Solomon. The books of the Maccabees have the same claim upon faith as the books of Moses; but their religious significance is less. The Old Testament is substantially the same book in both the Jewish and the Catholic collections; more important than the divergence in its contents is the agreement that it is sacred.

Or can we really speak nowadays of an agreement that the

Old Testament is a sacred book? It is easier to say what "sacred" has meant to our fathers than to say what it means to us. From early Christianity until the nineteenth century, all who accepted the Bible had no dispute about what made it sacred. Catholics and Protestants and Jews quarreled about its meaning, but not about its authority. For all of them, the Bible was sacred because it was the word of God. It was the word of God because God wrote it. Nor had they any doubt concerning the manner in which God wrote it; He "inspired" its human authors by dictating to them the words which they should write. Many thus regarded the Bible as a stenographic report of what God said to certain men, or told them to say; they did not write, they transcribed. Consequently, to quote the Bible in any passage was to quote "the words of God," what He said to Moses or to Paul. It was truly a golden age of theology, for the primary source of theology was as readily available as the dictionary.

What has happened to this simple and consoling belief, by which any man could pick up his Bible in full confidence that God had left for him in writing the very words which He had spoken to man? Many have thought that to abandon this belief was to abandon faith in the word of God altogether, faith that God had ever spoken to man; and, unable to find any other way in which they can think of the Bible as a sacred book, they have ceased to regard it as sacred. The enthroned Bible, the incense burned before the book of the Gospels, they think idolatry. Educated men, they say, do not and cannot read the Bible on their knees. We deplore their defection; but let us see what compelling reasons there are for the abandonment of the early belief in the verbal dictation of the Bible.

In substance, the belief in verbal dictation has been abandoned because it deprives the Bible of any human character. The stenographer contributes nothing to the letter which is dictated; in the same way, the men who wrote the books of the Bible contributed nothing, if they wrote what God dictated. Was it necessary to wait until the nineteenth century to see that the human character of the Bible emerges starkly from every page, that its writers left the impress of their personality, their times, their background, their limitations as much as any man who ever put pen to paper? Perhaps not, for there were learned men of centuries long past who perceived that the Bible is a human book; unfortunately, they did not carry their ideas to maturity, and they did not divert the course of scholarship. We cannot argue with an established fact.

Neither can we argue with the human character of the Bible; the most recent statement of the Holy See, in 1943, forbids us to do so, and imposes upon exegetes the task of studying the human character of the Bible: its authors, their times, the culture in which they lived, as a necessary step to the understanding of the Bible. The Holy See points out the truth of what has been taught in biblical schools for many years: that the Bible has many and close affinities with other literatures of the ancient Near East, and that to ignore these affinities is to close one's eyes to the meaning of the Bible. The Holy Father was not afraid to say that this knowledge of the Bible was impossible for men of earlier times; under such leadership, neither should we fear to say so.

When we thus affirm the human character of the Bible, we seem to make it more difficult for ourselves to understand its sacred character. For have not many religions their sacred books? The Vedas of India, the Avesta of Persia, the Sibylline books of Rome, and other such books of the ancient world were "sacred" in a way – although we must notice that we find no other book which claims to be the word of God; the Koran of Islam is an imitation of the Bible. Modern educated men, unable to accept the fairy tale of a divine book, have consoled themselves with the thought that the Bible is a "great" book, great in its content, great in its influence. They will not deny altogether that it is, in a manner, sacred; for they believe that it is the work of men of marvelous religious insight, men who were close to God and understood Him and His ways far better than does the ordinary mortal. The religious wisdom of these men, they say, deserves our veneration, and we should, even if less childishly than our forebears, humbly submit ourselves to their guidance in the way of God. The Bible speaks of God on every page, it views the world and man under the divine perspective; he who reads it feels that he hears God speaking to him "the words which are spirit and life." Is not this a truly sacred book which God has given to men, even if our understanding of its sacredness is more mature and more scientific than the simplicity of past ages?

All this is pathetically beautiful; but it does not give us a sacred book. For such a book is not the word of God; and we must, with Jeremiah, separate the precious from the vile, the word of God from the word of man. The faith of ages is folly, not simplicity, if the two are the same. We cannot pretend that is as easy for us as it was for the past; but modern theology has struggled manfully with the problem, and it presents an explanation which affirms both the divine and the human character of the Bible. Theology takes its departure from the words of Leo XIII in 1893: that God is the Author of the Sacred Scriptures; that the Holy Spirit assumed men as the instruments of writing; that He so moved them to write and so assisted them in writing that they conceived in their minds and faithfully wrote and expressed aptly, and with infallible truth, all that He intended, and nothing else; "in no other way," said Leo, "would God be the author of the whole of Sacred Scripture."

Let us dwell for a few moments on the idea of "instrument," which Leo XIII proposed as the key to the understanding of the divine authorship of the Bible. An instrument is an extension of the human body; the pen is an elongated finger; the knife, a sharpened fingernail; the hammer, a metal fist. The peculiar structure of the instrument gives it qualities which the human member does not possess. Yet without the movement which the human member gives it, the instrument is incapable of the action for which it is employed. Does the pen write, or the man? Obviously, the man writes, and the pen writes; but the man uses the pen, not the pen the man. We cannot say that the words on the paper are from the man, the ink from the pen; for the words on the paper are nothing but ink scratches. The man cannot write without the pen, nor the pen without the man; the man has, for his writing, made the pen a part of himself, an extra finger with qualities which his own fingers lack.

This is analogy, example, comparison; and, like all comparisons, it will fail in details. The man, one thinks at once, is a living instrument, capable of personal activity in which he is not an instrument; perhaps we should liken him to the ox which draws the plow rather than to the pen or the knife. But let us adhere to the likenesses. The ox cannot plow unless its strength be applied to the work by the man, and the man cannot draw the plow by his own strength. God cannot produce a human book without using a man; for a human book is, by definition, the work of a man. Nor can man produce a divine book; for this work, God makes the man a part of Himself, if the phrase be admitted. The man has a human mind, human sentiments, human experience, human language; these are the qualities which make it possible for him to produce a book. God takes the instrument, so endowed, and applies it to work, the work of writing; and by the use of this instrument He writes the book which He Himself wants written. He who puts his thoughts in written language is an author. But God submits Himself, so to speak, to the limitations of the instrument. One cannot carve with a brush, nor paint with a chisel. God cannot express thoughts which are beyond the mental capacity of the man who is His instrument; if He wishes to express other and more sublime thoughts, He must choose an instrument which is apt. He cannot express through the author of Wisdom the profundity of the book of Job, because the author of Wisdom is a less profound thinker. He cannot, through the author of Genesis, give a scientific account of the origins of the world, because the author of Genesis knew no science. He cannot write a fascinating story through the author of the books of Chronicles, because this dull author lacked both imagination and style. Yet God writes their books, for they are His instruments. The man writes, and God writes; but God uses the man. We cannot say that the thoughts are from God, the language from the man; for God uses both the thoughts and the language of the man through whom He writes.

This is not satisfactory in all details; for the idea of a human person as an instrument is unique, unparalleled, so that we might wonder whether the term is properly applied here. The use of the very human heart, of the mind and sentiments of an individual person, to express the thoughts of God seems a severe strain upon our credulity; yet to one who admits the creative power of God it is not impossible, however difficult it may be to grasp. Is He who made the eye without vision? Is He who made the mouth without speech? The man who writes under divine inspiration is not a stenographer; he is a living instrument, whose entire personality and experience, with his own peculiar gifts of mind and heart, is applied by God to express that which God wishes to say. The book is divine and human; God externalizes His mind through human thought and expression.

But the inspired book, in one respect, escapes the taint of humanity. As the ancients questioned neither the truth nor the authority of the sacred book, so modern believers accept the word of God as free from error. When God speaks, He does not lie and He cannot be deceived. This is the ancient faith; and modern man, however sophisticated he has become, cannot say that the word of God is deceitful or deceived. But does not the divine authorship which we have just sketched leave room for this human trait? If God submits Himself to the limitations of the instrument, does He not also accept this limit of the human mind, that it cannot attain infallibility? And would not this concession make it easier for the educated man to accept the Bible as sacred?

We wish to be honest with ourselves, and so we ought to attend to some of the reasons why the educated man finds it so difficult to believe that the Bible is free from error. From the beginning of modern science, scientific learning, with the brashness of the high school sophomore, has gleefully pointed out "scientific errors" in the Bible: the creation of the world in six days, the age of 6000 years for man, the immediate creation of the human body, the flatness of the earth, and dozens of others. The rediscovery of the history of the ancient Near East within the past hundred years has given occasion to charge the Bible with a heavy load of "errors" in fact: the chronology of the Hebrew kings does not even agree with itself, still less with the fixed and sure dates of other peoples; the story of the passage of the Hebrews from Egypt into Canaan cannot be harmonized with the known course of events in this period; the men of patriarchal times lived no longer than other men – and, again, dozens of others. Some of these are points of detail, perhaps, but where infallibility is in question, a single error in detail is one too many. These blasts have had a crushing effect upon many minds; for men are unwilling and unable to challenge the dogmatic assertions of those who show proved competence in their own fields. Scientific learning is terrifying to the layman; in its presence he is superstitiously aware of intellectual depths which the layman cannot penetrate. Now that the warfare of science and theology is several generations old, we can see that confidence in the Bible as a religious document does not long survive loss of confidence in the accuracy of the Bible in other respects.

We still wish to be honest with ourselves; and we know that the divine character of the Bible cannot be vindicated by denying the findings of modern science. The believer must be willing to admit the reality of the difficulties. At the same time, he must realize that error arises from misunderstanding; perhaps the Bible does not mean what we so easily think it means. St. Augustine advises us that we should rather admit that the text is not accurately preserved, or that we have not understood it, or anything, rather than admit that the word of God errs. The task of the interpreter who accepts the Bible as sacred is not rendered easier by his affirmation of its infallible veracity. He cannot hope that he will always reach an explanation of the Bible which will satisfy at once his faith and his honesty and his intelligence.

But he is encouraged in his task by the progress that has been made in the past hundred years. Many of the old heavy-handed assaults upon the Bible are now seen to be as ridiculous as the science which launched them. He knows that readers of the Bible, both believers and unbelievers, have often confused fiction and fact, imagination and vision, figure and reality, poetry and prose. He knows that the Bible speaks of natural phenomena in popular language, as all scientists do when they are "off duty," and that its accounts of past events are the artless and untutored stories of simple men, not the painstaking reconstruction of the modern historian. Because of these principles, to which an earlier age of theology paid less attention, he is not troubled when the Bible appears to be in error; and he does not create trouble for himself by making the mistake which that age sometimes made of appealing to the Bible as an encyclopedia of wisdom human and divine, the last court of judgment for every problem which confronts the mind. Rather he does his best to understand the meaning of the Bible as accurately as he can, assured that its meaning, when ascertained, will not contradict the truth. If he fails to answer every question which arises, he is not vastly perturbed; his principles assure him that an answer can be found, and he does not feel that it is his responsibility or that of his generation to solve all biblical problems.

We approach the Bible as a sacred book with the same veneration which our ancestors gave it, although we are more aware of its human side than they were. God wrote through the ancient Hebrews; the more we know of their habits of mind and speech, the better we shall apprehend the full meaning of the word of God. It is not the purpose of this book to deal expressly with this subject; but we shall, in fact, touch it, for much of what we have to say consists in pointing out the peculiarly Hebrew ideas of the Old Testament, and their significance for us. But a few generalities by way of introduction will not be out of place; they may help us to define the human character of the Bible more closely.

Let us first recall that the Hebrews, at no stage of their history, reached a point of civilization, of material and intellectual culture, which approaches the civilization of the modern world. The wisest of the Hebrews was ignorant of many things which are familiar to any intelligent sixth grader. The Hebrews antedated the tremendous intellectual movements of the philosophy of Greece, the politics and law of Rome, the theology of the Middle Ages, the natural science of recent centuries. These great movements have formed the modern world; their words and their ideas shape the thought and the speech of modern men who have never heard of them. To say that we enter another world when we open the Old Testament is an exaggeration, but not a great exaggeration. One must, as well as one can, put aside one's mental baggage to read these ancient books with intelligence and sympathy.

"Thought patterns" suggest an extremely complex subject; yet we must say something about them. Even at the elementary level, modern education introduces the student to abstract thought, inductive and deductive reasoning. The student hears of "the scientific method," even if most students never quite grasp it; but they are exposed to it, they learn to respect it, and they can easily detect its absence when it is so evidently absent as it is in the Old Testament. Modern control and use of natural forces was not known to the Hebrews, nor did the wildest fancy dream of anything like it; nature to them was mysterious and overpowering, and in it they sensed the activity of God Himself. Modern education, in whatever form we find it, is based upon a philosophy which it communicates to some extent, however slight, to those who pass through its process. The ancient Hebrews were pre-philosophical; the most ordinary patterns of modern thought were unknown to them. Logic, as a form of mental discipline, they lacked. Their language is the speech of the simple man who sees motion and action rather than static reality, static reality as concrete rather than abstract. It prefers nouns to adjectives, for it does not even like to make the obvious distinction between a substance and its properties. It sees reality rather as it is sensible than as it is intellectually apprehended, in its large outlines and in its superficial and palpable qualities. The sentences of the Hebrew are simple statements of subject and predicate, following one another with little subordination; for the Hebrew looked upon all propositions as having much the same weight, and rarely attempted that precise statement of the interrelation of propositions which is expressed by grammatical subordination. The language is repetitive, for repetition is almost the only form of argument and emphasis which the Hebrews knew. Johannes Pedersen has said that thinking, for the Hebrews, was "to grasp a totality"; for the modern man, thinking is rather an analysis of a totality.

The Bible is not read for the qualities which it lacks. It is read for what it is: simple and direct, aware of the urgency of concrete reality. Can it teach the modern world anything? one wonders. For we need not dwell on the fact that the Bible, and the Old Testament in particular, has not the place in modern Christianity which it had in the faith of earlier generations. The Salems, Sharons,

Bethels, Bethlehems, Gileads, Lebanons, Goshens, and the like which dot our maps, the Hezekiahs, Ezekiels, Jeremiahs, Isaiahs, Josiahs, Rachels, Rebeccas, Leahs which we read on the headstones of our country churchyards are witnesses to the familiarity of these earlier generations with the Old Testament. The hardy breed of conquering farmers who settled North America and left these names upon its face took the Bible with them wherever they went; and they would scarcely have thought of omitting their chapter a day any more than they would have omitted the evening meal. We know that the importance of the Bible in the religion of these people is derived from the Non-Conformist Protestantism of England and Scotland, and from the translation of the Bible known as the King James or Authorized Version, which is justly esteemed as a classic of our language. What has happened that the descendants of these earlier Americans, who live in towns with biblical names and bear biblical names themselves, have come to regard these names as exotic, like Powhatan and Mauch Chunk? How has the sacred book of their grandparents become something like Grimm's fairy tales?

If we study the place of the Bible in the English-speaking Catholic world, we have no such questions to answer. The single outstanding fact about the place of the Bible in the life of English-speaking Catholics is this, that no translation of the Old Testament produced in English by Catholics, except for one edition in 1635, was printed between the Douay Old Testament of 1610 and Bishop Challoner's revision of the Douay Old Testament in 1750. Plainly, Catholics were not buying the Old Testament, and hence it is probable that they were not reading it. Since 1750 the number of editions of Challoner's revision both in the United Kingdom and North America is large; but we do not find that its influence is visibly effective. The modern English-speaking Catholic is about as familiar with the Old Testament as the modern English-speaking Protestant, with this exception, that the Catholic is no less familiar with the Old Testament than were his ancestors. Some fairly obvious reasons can be adduced for this state of affairs.

The first and the most obvious reason is that the Douay Old Testament as revised by Challoner is neither a readable nor an attractive book. Even when the revision was first produced, it had little merit as a work of literary craftsmanship; add to this the generally cheap and horrible printing of the Bible, and you have a book that discourages even a high degree of good will. The fact that the Old Testament is the word of God is not enough to counter the repellent features of its English garb; for Catholics, trained in the fundamental principle of Catholicism that the Church herself is the teacher of the word of God, know that one need not read the Bible as a necessary means of faith and salvation. Another reason is that Protestantism, resting upon its own fundamental principle that the Bible is the sole source of the divine word, has, in a way, appropriated the Bible to itself; and Catholics, when they are not well instructed, may look at the Old Testament suspiciously as a kind of Protestant book. We smile at such things, but they have happened, and they still happen. Because Catholics have felt no need to read the book, and because the book repelled them even if they tried to read it, Catholics have left the Old Testament alone.

It is some small comfort to recall that the problem of the place of the Old Testament in Catholic belief and Catholic life is not new. Fifteen or sixteen hundred years ago Christians were asking whether they should read the Old Testament and for what purpose. The learned men of the Church in those days answered these questions in their own way and to their own satisfaction. But they saw the problem as it existed in their own times, and they attacked it with the resources which they had at hand; they did not work out a statement of the place of the Old Testament in the Church which can be applied without modification to all times and all places. For the problem recurs in subsequent ages; it takes new forms with changes in civilization and culture, and needs to be restated and solved in terms which are meaningful to the civilization and culture in which it takes its form. We shall have occasion to refer to some of these early works on the Bible; they will help us to understand the problem as it faces us. One may retort that the problem so posed is rather in us than in the Old Testament, and that we seek an understanding of ourselves rather than of the Old Testament. Perhaps this is true;

perhaps, if we understood ourselves, the Old Testament would be no problem. But the problem remains real.

We have spoken of the quality of translation; we now have solid hopes of better translations. The Old Testament of Monsignor Knox has been given us as a work of "timeless" English, a monument to be set up opposite the Authorized Version. We have no reason to enter here into a detailed criticism of this translation; professional scholars have done this in the proper time and place. Nor do we wish to appear ungrateful to Monsignor Knox, who has done more for the English Catholic Bible than any man since Bishop Challoner. If he has opened to many a book which had been closed, he deserves all honor. But we are obliged to state our opinion that the translation of Monsignor Knox does not fully realize the possibilities of translation into modern English. The Old Testament of the Archconfraternity of Christian Doctrine may realize these possibilities; what has appeared of this work gives ground for hope that it will do so. But the final verdict of the success and the value of any vernacular version of the Bible rests with the public.

The problem of the Old Testament is not entirely a problem of translation. Since the Douay Version appeared in 1610, the problem has been posed brutally but imprecisely in the stubborn refusal of Catholics to read the Old Testament, and it has not been solved by telling them that they have a duty to read it. More recently many have arisen — more numerous in continental countries than in North America or the British Isles — who have proposed the problem with laudable frankness and clarity, even if they have sometimes spoken with a heat which is less laudable. Surprising as it is, these men have been moved to speak by the tremendous progress in Old Testament study in the past hundred years. Since 1850, the literary and monumental remains of the ancient Semitic world have been recovered and interpreted with astonishing success. This was the world in which Old Testament history was lived and written; the monuments of this world have created entirely new possibilities for a "historical" interpretation of the Old Testament. During the same period, much work has been done on the literary origins of the Old Testament books: who wrote them, when and where they were written, how they were composed. The first duty of the interpreter of the Old Testament is to find the "literal sense," as it is called: just what the writer meant. Modern knowledge has made this easier by presenting a background for the words which the writer uses.

Now, it is this modern work on the Old Testament which many of our contemporaries assert is spiritually barren. They approach the Old Testament as the word of God, and they seek in it an increase of faith, hope, and charity. They find no such thing in the analysis of the sources of which the five books of Moses are composed, in comparisons between the laws of Moses and the laws of Hammurabi of Babylon, or between the Babylonian flood story and the story of Noah. They are not spiritually elevated by a more precise chronology of the Hebrew monarchy, or by comparison of Canaanite and Hebrew artifacts found in the ruins of ancient Palestinian cities. Many Catholic writers have been concerned with defending biblical inerrancy, the validity of Old Testament history or of Old Testament predictions of the Redeemer. Necessary as these arguments may be, not a few critics allege that they are of no meaning or value to the Catholic faithful, who are not interested in these disputes, and whose supernatural life will not grow by acquaintance with the discussions of the biblical schools.

Again some small comfort is at hand, if misery loves company. Many Protestant writers in recent years have given voice to their disappointment with merely scientific learning about the Bible. Protestants for whom the Bible is still the rule of faith are deeply disturbed at the failure of modern biblical science, as they say, to contribute anything to religion. They ask for a return to a frankly theological treatment of the Bible; they believe that the Bible is a living message, and they fear that the message is no longer relevant, as it is now presented. They do not desire that the study of the Bible become unscientific; but they wish biblical learning to speak with conviction to men about their life and their affairs, or, at least, to let the Bible speak to men.

It would be surprising – indeed, shocking – if the Old Testament meant less to us the more we know about it; but this is what the recent complaints amount to. However, we cannot annihilate a complaint by saying that it should not be made. Learning is not of itself directed to spiritual progress. We have to ask whether Catholic work on the Bible has been directed to spiritual progress. We are inclined to agree with the complaint that it has not. But shall we, therefore, agree with those who say that we ought to turn back the clock, abandon any effort to synthesize our learning with our spiritual life, and return to the methods of biblical interpretation which were employed before the modern knowledge of the Old Testament world was revealed? For this is what some of our contemporaries have proposed. The age of the Fathers of the Church, they tell us, poor as it may have been in biblical learning compared with modern times, was far richer in spiritual insight into the Old Testament. They think that we would do better to abandon our effort to learn what the Old Testament means — or, at least, leave this work to scholars — and ask ourselves what it means to us. This we shall answer, they say, as the Fathers did: by seeking resemblances between the Old Testament and the New, by looking at the Old Testament as the New Testament in type, figure, mystery. It makes little difference, it seems, whether the resemblances, types, figures, mysteries tell us the true meaning of the Old Testament; they are to be tested only by their spiritual relevance.

Not many, we think, will follow this lead. It is rarely progressive to turn back the clock. And it is hard to explain how indifference to the true meaning of the Old Testament is not a rejection of the Old Testament itself. The spiritual fruits which will be gathered in this way do not grow from the Old Testament; they sprout from the spiritual ingenuity of its commentators, who make the Old Testament an occasion, a springboard from which they soar into flights of spiritual speculation. Such flights can be admirable; but why should they start from the Old Testament rather than from any other point? Nor is the spiritual value of such speculations always apparent. We do not wish to seem contemptuous of this method of handling the Old Testament, which has been so long honored in the Church; but we cannot see that it is the key which will unlock the spiritual riches of the Old Testament.

Those who propose this approach to the Old Testament as the approach of the Fathers forget, it seems, that the Fathers who used it, such as Origen, thought of it as an exposition of the true and highest meaning of the Bible. They did this because they had an idea of the meaning of the Bible which we can no longer share with them. Were they to study the Old Testament from our point of vantage, they would still try to find the true and highest meaning of the Bible, its meaning for Christian belief and for Christian life; but they would do it by new means. They would bring their learning to bear upon the subject and try to illuminate the sacred books with all the light they could borrow from human science.

But neither do these considerations remove the complaint that much modern work on the Bible is spiritually barren and insignificant. I have said elsewhere that this seems to be a failure of those who practice biblical science rather than of biblical science. The object of science is the discovery and the understanding of truth; we do not see how truth can be an obstacle to the spiritual understanding of the Bible, how it can make the Old Testament spiritually less significant. We believe that Catholic interpreters have often been more concerned with defending the Old Testament than with explaining it, more concerned with justifying it to unbelievers than to believers. They have made the Old Testament a battleground, a proving ground, but not the ground from which one ascends to God. Are they, perhaps, not sure that it is at the base of the spiritual ascent? In consequence, we are now urged to consider that there is no spiritual value in the Old Testament except where it exhibits – or shall we say conceals – identity with the New Testament.

We must, of course, admit that the Old Testament has no other spiritual value for Christians than its identity with the New Testament. But what kind of identity do we mean? We do not believe that it is necessary to flee to types and figures, to some higher or fuller sense, to reduce the Old Testament to a shadow of the New, in order to find spiritual meaning in the Old Testament. The Old Testament is a collection of religious writings; this is its primary interest, and this is the only interest it has ever had for the world at large. The religion of the Old Testament is the relationship between the Hebrew people and their God, as they experienced it and as they described it. If this relationship has no spiritual significance for our faith, then the book means nothing to us, however diligently we look for something as a substitute. Modern studies have made this religion more intelligible, under certain aspects, than it was in earlier ages; until we have looked at it again, under the light of recent studies, we cannot be sure that it has no significance for us. We shall, indeed, see it as identical with the New Testament; but it will be an identity of spirit, of ideals, of development, of hopes, of values, of one God and one humanity.

We believe the Bible can teach the modern world something, if the modern world knows that it is hopelessly entangled in its own complexity. The Bible will say little, and it will say it simply; for it cannot add to the complexity of modern thought and modern life, and we will not read it for this purpose. What it has is a firm grip on reality which enables it quickly and surely to discern the true from the false, the genuine from the sham, good from evil. It knows nothing of fine intellectual speculations and elegant language which vest the nakedness of evil with some spurious good. It is concerned with things, not words. The human character of the Bible, its Hebrew realism, merges, in a way, with its divine character; for that reality which the Hebrews saw most concretely and immediately was the supreme reality: God. Even modern Christians, unless they be endowed with unusually great faith or unusually great simplicity, are affected by the wall which philosophy and science have, whether they wished it or not, erected between men and God. The wall is not impassable; God is a neighbor, but the wall keeps Him in His place, and preserves us in ours. God can be reached, but one must climb the wall or pierce it; for it does not lead to Him, and, if one looks only at the wall, one will not see Him. We think of the men in Plato's cave, who did not believe in the world of light, and could not bear it when they were exposed to it. We would find the world of the ancient Hebrews ignorant of much that we take for granted, crude almost to the point of barbarism, narrow and provincial, uncomfortable for both mind and body; but it was a world in which men felt they could reach out and touch God. If we could gain some of this sense of the divine reality, we should have heard whatever spiritual message the Old Testament has for us. The Bible is a sacred book; it comes from God, and it brings God to us.

GOD SPEAKS TO MAN

THE religion of the ancient Hebrews was based upon the belief that God can and does speak to man. Were we to count the number of times when God is said to speak to man in the Old Testament, we should find that they are scarcely less than the number of pages in the book. We can, it is true, draw a line after which the Old Testament books contain very few such allusions; it is the Great Divide of Hebrew history, the period of the Exile, roughly 587–536 B.C. When Ezra returned to Jerusalem from Babylon, he brought with him "the book of the law of the Lord"; but it is not said of him, as it was said of the prophets, "The word of the Lord came to Ezra." His near contemporaries, Haggai and Zechariah, received the word of the Lord; but there is a difference between them and the men of a century or two before. Judas the Maccabee and his companions, faced with the problem of what to do with the stones of the altar which had been polluted, put them away in a suitable place until a prophet should come and tell them what to do; the author, as well as Judas and his men, four hundred years after the Exile, seems sadly aware that the age of prophecy is past.

Can we trace anything like this belief in the religions of the ancient Semitic world? Revelation they knew, and chosen individuals, the vessels of divine revelation, they knew. Two thousand years before Christ, Gudea, the ruler of Lagash in Mesopotamia, learned in a dream the plan of the temple which he should construct. The diviners of Mesopotamia ascertained through the occult arts the intentions of the gods, and thus advised men how to meet the future. A seer of Ashurbanipal of Assyria had a dream in which the goddess Ishtar of Arbela gave him a message for the king. In the eleventh century B.C., an Egyptian ambassador to Byblos in Syria tells how a god seized a young man of the court of the king of Byblos, so that he spoke as one inspired; many scholars think they see a kinship between the young enthusiast and the Hebrew prophets. Monsignor Ronald Knox has recently studied religious enthusiasm and found it to be of wide, almost universal diffusion. The Hebrew belief that God speaks to man appears to be, at first glance, a manifestation of a universally human religious instinct.

Historians of religion, of course, have no difficulty explaining the phenomena of divine communication in ancient religions: it was a fraud or a superstition or an accepted convention. Men have always believed that the will of the gods was not altogether veiled from their sight; in one way or another they have sought it, and they have often believed they have found it: in the babblings of a fanatic, in the movements of the stars, in the liver of a sheep. One thinks that the logic of events would render this superstition entirely incredible, and it does; but the superstition persists. For even in the most debased forms of religion, the will of the gods is the factor of supreme importance in life; if it cannot be ascertained, then unbelief is the only attitude possible to a thinking man. If the will of the gods cannot be ascertained, it is entirely insignificant; if the gods were concerned with what men did, they would make their will known. Many of our contemporaries, aware of this, and aware also that the study of religion shows the human origin of many alleged divine communications, have renounced any belief that the will of God effectively touches human life. If this be true, then the Hebrew religion is based upon a falsehood; and it is a mere accident that the beliefs of the Hebrews have any more value for modern man than the beliefs of the headhunters of the Solomon Islands.

It is not our purpose to demonstrate that the Hebrew belief is sound, but merely to set it forth. It is important, however, to realize that the Hebrew belief that God speaks to man is fundamental. One cannot accept some of the Hebrew beliefs as valid for modern man and abandon the basis upon which they are proposed; for this leaves them precisely baseless, unfounded. One would then accept them because one likes them, or because they are in accord with what one believes already on quite other grounds. One finds the words of the Hebrew Bible appropriate to express one's own thoughts, or the thoughts of one's philosophy or theology, but not the thoughts of the Hebrew Bible. The words of the Bible are often torn from their context to ornament a system of thought or of belief which is a human invention.

If we examine the Hebrew belief in divine communication, we cannot fail to notice some obvious features which do not appear in other religions. The first is the large place which this belief occupies in Hebrew religion. Hebrew history, from the patriarchs to the fall of the kingdom of Judah, exhibits a series of men who claimed attention for no other reason than this, that they spoke in the name of the Lord. They recommended themselves not for their learning, their experience, their wisdom, their power, but for this only, that the word of the Lord had come to them. We find no such history in other religions, especially in those which were nearest to the Hebrews in time and place; this series of men arose in imitation of no one.

A second feature is the content of what these men spoke. If one goes through the divine communications of other religions, one sees that men's curiosity is less about the will of the gods than about the future. Not what the gods want them to do, but what is going to happen is the question which they addressed to their diviners. The Hebrews who spoke in the name of the Lord have no answer to such questions. The law and custom of the Hebrews prohibited the practice of the occult arts, the accepted and ordinary means of ascertaining the divine will throughout the ancient Near East. What these men had to say about the divine will was totally different. They proposed the will of the Lord as determining every activity and every department of human life, regulating it according to a moral standard which rose above anything which the world had yet seen. They spoke of the future, as we shall see; but they spoke of it to threaten evil if the standards of conduct which they set forth were not maintained. The priests and the diviners of the ancient Semitic world generally knew and kept their place, and did not attempt to direct the political and economic life of their people. It did sometimes happen that priestly circles, because of their wealth or superior knowledge, or because the power of superstition is very great, succeeded in acquiring control of secular affairs. But, when it happened, the priests succeeded to a secular power, which they employed for secular ends. Look again at the men of the word among the Hebrews. They remained outside secular ends and means. Power and influence they wished and they possessed, but it was not secular power. If they collided with secular power, it was a collision of two orders, not of two competitors in the same order. They proposed religion, the will of the Lord, as the supreme regulative power of all human activity. There were no others in the world of their time who did so.

A third feature which exhibits itself is the manner in which these men spoke. If we grant that Ezekiel had his trances, and that Elisha called for a minstrel before he spoke the word of the Lord, we can still see, without any need for discussion, that the Hebrew prophets spoke the word of the Lord with none of the external trappings of the seer and diviner of the ancient world. There is no abracadabra, no ranting and raving, no witches' brew from which they educe their mystic knowledge. They speak with passion, but not in a frenzy; they are in full possession of their minds. There is no sign of any adaptation of their message to the desires of their listeners; rather there is a studied effort to run counter to existing practices and prejudices, to overturn accepted conventions. They claim to be the spokesmen of the true and highest traditions of their people; but they are revolutionaries, come, like Jesus, "to cast fire on the earth," and "to bring not peace, but a sword." What seer or diviner of Egypt or Mesopotamia was hated for his message? Do we hear that any of them took and maintained a position in pertinacious hostility to king, nobles, wealthy, commoners at the hazard of his goods and his life? A classification which will include the Hebrew spokesmen of the Lord with the pliant priests and diviners of the ancient world must be broad indeed. Surely, we think, there can be no single explanation of two types of men so different. Surely there must have been factors operating in the Hebrew religious world which were not present in the ancient Semitic world at large.

Shall we find these factors in the "peculiar religious genius" of the Hebrews? We must not underestimate the creative powers of the human genius. The sophists of the Athenian market place did not produce Socrates. What makes the history of the human race differ from the history of the anthropoid ape is the rare but recurring emergence of men who can break out of the framework of their times and initiate a new departure: anonymous heroes like the men who invented the wheel and the alphabet, men better known like Socrates and Isaac Newton. The homely proverb has it that he was a bold man who first ate an oyster. More likely he was a hungry man, but necessity mothers boldness as well as invention; shall we suppose that he too was a bold man, driven by the necessity of some guidance for human conduct, who first arose and announced: "Thus saith the Lord"? Let us admit that the Hebrews had a peculiar religious genius to this extent, at least, that no other people has produced so many men who spoke as these did, and whose words have echoed so far: "their voice goes through all the world, and their words to the end of the earth." The Greeks also had a peculiar genius for philosophy, and abstract thought is their gift to the world. We Americans are accused of a peculiar genius for the machine; certainly no other people has given the world so many gadgets. No, the "peculiar religious genius" of the Hebrews is an attested fact. The question is: to what shall we attribute this genius?

Perhaps the question is idle, as meaningless as if we were to ask to what we should attribute the philosophical genius of the Greeks, or the military genius of the Romans. It is the essence of genius that we cannot account for it. But we must notice that the "peculiar religious genius" of the Hebrews can be found in a few men only. These men habitually accuse their countrymen of a peculiar obtuseness in matters religious; they are "dazed, blind, drunk, reeling, wrapped in deep slumber, with eyes closed and heads muffled," a people that does not hearken to the word of the Lord. It is incomprehensible how one can attribute the words of the prophets to a collective religious consciousness and think of them as the flowering of a folk creation. The prophets, it is true, had never heard of such a collective consciousness; the point is that their words are a denial of any such collective creative genius, and this apart from the fact that the prophets themselves attributed their words to the Lord. We grant that the world has long been afflicted with men who claimed to be divine emissaries; but even the most broad-minded student of the history of religion does not wish to put the Hebrew prophets in the same class with Buddha and Mohammed. Again, the differences are far greater than the similarity. Should it not be within the compass of a peculiar religious genius to distinguish between the divine and the human? But we must not oversimplify. After all, we ought to consider the suggestion that the claim of the Hebrew prophets to speak in the name of the Lord is no more than a manner of speaking, proper to their culture. They were ignorant of psychological analysis, and perhaps what they call "the word of the Lord" can be explained, by careful analysis, as immanent: the product of their own minds, of the mysterious processes of genius, whose nature eludes even its possessors and is, consequently, attributed to some superhuman agent.

To satisfy ourselves about what the Hebrews meant, we shall have to look more closely at the great body of Hebrew letters, in which God speaks so often. We may, for the moment, omit the conversational level on which God deals with man in the first few chapters of Genesis; the Hebrews, like all other peoples, thought that things were quite different in the beginning from what they are now. The significance of this Hebrew belief is important, and it will be considered in its proper place; but it is not relevant to the question which faces us now. Let us rather remove ourselves to the time of the patriarchs: Abraham, Isaac, Jacob. These are historical figures, at least in the sense that they lived in historical times; we know the geography of the places in which they dwelt; we know a great deal about the kings and peoples of their times, and the spade of the archeologist has uncovered the remains of city walls and houses upon which their eyes could have fallen. It was the tradition of the Hebrews that no man knew the Lord when He said to Abram, "Leave your land, your relatives and your clan, and go to the land which I will show you." It was the same tradition that the Lord blessed the patriarchs and promised to bless more abundantly the great people which should spring from their loins. To them God speaks or appears, in what form we cannot say, or is seen and heard in a dream, and, in one startling episode, stops and dines with Abraham as a guest. In such episodes as Abraham's hospitality or Jacob's wrestling or Moses at the burning bush, the story unfolds itself with such convincing realism that we forget who is involved, and we are suddenly shocked to recall that it is the Lord God who is an actor in the story. The gods of Homer also mingled with men; but the gods of Homer were frankly human, charming rascals. What, we wonder, was the form and the voice and the manner which was in the minds of the men who told such things of the Lord? For the moment, at least, we cannot determine this; but it is clear that the Hebrew tradition represented the patriarchs as enjoying an easy familiarity with the Deity such as few men have ever been believed to enjoy. And this easy familiarity was at the basis of the Hebrew belief, for the Lord made Himself known to His people through the patriarchs; they felt themselves the heirs of the promises which He made to Abraham, Isaac, and Jacob.

This easy familiarity was continued with Moses, the true founder of the Hebrew nation. Of him more often than of any other is it said that God spoke to him. The traditions of this familiarity are not entirely of one piece; for, while "the Lord used to speak to Moses face to face, as one man speaks to another," "mouth to mouth, plainly and not in riddles," it is also said that Moses was permitted to see only the back of the Lord, and not His face. Of Moses are related the striking visions of the burning bush and of Sinai; not only did the Lord give Moses the two tablets inscribed with the law, but a whole collection of law which no two tablets could contain is ascribed to the Lord Himself, to be enunciated through Moses. Throughout the journey from Egypt to the land of Canaan, the Lord appeared to Moses in every crisis; and when the Lord threatened to destroy this rebellious people, Moses argued and pleaded on their behalf until the Lord relented and showed mercy. Again, we wonder what form and figure lies behind these stories, or what could be meant by the "face" and the "back" of Him whom no man can see; but these questions do not alter the fact that Moses is certainly represented as the spokesman of God, and that his impact upon the history of Israel, and through Israel upon the world, is that of a man who brought God to his fellow men. To understand Moses as anything else is to rewrite the early history of Israel; and this has often been attempted.

We may pass over quickly the turbulent century or two known as the period of the Judges, when every man did what was right in his own eyes; we pass it over with some regret, for we omit the picturesque stories of Gideon and of the parents of Samson. We pass over Joshua even more easily, for tradition described him as a lesser Moses. But with the beginning of the Hebrew monarchy under Saul and David we enter the period of the prophets; and prophecy is a unique Hebrew phenomenon which demands some consideration in detail. We lump together under the one word "prophecy" a great many diverse personalities and incidents which might perhaps be better distinguished; but we are thinking here of the one thing which was proper to prophecy: the word of the Lord. "The word of the Lord" is the consecrated phrase which describes the experience of every man who is called a prophet. The name is given to men as different as Samuel, who would recover lost articles for a small fee, and Isaiah, whose stately dignity did not prevent him, at the word of the Lord, from walking naked and barefoot through the streets of Jerusalem, and Elijah, who dwelt solitary in the wilderness and wore a rough garment of animal skin, and Elisha, who cursed small boys. They are a strange and not entirely attractive group of men, these prophets, and they are not all cast in heroic mold. It is worth notice, and we shall have to recall it again, that the word of the Lord did not ennoble him to whom it came; the Lord can slay a thousand with the jawbone of an ass. It was not by the flash of intelligence or of character that the prophets affected history, but by that two-edged sword, the word of the Lord.

The bare words, "the word of the Lord came to X," do not tell us much about the experience itself. To discover what the words mean, we shall have to find some more circumstantial accounts of what befell the prophets. The material for this, while not abundant, is ample enough to take us a good part of the way. We have the story of the call of Samuel; the Lord called him while he slept, and the boy thought it was the voice of the old priest Eli in the adjoining room. We have the magnificent experience of Elijah on Mount Horeb; the prophet heard a mighty wind, felt an earthquake, saw the flash of lightning, but the Lord was present in the barely perceptible movement of a gentle breeze. We have the story of Micah ben Imla, who saw the Lord with all His heavenly retinue. We have Ezekiel's vision of the marvelous chariot upon which the Lord sat enthroned. But we shall find out most about the mind of a prophet if we consider the experiences of two men, Isaiah and Jeremiah.

Of Isaiah is related what is called his inaugural vision: the experience by which he knew himself commissioned as a prophet, in which he first received the word of the Lord. He was in the temple, and he saw the glory of the Lord: the swish of the skirts of the robe of a gigantic enthroned figure, the sound of heavenly beings chanting, "Holy! Holy! Holy!" and he felt himself doomed, for he, an unclean mortal, knew he was in the presence of Divinity. Yet when a voice asked of no one in particular, "Whom shall we send?" he could not help answering, "Here I am; send me." And there follows a commission to speak the word of the Lord which is itself a brief summary of what the prophet subsequently said. With his lips cleansed by a burning coal in the hands of a seraph, he is fit to speak the word of the Lord.

Now, there are those who would see in this a story entirely imaginary. The invisible Lord is not a robed figure of gigantic proportions. It is a strange seraph which would need tongs to pick up a red-hot coal, and a strange coal which would cleanse the prophet's lips without searing them off. Isaiah was not unskilled in creative imagination; the hot coal symbolizes very well the contrast between the impure lips of man and the pure word of God. And we have no reason to deny that Isaiah clothed his inaugural experience in imaginative vesture. But we should not make the mistake of thinking that he himself created the idea that the Lord had called him to be a prophet. Critics often forget that, if God is going to communicate with man directly, there is almost certainly going to be some psychic disturbance; for the experience can scarcely be called normal. If a severe blow can make one see stars, we hesitate to say what a man would see if God spoke to him. All who have had the experience attest that there was a psychic disturbance. For Isaiah, the psychic disturbance resulted in a lasting sense of the profound gulf between the holiness of God and the unholiness of man, a gulf which only the Lord can bridge. Behind his words one can always discern the sublime and dimly seen figure of the vision, the thrice Holy One; here is the conviction that gives force to his words. He spoke of this as no one else had spoken; and he tells us, very simply, that he so spoke of it because once in his life he had seen the Lord and known, as he could not otherwise have known, what the holiness of God means. If this be delusion, let us have more of it.

Jeremiah, too, had an inaugural vision, but he saw not even the skirts of the robe. He heard the Lord tell him he was predestined to be a prophet; far from volunteering, he pleaded youth and slowness of speech. The answer was: "Go wherever I send you." Then the Lord gave him speech; the Lord touched his mouth, and put His own word in the mouth of Jeremiah. This vision, too, leaves its impress on the career of Jeremiah; for he is not only a man with a message, he is a man under compulsion. Again and again he expresses his own loathing for the hateful message he has for his people, that they are perishing by their own wickedness. Again and again he complains of the hatred and persecution which the word of the Lord brings him, opposition he would gladly end by keeping silence. But he cannot keep silence; for "the word of the Lord is in my heart like a burning fire; I am worn out with holding it, I cannot endure it." And, when his courage nearly fails, he senses of a sudden that the Lord is with him, keeping him, as the Lord promised him in the inaugural vision, "a fortified city, a column of iron, a wall of bronze."

More than this Jeremiah tells us; for he is almost the only one of the prophets to speak of what we now call "false prophets." They too claimed the word of the Lord; and we cannot tell now whether they were the sincere victims of their own delusion or dishonest pretenders. But they called themselves and were thought to be prophets. Jeremiah knew that they felt no compulsion such as that under which he suffered. They ran when they were not sent, they prophesied when the Lord had not spoken to them; they had not stood in the circle of the friends of the Lord and heard His words. They prophesied the delusions of their own mind, lies in the name of the Lord. If the prophet has a dream, let him tell his dream; if he has the word of the Lord, let him speak the word of the Lord.

All these things indicate that Jeremiah was not unaware of the problem of the origin of the word of the Lord, as it has been raised by modern scholars; he was troubled by the possibility that men can believe that their own thoughts are the word of the Lord. Was it possible that he himself was so deluded? Against this possibility he had only that overpowering sense of "otherness" in the word of the Lord; and he knew, as one knows his own mind, that those who gave him the lie had no such sense of compulsion. Yet how could he prove it? To those who challenged his commission he gave a response that seems remarkably feeble: earlier prophets who had threatened evil had usually been right, and those who had said that all is well had usually been wrong; therefore let us wait and see. Not spectacular, this, and scarcely to be compared with the story related of Samuel, who, at a much less critical juncture of Hebrew history, called upon an unseasonal thunderstorm to justify himself; much less impressive than the story of Elijah on Mount Carmel, who challenged the Lord to prove Himself God by lightning on demand. Was the hand of the Lord shortened in the days of Jeremiah, or was Jeremiah of so much less faith? In any case, the answer of Jeremiah is more reassuring than thunder and lightning because it is so genuinely human. It is as certain an attestation as we could wish of the tremendous integrity of his character, the thing that separates him decisively from the false prophets; if anyone ever tried to separate the precious from the vile, the word of the Lord from the word of man, it was Jeremiah, who was flogged and imprisoned because, despite the revolt of his whole being, he could not escape the compulsion that it was the word of the Lord. Let critics join him in his muddy cistern before they quickly judge that he, like the false prophets, could not tell the word of the Lord from his own psychic processes.

We are, of course, faced with the question of analogy. We Catholics believe that Ridley and Latimer were in error; yet Latimer urged Ridley to play the man, and they died bravely for their error. Courage and integrity of character are not found exclusively on the side of truth; men have died bravely for error, as they have surrendered cravenly in defending the truth. Yet there is something about the experience of Jeremiah which puts it into another class. Whether for truth or for error, men must convince themselves that their beliefs are true before they will put forth their all on their behalf; the testimony of Jeremiah is that he did not convince himself, but was convinced by another. His doubts were never resolved, they were simply smothered. He was an unwilling witness. He was strong, but not with his own strength. One cannot think that he, like many others, stuck to his task because he was unwilling to reverse his whole life and admit that he had been wrong all the time. There was nothing he would rather do.

We should not rashly extend what we say of Jeremiah to all those whom we call prophets, even if he himself expresses an awareness of continuity with the prophets of the past. Yet there is a community of idiom among them – "The word of the Lord came," "Thus says the Lord," and a dozen such set phrases which occur in all the books of the prophets. There is a community of visual and auditory allusions to heavenly sights and sounds. Most striking of all, there is a community of content, obvious if one reads the books, which we shall have to discuss at length in later chapters. Thus we have little evidence of such an inner conflict in other prophets as we have in Jeremiah; but we have no reason to think that the prophetic diction in them expresses anything else than the same overpowering sense of otherness. With Jeremiah, we can be sure that the man who lacked this sense was no prophet.

But there were other channels also among the Hebrews in which God was deemed to speak to man; we have to look at these somewhat carefully, for it would be a mistake, it seems, to put them on the same level with prophetic consciousness. What was the mysterious device called "Urim and Thummim," mentioned several times in the stories of Saul and David? One "asked the Lord," and the Lord answered through Urim and Thummim. From the nature of the questions and the answers, it is clear that this device was oracular, quite similar to the oracular devices of the diviners; and we have no reason to think that it was other than a survival of primitive usage, through which the Lord was thought to unveil the future, probably by the casting of lots. Here we have a combination of popular superstition and a conventional manner of speaking. The device was no more and no less a revelation of the will of the Lord than the modern Christian device of seeking the will of God by opening the pages of the Bible at random. The Urim and Thummim do not appear after the time of David; in a more enlightened age there was no room for this primitive device. It seems evident that it would be a false logic to compare this device with the prophetic consciousness.

The priests also were channels through which God spoke to men. They possessed the traditions of the law and custom through which Hebrew worship and Hebrew life were regulated. This was "the law of the Lord," for the Lord had given it to Moses. Yet, with changing social and political conditions, new problems arose to which the old laws gave no solution. In such instances, one consulted the priests, and their answer was an answer of the Lord Himself, for they spoke in His name. If their answer became an integral part of the law and custom, it was incorporated into the code, and became a part of the law of the Lord. Did the priests speak in the name of the Lord as the prophets did? Hardly;

for in the priests we have the basis of a conventional manner of speech: the priestly authority. They spoke with the authority of their office, they interpreted the law of the Lord, or answered questions, or adjudicated disputes according to the law of the Lord. They expressed the will of the Lord much as the religious superior expresses the will of God to his subjects; but they do not exhibit that sense of otherness which we find in the prophets.

But we do meet the question: in what sense is that body of law which is contained in the four latter books of Moses "the law of the Lord"? Are we to extend the story of the two tablets, "written by the finger of the Lord," to cover that vast bulk of precepts and prohibitions? Open the book of Leviticus at random, and we meet such a sentence as this: "Say to the sons of Israel: The following are the creatures that you may eat, of all the animals on the earth: any animal with a cloven hoof that chews the cud you may eat"; and there follows an enumeration in which the hare is called unclean because it has not a cloven hoof, although it chews the cud! The picture of Moses writing this unbiological sentence at the dictation of the Lord is one at which the most devout mind is startled. One thinks of the words of St. Paul: "Is God concerned with oxen?"

But there is more to the question than this. Since the beginning of the twentieth century, many codes of law, some almost complete, have been recovered from the ancient Semitic world of which the Hebrews were a part. When these are read, similarities in detail with Hebrew laws appear which approach very closely to identity. The law which required the man who seduces a virgin to pay the marriage price and marry her is not even a wise law, by modern standards of conduct; it may have been wise in the ancient world, but could not God leave the ancients to settle such problems in their own way, as He leaves us to settle ours? A large number of Hebrew laws are obviously derived from the common law of the ancient Semitic world. In 1902, there was discovered at the site of ancient Susa a massive column of hard stone on which were inscribed the laws of Hammurabi of Babylon, who was a near contemporary of Abraham, four to five hundred years before Moses. In several dozen instances, the resemblance between the code of Hammurabi and the Hebrew codes is very close. Some have thought that the law of Moses not only used the code of Hammurabi as a legal source, but also imitated it in its account of the stone tablets. This impression is not correct; Hammurabi is grateful to the gods for giving him the kingdom and maintaining his power, but he does not attribute the laws to them.

It must be granted that the attribution of the mass of material called the law of Moses to the dictation of God Himself has made it extremely difficult for many to accept any idea of God speaking to man in the Old Testament. And since this attribution was a theological commonplace for many centuries, it was hard to see how it could be abandoned or modified without abandoning what we have called basic in the religion of the Hebrews: the belief that God can and does speak to man. Modern studies of ancient legal collections enable us not only to put the "law of Moses" more clearly in its historical perspective, but to explain it as "the law of the Lord" without fearing that we stultify ourselves. The Hebrew law is a collection of collections, an amassing of laws and customs which arose in various times and places, and which were ultimately gathered in a single corpus under the name of Moses, the Lawgiver. How many of these laws go back to the time of Moses modern criticism has not determined in detail, and it probably never will. But we can see that the picture of Moses receiving all these laws from the hand of the Lord is imaginary, the figured idealization of his position as the emissary of the Lord and founder of the Hebrew commonwealth.

Do we thereby take away from Moses the authority which Hebrew tradition accorded him, and put him in the limbo of legend with Minos of Crete and Arthur of Camelot? Before we do so, let us recall that without Moses there is no such thing as a Hebrew people or a Hebrew religion. Moses in Hebrew tradition is the man through whom the Lord and the people were joined. If Moses did not exist, to borrow a phrase, we should have to invent him. The religion of the Hebrews is a singular episode in the history of man's quest for God, and it demands a singular cause. Hebrew tradition gives us Moses, and we had better take him. In the long line of spokesmen of the Lord who pass through Hebrew history Moses is the first and the greatest. If he was not of the prophets, then there were no prophets, for they all presuppose him. His story raises questions which the story of Jeremiah does not raise just because he was the first. There is no comparison between the story of Jeremiah, partly autobiographical and partly collected from contemporary or very nearly contemporary accounts, and the stories of Moses and the patriarchs. Moses has acquired a halo and a haze of glory in the tradition; his often told story has been overlaid with such touches of grandeur as attach themselves to every great historical figure. It seems unsound to attempt a precise analysis of the Hebrew idea of divine communication on the basis of such stories as that of the burning bush or the Sinai theophany, stories which have been embellished by the vivid imagination of the popular storyteller. On the other hand, the story of Moses, however it be understood, exhibits the same sense of otherness which we find in the prophets; to remove this is to remove Moses from history altogether.

There is yet another way through which the Hebrews found that God spoke to men, and this is through the wisdom of the sages. The book of Proverbs tells us that "the Lord gives wisdom; out of His mouth come knowledge and reason." The same idea is expressed in the story of Solomon, the very model of the wise man, who asked the Lord for wisdom rather than riches and honor, and received it; for his prayer was itself the proof of his wisdom. Evidently, however, we are not dealing here with an experience like that of the prophets. What the wise man says is the fruit of the Lord's gift, but it is the word of the wise man; the wise man will deliver his wisdom to his son, and the wisdom of the ages will be accumulated. Without doubt the Hebrews believed that such a blessing as wisdom was a gift of the Lord, and this belief also has its significance; but they do not speak of wisdom as the prophets spoke of the word of the Lord.

This sketch of the Hebrew idea of the communication of God with man has, up to this point, left us with an irreducible core of belief in something which we have designated "an overpowering sense of otherness." It is more than this; but how much more depends on our answer to some further questions. Must we suppose that Jeremiah heard the sound of a voice impinging upon his ear from some invisible source? How could Isaiah see the skirts of the Lord's robe, when he knew as well as we do that the Lord is invisible and has no robe? We spoke earlier of the convincing realism of many of the accounts of the conversation of God with men. Does this realism force us to admit that God did, in the obvious sense of the words, "speak with Moses face to face, as one man speaks to another," or that God took dinner with Abraham, and debated with him the fate of Sodom? No believing Christian can doubt the condescension of God; for if He has condescended to become a man, there is no loss of dignity in speaking with man. But the believing Christian is not less a believer if he wishes to know more exactly how the divine communication became perceptible. Did the prophets, as they spoke the word of the Lord, repeat phrases which they heard ringing like a bell within them?

The last question is the easiest to answer. If the prophets spoke in this way, it is strange that they should speak each in his own language and in his own style. If the Lord spoke to Isaiah in this crassly material manner, then He spoke exactly as Isaiah would speak to himself; and the same is true of each individual prophet. We meet again the obtrusive human element, which forbids us to make men lifeless tools of the divine. God uses them in the manner proper to their nature; that is, He uses them as they are, to the full extent of their distinct personality, their powers of mind, heart, tongue. That the prophets parroted what God dictated is as impossible as the idea that the writers of the sacred books were unthinking stenographers.

We may find a key to the things which the prophets saw and heard if we look to the experiences of Christian mystics. This strange phenomenon of communication with the world of the supernatural has been constant in the history of Christianity. There has been much pseudo-mysticism, perhaps more than we know, and the Church never speaks a final word about the mystical phenomena which are attested. She has no real test of the genuinity of the phenomena except her own faith and the performance of the mystic; if the alleged mystic leads a truly Christian life, if the mystic exhibits heroic Christian virtues, then there is no reason to doubt that the mystic has experienced God in an extraordinary manner. Yet even the true mystic may be occasionally deceived, and no one is more aware of this than the mystic himself. It is remarkable how some pretenders have been able to deceive wise and holy men by false claims to mystical experience, perhaps for many years. There is little in the mystical phenomenon itself, even when it appears in such sober and reasonable people as St. Teresa of Avila or St. Francis de Sales, to prove that it is what the mystic believes it to be, or claims it to be. Many Christians have a fanatic curiosity for novel revelations, and there are always those who for vanity or for gain will satisfy them.

Now it is immediately obvious, if one looks at mystical phenomena, that there is a startling diversity in its character in different people. One cannot imagine St. John of the Cross having the experience of St. Margaret Mary Alacoque, or St. Ignatius Loyola speaking of God in the manner of St. Therese of the Child Jesus. Even in the mystical experience, God is, so to speak, refracted through the personality of the mystic, and apprehended according to the capacities of the one to whom He reveals Himself. We see this diversity in the sensible and external effects of the mystical experience, and so the mystics describe it. They also see things and hear things, their members are affected, they may be rendered unconscious. The mystics tell us that such things are a sign not of holiness, but of the weakness of human nature, and that the highest experience of God is elevating and inspiring, without any external disturbance. They do not confuse the sights and sounds aroused in their sensible perceptions with God Himself; at least, they do their best to avoid this confusion, admitting that it is easily possible and that it often happens. The experience of God, they tell us, is indescribable in human language; the more easily it is described in sensible image, the farther removed it is from the reality. But the experience of God has a tremendous effect upon one's life, giving it new perspective and purpose, new strength and endurance. The Church, as we have seen, judges the genuinity of these experiences by performance. If there is no change in the life of the mystic, the Church is not much interested in the external phenomena, however spectacular they may be. She does not wish Christian holiness to become a sideshow.

If, then, we view the experiences of the prophets in the light of what we can learn from Christian mysticism, we see that the phenomena found in the prophets are of a piece with those found in the mystics. "The word of the Lord" is the shattering experience of the divine reality, with repercussions in the sensible and emotional activity of the prophet. But, just as the mystics do not confuse these sensible and emotional reactions with the experience of God Himself, neither should we, in reading the prophets, identify these peripheral fireworks with the prophetic experience itself. They are not the divine reality. If we look for the transformation of the prophet, the alteration of his life into new dimensions and a new perspective, we see it beyond doubt, especially in Jeremiah. To the prophets we may apply the test of performance, although we should note again, as we remarked above, that the word of the Lord does not of itself ennoble one. There were small and imperfect men among the prophets, as we shall have to point out, just as there have been many whose mystical experiences we can hardly doubt, although the experiences did not raise them to the level of heroism. Even so moving an experience as mysticism does not force men to do that which they really do not want to do; and even "the word of the Lord" did not make a man that which he really did not want to be.

We seem to have reduced "the word of the Lord" to something indescribable, and so to have brought ourselves up against a blank wall. Certainly there is something in the supernatural which ultimately escapes analysis; there is a frontier beyond which experience and analogy cannot pass. But the supernatural does not elude our grasp altogether. This experience of which we are speaking is described by those who know it as a knowledge of the reality of God more profound than is possible by faith or by thinking. It is an awareness of His present and immediate reality in the prophet himself, in the world, in other men, in the course of nature, in the course of human events. It is a marvelously keen perception of the living personality of God; to this thought we shall have to return, for it is one of the most striking features of the Hebrew belief in God that it always sees God with sharply defined personal traits. It is a sense of the divine immediacy which is at once terrible, since it made Isaiah fear for his life, and consoling, since it made Jeremiah secure because the Lord was with him as a dreaded warrior. We cannot call it vision, and we cannot call it hearing or feeling, for God cannot be perceived on the sensible level; God is perceived in what St. Teresa called the interior of the soul. But we cannot, unless we reject all the evidence there is on the question, reduce this experience to any kind of normal sensible or intellectual activity. Without exception, this knowledge of God, wherever it appears, is described as something impressed upon the soul by an overpowering agent outside the soul itself, who thus makes Himself unmistakably known as a human person makes himself unmistakably known.

Such a terribly immediate awareness of the divine alters entirely one's habits of thought. The prophet has a sharper perception of the difference between good and evil, and a finer insight into the unspeakable consequences of human malice. In a way, he comes to share God's attitude toward good and evil. Because he sees the divine reality so clearly, he sees human life as a process tending toward a term, which is God; and he knows that this process must be directed by God, not by man, a direction which man cannot finally avert. He sees the urgency of the divine imperative which governs human life, for he sees this imperative in the will of God as he has felt it. The sense of the divine reality is a glowing light within his mind, casting its beams upon everything which falls within the scope of human knowledge, bringing out each object in sharper focus; in the clarity of this light he sees things somehow as God sees them, and he formulates his words, "the word of the Lord," with all the intensity of feeling and language which he has at his command.

This, indeed, may not be "revelation" in the accepted sense, and we do not intend to speak of revelation in this sense; we make an effort — slow and stumbling, we know, but an effort — to reach into the psychological wellspring of revelation, to enter into a mind where God meets man "face to face." Here one feels that one is an intruder. But our modern sophistication has forced us into many places where our fathers feared to tread; if we do not attempt some analysis of the psychology of prophecy, others will do it for us. There are many modern studies of the subject, few of which are in even substantial harmony with Catholic belief. What we think we have found in the prophet's mind is, we believe, not that which one finds in great creative minds. The processes of genius, as we have noticed, are not easily analyzed; the possessor of genius cannot easily explain the brilliant intuition which is the mark of his gift. We do not mean to call the prophet's insight into God and the world and human nature a "brilliant intuition"; for a brilliant intuition lacks the overpowering sense of otherness which is the mark of the prophet. Socrates said that he was impelled to speak to the Athenians by a "demonic being"; he left it purposely vague and tantalized us beyond patience. Was he merely exercising the famous Socratic wit, and prodding his adversaries, who thought themselves the defenders of piety and orthodoxy, with the hint that he also had an other-worldly guide? Or did the phrase mean any more than "the devil in me"? In any case, it is merely a passing allusion in the life of Socrates; and we really should not make the comparison.

It is worth our attention to notice how this sense of "otherness" appears in the identification of the prophet with the Lord. More often than not, the prophets deliver the word of the Lord in the first person; usually with an introductory formula, but not always. If the prophet begins to speak in his own person, he will easily lapse into speech in the person of the Lord. This does not, as we have seen, indicate that the prophet was echoing an inner voice; but it does indicate the close communion with the Lord which was the fruit of his mystic insight. We have said that the prophet shared, in a way, in God's views; he knew that his thoughts were clarified by that divine illumination, his emotional response was a human expression of the divine attitude, and he spoke the word of the Lord with a full conviction that he was one with the Lord in whose name he spoke. This exhibits the mystical character of his experience, and at the same time shows the gulf which lies between the word of the Lord and the brilliant intuitions of creative genius. Genius is self-conscious, aware and proud of its power; it does not lose itself in identification with another, even if that other be God. In the prophets we constantly strike against that hard core of "otherness," the sense of something real and objective which is not themselves. Modern writers sometimes speak of the "irrational" in the prophetic consciousness, and the word is apt, if properly understood. The irrational is that which cannot be resolved into its component parts, which is beyond exact calculation; it is something which normal experience and scientific analysis cannot account for, and that something is God.

Shall we call the prophets abnormal? Many modern students of the prophets look for the key of the prophetic experience in abnormal psychology. This approach is not very flattering to the prophets, for abnormal psychology is the study of the malfunctioning of the mind. In this sense, certainly, we do not like to have the prophets called abnormal; and we do not believe that any analysis has shown them to be abnormal, in the technical sense of the word. Mental disorders are classified in certain patterns; the layman will say simply that his neighbor is crazy, but the clinical psychologist will put a name to what he observes. If the prophets are abnormal in the technical sense, then they ought to exhibit certain symptoms and certain patterns; and these the analysts have failed to give us. An isolated instance of abnormal behavior, if it were a sign of mental disorder, would have us all behind bars; for normal mental and emotional stability is far from a perfect equilibrium. The application of such principles to the prophets is ridiculous, and perhaps we should not mention it, except to show how far men will go rather than admit the personal intrusion of God into human life and human affairs.

But the prophets are abnormal in the popular sense of the word, just as genius is abnormal; and if the line between genius and insanity is very thin, as we hear, then perhaps the line between prophecy and insanity is very thin also. Genius does not appear except in persons of extremely delicate sensibilities, and their very sensitivity, which is their strength, is also the weakness which makes it possible for the mind to break down. No doubt the word of the Lord could come to the dull and unimaginative and unfeeling person whom we usually call "normal," but it seems that it rarely did so, if at all; and if it did, its utterance would be comparatively dull, unimaginative, and unfeeling. The fire of Amos burns low in Haggai; and we have all heard the words of the Gospels, which are spirit and life, reduced to intolerable dullness by spiritless preaching. We could infer for ourselves, even if we did not have the introspection of Jeremiah to inform us, that the word of the Lord was a dreadful psychological burden, mentally and emotionally fatiguing; and we should not be surprised if nature occasionally bent under the strain. Prophecy, again like genius, made its possessor a lonely man; the singularity of his psychic processes isolates him from his fellows, for there is no one with whom he can share his thoughts and feelings about the thing to which his life is dedicated. The prophet cannot expect understanding and sympathy from his fellows; he is closer to the Lord than he is to any man.

We have attempted to sketch here something of the way in which God speaks to man: to put the Hebrew belief that he did so into our own language. We believe that God did speak to man, but we have observed that it is not our primary purpose to argue this point; we are more concerned with showing that this belief cannot be analyzed out of the Hebrew faith without essentially altering our own estimate of that faith. We cannot escape, in the Old Testament, the pervading conviction that God intrudes Himself into the minds of men in an extraordinary but thoroughly objective manner, and that men, possessed of this awareness, become His spokesmen. They remain men, and they sometimes remain men who are petty; but Hebrew faith in the Lord God is meaningless apart from this fundamental belief, that they knew Him at all only because He spoke to them.

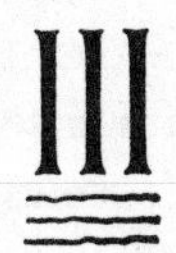

THE GODS OF THE SEMITES

IN FORMER years, one could read and study the Old Testament by itself, without much concern for anything outside it. It was the only written document from its period of human history, and it admitted no comparison, no criticism from any other source. The Canaanites, Babylonians, Assyrians, and others who appeared in its pages were known only from the Old Testament. It was easy to imagine the Hebrews as a monastic group marching through the desert under the leadership of a mystic abbot and establishing themselves in Canaan – after thoughtfully emptying the land of its inhabitants by a total liquidation – in peace and recollection. There, unfortunately, they permitted themselves to be corrupted, as the decadent monasteries of the Renaissance grew lax, and fell into the worship of idols after the manner of the Canaanites – who must have sprung from the ground, for the sword of Joshua spared neither man, woman, nor child.

History has taken the Israelites out of this isolation and re-created the world in which they lived. Assyria and Babylonia have yielded their ancient cities to the digging of the archaeologist, and have given us some of their literature, vaster in extent than the literature of Israel. A hundred years ago Sargon of Assyria was unknown except for a single mention of his name in the Bible; now we know more about him than we do about the Hebrew kings Ahaz and Hezekiah, his contemporaries. The passage of the Hebrews from Egypt into Canaan was no problem when nothing was known of the history of either country; now their history is known, and the exodus cannot, as yet, be fitted exactly into any historical scheme which can be erected on the data at present available, although we can place it within a century or two. That it will be fitted into some scheme we do not doubt, but we think it will not be the same straightforward account which we once had. Ancient Hebrew and Canaanite cities also have come out of their tomb. We have learned that the Hebrews were not a culturally creative people; in such things as arts and crafts, houses, and household vessels they were content to use the skills of others. Their political history shows them, except for a few years, as a football in the power game of greater nations; their external political life and their internal social life were substantially affected by the decisions of others over whom they had no control. We do not imply that the historian's view of ancient Israel is essentially altered from what it used to be. Hebrew traditions, placed against the background of the ancient Near East, take their place harmoniously in a larger pattern of history. This pattern illuminates Hebrew history and is illuminated by it. Points formerly obscure are now clear, misunderstandings can be corrected, gaps can be filled.

If the history and the culture of the Hebrews are perfectly intelligible only as a part of a larger historical and cultural pattern, then we may expect to find that this is proportionately true of their religion also. Religion cannot and should not be isolated from human life as a whole; and religion, as the Hebrews understood it, pervaded every human activity. If the culture of their neighbors imposed itself upon them, it is impossible that the religion of their neighbors should not have affected their own. It is true that we must distinguish between the religion of the Hebrews and their general culture. We have said that the Hebrews were not culturally creative; we have already seen that their "religious genius" is an acknowledged fact. But this genius did not operate in a vacuum; it must have been subject to the influences which affected their culture as a whole. The religion of the Canaanites and other Semitic peoples, like their history, was once known only by casual allusions in the Old Testament. They can now be studied in themselves, and they ought to be.

This is our apology for introducing a sketch of the religion of the Semitic peoples before we pursue further the religious beliefs of the Hebrews; for much of Hebrew belief is meaningless except as a response or a reaction to the religions of Mesopotamia and Syria.

We said that, until a hundred years ago, the religions of the ancient Semitic peoples were known only by casual allusions in the Old Testament, and in a few writers of classical times whose veracity was not above suspicion. It should be noted that our present knowledge enables us to recognize an even greater number of allusions which were hidden before. The ancient writers are shown to be better informed than they were formerly thought to be. The obvious allusions in the Old Testament to Canaanite religion, despite their number, are limited to a few items. The vice most frequently mentioned is idolatry. We hear of the "abominations" of the Canaanites, but the Old Testament does not tell us what they were, except where the word most obviously designates the image of a god. It mentions gods whom it lumps together as "baals," male deities, and "ashtaroth," female deities, but it tells us nothing of their character. We learn that the Hebrews worshiped at the "high places," but we do not learn what they were. We read of human sacrifice, especially of the sacrifice of children, "to Molek"; in this word some modern scholars think they recognize the Hebrew and Canaanite divine title of "king," others see in it the technical name of the sacrifice. We hear of sacred prostitutes, and demons, and the horses of the chariot of the sun-god, and the sacred stone, and the sacred pillar.

These allusions are now seen against a background which gives them completely new clarity. The religion of the great cities and states of Mesopotamia began to come to light about a hundred years ago, and new discoveries are still being made. This was not the religion of Canaan; but there are certain basic beliefs and practices which run through both religions, even though they differ in detail. The religion of the Canaanites themselves was first revealed in Canaanite sources in 1929. In that year, near the Syrian headland called Ras Shamra, were discovered the remains of the ancient Canaanite city of Ugarit, in a splendid state of preservation, dating from 1400 B.C., before Moses was drawn from the Nile. For the first time the literature of Canaan was known, a literature which must have been as extensive as that of Mesopotamia. An unexpected find was that a large portion of this literature was religious, containing a number of Canaanite myths. The similarity between these myths and the myths of Mesopotamia was at once apparent, and equally apparent were a number of items which lay at the base of biblical allusions. Scholars are still exploring this material, and it has not yet been put into definitive form; indeed, there is no reason to think that all of the literary remains of the site have been uncovered. But what has already been made available is enough to show us the true religious background of the world of the Hebrews.

We have learned that the vice of idolatry, which is so often mentioned in the Old Testament, has to be understood as the Hebrews understood it. Neither the Canaanites nor the Mesopotamians were idol worshipers in the gross sense of the word; the deity was thought to be in the idol in a certain sense, and the idol was treated as the deity, but the deity himself was, in the mind of his worshipers, a distinctly personal being. The Hebrews scoffed at the idolatry of their neighbors because they knew that there was no reality behind the idol; those who thought they were worshiping their god were actually worshiping the image, because there was nothing else to receive the worship. It was an ingenious conceit, perhaps, but a striking way of denying the reality of the gods of the nations.

Perhaps the Hebrews oversimplified; for there was a reality behind the image, even if it was not the reality which was thought to be there. The religions of the ancient Semitic peoples were nature-religions; the deity was identified, in one way or another, with the forces of nature, and these peoples never went behind these forces to the idea of a being outside nature, beyond it, above it. Because the forces of nature are many, the gods also were at times in conflict; and there was no one to impose order from above. To the prescientific man, nature is mysterious and fearful; it blesses, but it can also strike catastrophic blows. Here is evidently a higher power, beyond the control of man. The prescientific man identified these mysterious powers with personalized beings like himself, and worshiped them as gods; he worshiped the creature, not the creator, and found his gods in the material things of the universe, not in the spiritual. We would not wish to make this statement too sweeping, as though the gods of the ancient Semitic world had no moral significance. Man is conscious of a morality within himself, and if he believes in gods at all, he believes that the will of the gods is turned to what he thinks is right and good. But the strength of that divine will for good will be no greater, in his own mind, than his own will for good; and thus the moral life of man, like the physical world, is, as Thorkild Jacobsen has called it, "an uneasy equilibrium of conflicting forces." This uneasy equilibrium is reflected in the world of his gods, who exhibit the same moral conflict which man sees in himself. Since he has not escaped the limits of the visible world, he cannot conceive of a being in whom this moral conflict does not exist. So the moral will of the gods was like the moral will of their worshipers: substantial enough in the essential morality without which social life is impossible, but subject to many hostile influences, guided by a perception of right and wrong which was obscure, and not proof against breakdown and corruption. The moral will of the gods was not the dominant note in the religions of the ancient Semitic peoples, and hence we may classify these religions, as we have done, as a worship of the material universe.

The worship of the creature is superstition, and the extreme form of superstition; but, for purposes of convenience, we distinguish between the worship of beings which are conceived as personal, however distorted the conception of divinity may be, which we call religion, and the belief in occult impersonal forces, which we call magic. Superstition, in this latter sense, ran through the whole Semitic world. The world was not only full of gods, but also full of demons, both good and evil. The scope of action of the demons was less cosmic than that of the gods. One could attribute a toothache, a nightmare, spoiled food to a demon; but a storm, a plague, a drought was the work of a higher being.

The more petty evils of the demons could be met by magical means; and the tremendous mass of magical literature which Mesopotamia has left us is a pathetic witness to the superstition of one of the most intelligent, ingenious, and charming peoples which the race has developed. Bouché-Leclercq concluded his researches into Greek astrology with the desperate remark that it is not a waste of time to study how other people have wasted their time. But there is an interesting feature in magic, all the same; for it is man's first effort to control nature. It has been said, wittily and wisely, that magic is the science of the primitive, as myth is his philosophy; and if the scientist is indignant when he is reminded that he is the medicine man of the modern world, he will do well to recall that the medicine man dealt better with some human problems than the scientist has dealt with them. Man does not worship what he thinks he can control; the demons were feared, not worshiped. But the greater, more mysterious, more unpredictable, and entirely uncontrollable forces of nature could not be handled by occult means; they could be approached only by rendering propitious these personalized higher beings who could, like men, be friendly or hostile, depending on how one treated them.

A powerful being is most readily appeased by the profession of submission, accompanied by a gift. He is pleased when his excellence is praised; if angered when he is offended, he can be placated by apology and a petition for pardon. This is the universal human response to the higher beings in which man believes, and it creates the ritual of adoration and sacrifice, praise and atonement. This ritual appears in ancient Semitic religion, and it appears in Hebrew religion; we shall speak of it in its due place. But it is not this part of ancient Semitic religion which most affected the religion of the Hebrews. The point of clash between the two is found in a feature which the Hebrew religion rejected without, perhaps, really knowing why, except that it was altogether out of harmony with the character of the God who had spoken to them; this is the cultic myth, to give it its proper name, and of this we must speak.

We quoted above the remark that myth is the philosophy of

the primitive. This witty remark must be qualified, if we are to speak precisely. Philosophy professes to be a synthesis of intelligible reality constructed by the human mind; it proudly admits no dependence on anything else. The prephilosophic mind is, in its simplicity, unaware of its power; and the myth, while it is, of course, the construction of the human mind, is thought to be given from above. Since the forces of nature are hypostatized in personal beings, the interplay of the forces of nature is seen as the interplay of personal beings; and the course of nature, as it affects man, is determined by the relations of these beings to each other. Modern scientific man speaks of the "course" or the "cycles" of nature, and never doubts that nature will follow its demonstrated pattern, for there is nothing which will disturb it. Even what we call disturbances of nature are the results of causes acting according to their known and predictable properties. If moist warm air meets cold dry air at the proper temperature and pressure, the result will be a hurricane which can destroy thousands of lives and wreck whole cities in a few minutes. While the victims of the storm are picking up their bricks and their bones, the meteorologist will observe how the storm followed its plotted course. The hurricane is no less destructive for us than it was for the Mesopotamian, but it is less fearful, because it is not personal. It would be false to say that the ancient Semites were unaware of the cycles of nature; they did not plant in midsummer and expect to harvest in midwinter. But they had never analyzed the cycles of nature in such a way as to see that they followed with necessity from given conditions. Each time they recurred, they recurred because of the meeting of the wills of higher beings; they were an effect of the celestial drama of the gods which we call myth.

The cultic myth is the ritual expression of this belief. In order to assure the regular and beneficial recurrence of the celestial drama, man must enact this drama himself; and so, through the official representatives of the gods, he performs a series of symbolic actions which portray the adventures of the gods. Once this is done, man has done all he can do to insure his survival. There is no cycle of nature which is more significant to man than the cycle of fertility. The recurring interplay of sun, rain, wind, soil, seed, and the other things which bring forth food is life, and the failure of this interplay is death. In ancient Semitic religions the myth and ritual of fertility occupied the central position; and this myth and ritual is at the base of most of the allusions to Canaanite religion in the Old Testament. From these allusions alone the true character of this myth and ritual and its central position were never known.

In one form or another, the myth and ritual of fertility appear throughout Mesopotamia and Syria; and we ought, if we wish to be precise, to point out the variations which can be seen. But we can limit ourselves to the basic ideas; the Hebrews, who were acquainted with more than one form, were not too careful in distinguishing one form from another. At the bottom of the myth was the belief that the annual cycle of fertility was an annual renewal of creation; the earth was produced anew each year. So most modern scholars interpret the myth; some would extend the cycle over a period of years (seven), but the essence of the myth and ritual lies in the cycle and its renewal, not in any definite period of time. Creation, in ancient Semitic religions, was a cosmic struggle; a primitive chaos, personified as a monstrous being, was subdued by the creative deity, who made the world from the remains of the monster. The annual cycle is a production of life from death; and the god who produces fertility must himself die. Chaos, in the world of nature, is victorious in its turn; but the creative deity will rise from death and smite his enemies. Fertility is the union of the male and female principles; for the ancient Semitic peoples, sex was as primeval as nature, as divinity itself. And so the god of fertility was of necessity accompanied by his consort, who is the deification of the most mysterious powers of fertility. She is the ideal woman, combining in one figure the two things which the ancient Semitic peoples saw as the most desirable qualities of her sex: virginity and sexual fulfillment. The victory of the god over his chaotic enemies was followed by his union with his consort, which renewed the source of fertility.

We have simplified the myth in this sketch. We say nothing about the great god El, the father of the male and female fertility deities, because he is relatively inactive in the myth, although his name is often given to the Lord whom the Hebrews worshiped. We say nothing about Asherah, the consort of El, although we recognize in her name the title which the Hebrews gave to the wooden stake which represented the female fertility deity. In the name of the fertility god, Aleyan Baal, we find the god whom the Old Testament mentions so often. His consort Anath, on the other hand, rarely appears in the Old Testament except in place names; more often we meet Ashtart, whom the Greeks called Astarte, a goddess identical in character. W. F. Albright has remarked that the Canaanite gods possess an extraordinarily fluid quality, and that their names and functions may be easily interchanged; for this reason, the essence of the myth is more to our purpose than the precise identification of the parts which the various gods play in it.

This is the myth, as we can reconstruct it from the literary remains of Ugarit; these remains are not complete, and the proper order of the various portions of the literature is not yet altogether certain. We can supplement the myth of Ugarit to some extent from the literary remains of Mesopotamia, which are also incomplete; we run the risk of contaminating the sources if we do this in detail, but we are fairly safe in tracing the basic pattern. We do not have the rubrics of the temple ritual for Ugarit, and we have them only in fragments for Mesopotamia, so that restoration of the ritual is, likewise, largely conjecture. We cannot be sure that, in civilized times, the death of the god was enacted upon a ritual human victim; there is little doubt that this was the primitive form of the ritual. We have no doubt that the union of the god and the goddess was represented by two members of the sacred personnel, the high priest (or the king) and a priestess. We have no doubt that the worshipers also took part in this representation by union with the sacred prostitutes, who played the part of the goddess, and that this action was communion with the gods, the forces of fertility. The "high places" must have been the stage of obscenity which revolts the imagination; it is not difficult to understand the fascination which the myth and ritual of fertility had for the Hebrews, and the horror which it aroused.

We have noticed that the Hebrews, like other ancient Semitic peoples, viewed reality in its sensible and concrete forms, and shunned the abstract and the immaterial. If myth was the philosophy of these peoples, it might repay us to formulate the implications of this cultic myth in the abstract form which we prefer, in order that we may feel its impact; it is much more than promiscuous sexual license under the auspices of religion. And these are the philosophical propositions which it expresses in myth and ritual: the supreme good, the good life, consists in the satisfaction of human material needs. This is all we ask of the gods, and this is all they can give us. They bless us in full when they satisfy these needs not only in the minimum necessary for survival, but in abundance, so that we enjoy not only the simple life, but also the material comforts of life. We ask of the gods more than meat and drink; we ask wealth, to that degree which will enable a man to purchase every satisfaction which he craves. The highest of all pleasures is the pleasure of sex; life offers nothing finer, nothing which so raises a man to the level of the divine. Consequently, the difference of the sexes exists only that the male may have this supreme satisfaction; woman is his possession, and her noblest function is to satisfy his sexual appetite. When she does this, she is a goddess; otherwise, she is a high-grade domestic animal, a drudge, not fully a human being. Society exists, under the patronage of the gods, to create the conditions in which this good life may be attained. We must have law, order, restraint, but only to that degree which will prevent human crime from corrupting the good life of the group; the important thing is that law and government should protect wealth, material goods, and should make it possible for every man, within the limits of his capacity, to enjoy himself as he desires. But the power which puts these good things within a man's reach should not be restrained, and law and order should not protect the weak; for ultimately it is power that makes the good life possible. Such is the life of the gods, and such, when the gods are well disposed, is the life which they offer to men.

All this, we think, is implicit in the cultic myth of fertility. When this ancient belief is thus formally proposed, it does not sound altogether unfamiliar to modern readers; one might conclude that our technical advance over the men of ancient Mesopotamia and Syria is far greater than our intellectual and spiritual advance. One suspects that many modern Europeans and Americans, if transported suddenly into the Babylon of the second millennium, after an initial adjustment to inconveniences in such things as language, travel, and plumbing, would find themselves spiritually at home; they would never feel at ease with the ancient Hebrews.

We seem to have tagged the religion of the ancient Semites as secularism, pure and undefiled; and if we were so to simplify its designation, we should not grossly exaggerate. For if we go on to consider the gods as expressions of the political and social sentiments of the ancient Semites, we shall find that we remain in the same sphere of ideals. For the gods were more than personified natural forces; they were also personified human forces, if we may use the expression, and of these human forces the force of social cohesion demands our attention. I use this somewhat precious term because modern terms like race, state, or nation can be transferred to the ancient Semitic world only with great caution; for social groups were not the same in that world, although, of course, the fundamental human relations have not changed. The ancient Semitic world, again to employ a modern term, was collectivistic in this sense, that the individual person did not have the importance which we like to think he has in modern democratic society; the dignity of man, personal liberty, and such catchwords would have been idiot's jargon to the men of Mesopotamia and Syria. To them, life was in the first place survival, and survival was inconceivable outside the group. They did not philosophize about the constitution and structure of the social group, but accepted it as it was, just as they accepted the structure of the physical world. Society also was a higher power, the collection was more than the sum of its individual parts; this higher power was personalized into a god, and the power of society came down from heaven to earth and took up residence in the human representative of the gods, the king.

There is no inner connection between the forces of nature and the power of society. If Marduk of Babylon was originally a solar deity, as some scholars used to think, then we can see no reason why the god of the sun should be the god of the city. For the sun shone no more on Babylon than it did on Ur, yet the god who was invoked as the patron of Ur was the moon-god. Such connections, as far as we can judge, are merely coincidental; the function of the god as the embodiment of a social group was independent of any natural significance he may have had, and the more important the social group to which he was attached, the less significant his natural character becomes. He is primarily a national god, the embodiment of the social entity which worships him, and sees in him the deification of themselves in their societal unity.

Nowhere in the ancient Semitic world can we see this better than in Assyria, whose god, Ashur, bore the same name as his people and the city where his temple stood. He is a strangely impersonal god, a conqueror, like his people; it is he who leads them in war and gives them the victory. He embodies the ruthless efficiency of the conqueror, the hard indifference to the fate of those who fall beneath his military machine. The people and the god suited each other perfectly, for in worshiping Ashur the Assyrians worshiped themselves as a conquering state. Indeed, no other people could worship Ashur; rarely has a national spirit been so aptly hypostatized, and we are probably not far wrong in finding in this religious expression of national ambition an important factor in the tremendous expanding drive and supreme military success of the people who marched behind the winged disk of Ashur.

It is not a mere coincidence that the Assyrians invoked the storm-god more frequently than did other peoples. The storm is fearful and destructive; the ancient Semitic peoples were aware that the natural forces which make the ground apt for cultivation were the same forces which brought wind and flood to wreck cities and drown their crops. The storm-god was a deity to be feared and propitiated from a respectful distance. But to the Assyrians this deity, whom we see in ancient art standing masterfully upon a lion, girded like a warrior and brandishing a handful of thunderbolts, was an incarnation of themselves. Well they might think so; the armies which swept across Asia, leaving burned-out cities and piles of heads, were the scourge of their time. Any ancient nation, of course, marched behind its gods to war; it happens that in Assyria we have the most warlike people of the ancient Semitic world. But the Assyrians did not differ from their neighbors in their belief that the function of the gods of the state was to give victory by any means and in any circumstances. "Conquer we must, for our cause it is just" would have been more idiot's jargon to the men of those times. For them, too, the gods were on the side of the big battalions. If a people were defeated, then its gods had been proved weaker than the gods of the conquerors, and were carried off to grace the temple of the conquering god; by a courteous fiction, it was assumed that they had abandoned the defeated and delivered them to their conquerors. A god who lost his local seat had little chance of survival. As in nature, war was simply a conflict of forces, and the right cause was that which prevailed.

It is perhaps worth our notice that the gods of war were not exclusively male. The Assyrians venerated the mother goddess, Ishtar, as a military heroine who, with Ashur, led their armies; Anath, the virgin consort of Aleyan Baal, waded in the blood of the slain up to her waist and exulted like a drunken woman. "Blood lust" is not a mere figure of speech; and there is a strange perverse connection between the satisfaction which Anath and Ishtar personalized and the satisfaction of sadistic cruelty. We sometimes wonder whether the conquests of the ancient Semitic world were as bloody as their own records tell us; but when we see this horrible female with a murderer's sword in her hand, we are forced to conclude that such conquests were not merely *Schrecklichkeit,* not merely calculated policy, not the exaggerations of propaganda – which the ancient world also knew – but the mad orgasm of a lust for blood. And this human force also, a higher power beyond the control of man, was personalized into a goddess.

So the ancient Semitic world knew how to deify the state; and as long as it deified the state, any development of the idea of the dignity of the human person, of the essential personal liberties, could not occur in that world. The state was what we see it implied to be in its conquering wars: a means of producing wealth, of acquiring slaves and plunder in order that its citizens might enjoy "the good life." The deified state rendered sacred the acquisitive activities of the social group, as the cultic myth of fertility rendered sacred the animal satisfactions of the individual man. Each idea arose from the conception of something as necessary: social life and the production of the necessities of life. And each ended in a god, because men esteemed these things as the supreme good.

The gods of such a society could not have been different from the men of that society; they were basically unprincipled. They were mysterious and unpredictable, not only with the mystery of natural forces – which man, by scientific investigation, can largely remove – but with the mystery of the unstable human will, which is never less fixed than when it is fixed upon itself. Caprice was essential to the nature of these deities; they offered no true security in any of the things which they promised. They could always betray their worshipers, and their worshipers knew it. When the Mesopotamian poet said: "What seems good to man is to the gods evil; what seems evil to man is to the gods good," he gave voice to more than a momentary impatience. The ancient Semitic world had from its gods no definition of what is good and what is evil; it pursued the things it thought good, dimly aware, if it took time to reflect, that it did not know whether these things were good or evil. Within its limited horizon, how could it have known? The capricious will of the gods was a true counterpart of the intellectual and moral instability of the world which worshiped these gods; for a world in which nature and man are the supreme good is an essentially unstable world.

We have, no doubt, emphasized the unpleasant aspects of the ancient Semitic search for God, a search in which they found only themselves. We could have paid more attention to some of the expressions of a nobler religious sentiment, of a sense of obligation to do right; but these things do not come from the religion of the ancient Semitic peoples. Spontaneous eruptions of a certain ineradicable human decency appear even in the most improbable environments. The essential features of ancient Semitic religions were directed to the extirpation of that human decency, as far as it is possible; these features finally brought ruin to their religion and to the society in which it arose and to the individual members of that society. Their cities have lain dead and buried for thousands of years beneath the sands of an arid plain; these sands cover the once fertile fields where the cultic myth of fertility found its annual fulfillment. Those who look for the irony of history may find it in this, that Marduk and Ishtar still promise wealth and the good life; for their fields hold one of the richest deposits of oil in the world.

We have sketched these beliefs of the ancient Semitic world, and tried to put their implications into form, because the Hebrew religion was born and grew up in the world of these gods. The Hebrew people was never a stranger to these gods; it was in almost constant touch with them. The Hebrew religion gave these gods nothing, but it took from them, it responded to them with its own intrinsic strength, it assumed a form shaped, to no small extent, by the blows and caresses it received from these gods. The Hebrews were racially, ethically, spiritually akin to the men of Mesopotamia and Syria; if the Hebrews could have had their own way, their gods would have been the gods of their neighbors. Once we have seen these gods, we can never think that the Lord was one of them; we cannot fail to see that He was totally different, that He was not the incorporation of the ideals of a people or of the forces of nature, but a vital personality who intruded Himself into the world of the Hebrews.

THE HEBREW STORY

WE MUST return to a remark which was made previously: the remark that the Hebrews were not a culturally creative people, although their "peculiar religious genius" is universally acknowledged. The remark might appear to need modification because the Hebrews did create a literary form which has no parallel in the ancient Semitic world. But since we believe that this creation should be attributed to their "peculiar religious genius," the remark may be allowed to stand. This literary form is history, to give it the most obvious name, although "historical writing" would be more precise; for we shall have to explain immediately that it does not mean what we think it means, that it is not history in the modern sense of the word. Perhaps we shall approach our problem more effectively if we take up this last point first.

In the modern world of learning, history is called a "social science." Science is nothing if not exact knowledge; the social sciences are often regarded as spurious sciences because their objects do not admit the exact measurement and observation which are the methods of the natural sciences. The object of history, which is the actions of human beings in groups, eminently escapes exact observation and measurement. History is called "the remembered past"; not the past as it was, but as it is remembered, and history cannot surpass the limitations of human memory. History cannot make the past present again, even if it tries to do so; an exact reconstruction of past events is out of its reach, because the human memory does not retain the past exactly.

History must be satisfied if it can reconstruct the memory of the past; then, by comparison and criticism, it can construct, from the items of individual memories, a collective memory which will restore to us as much of the past as memory has retained. It is this rigorous and methodical comparison and criticism which distinguishes the historian from the storyteller; for the storyteller is interested in the memory of the past only as it is a story, as it has some fascination for himself and for those to whom he tells it. The storyteller is not interested in the exploration of truth for its own sake; he does not think of himself as contributing to the sum of human knowledge. Unhistorical people – and most men are unhistorical – quickly forget those features of the past which are not or cannot be included in a story. The storyteller is not even interested in giving us all that is remembered of the past; he is interested only in those memories which constitute what we call a story.

It is an obvious fact, which anyone can attest from his own experience, that the human memory is reliable only up to a certain point, which some men reach more quickly than others. If we wish to be certain about what we have seen and heard, we put it in writing, which cannot be affected by further personal experiences. Without written records, which take away the personal and the variable element in recollection – although they do not take away the same element in narration – the modern historian does not think there is any possibility of history; for he knows that the memory which is transmitted by word of mouth cannot preserve itself in that form which he thinks necessary to reconstruct the memory of the past. Unless the story acquires a fixed form – and it can be fixed only in writing – it is smoothed, polished, embellished in every repetition; it loses some details in every transmission, it acquires others from the imagination of the storyteller. For the storyteller is not satisfied with a bare recital of names; his characters must live, and their actions must take on movement and realism. Therefore he tells what they felt, what they said, what they did, what they wore, and such things, even though he has no memory of these details. Were he a historian, he ought not to do this; but he would stand astonished if we were to tell him so. I, he would tell us, am a storyteller, not a historian; I do not know what you mean by historian. If people want lists of names and dates, let them look at the royal archives; I tell them the story.

It is a fact that the modern idea of history does not go back beyond the Greeks, if it goes back that far; and it did not exist in the ancient Semitic world. The men of that world told the story, because it was the only way they knew in which the past could be reported. If we go back to a time when there were no official archives, then the past lived only in the story; and when men first began to write down the remembered past, they had only the official lists and stories as sources. Neither of these is what we call history. Geography and chronology are the eyes of history; if the modern historian cannot tell you when and where something happened, he will not call it a historical event, although he does not thereby deny that it happened. He means that it has no "historical record." But the storyteller is satisfied with "Once upon a time, in a country far away . . ." And why should he not be? What man or woman, even in these days of historical science, is unacquainted with the folklore of his family, his town, his parish, and the company for which he works? These are the stories which pass by word of mouth from generation to generation: not history, nor yet fiction, even if they are memories fleshed out by creative imagination. They are a part of the remembered past, the stories of those who are not great enough to have their history written, too great to be entirely forgotten.

We should not forget that the story preserved by oral tradition is not at all the same thing in a civilization which studies history and in a society in which men write little or not at all. We have studied these stories more closely in modern times, and we no longer look at them with the skeptical contempt which earlier scholars gave them. When the past is preserved only in story, the group memory shows itself more tenacious; we moderns are careless in telling our stories, because we know that anything really important will be put in writing. The ancient storytellers could preserve an account, even word for word, with more fidelity than we would think possible. Homer used to be thought little better than a fairy tale; now we know that he told us a good deal about the fall of Troy. Homer, of course, would not take this as a compliment; he wanted to be heard for his story, and not for any "historical facts" he might happen to relate. Let others write the history of the fall of Troy, if they wish; he sang its story, and he could not have written its history had he wanted to. But the modern historian knows that the stories of ancient times tell him far more about the remembered past than historians used to think.

Some are disturbed when they hear that the Old Testament gives us the stories of the remembered past of the Hebrews. Others greet these stories with the same skeptical contempt they give all stories, and deny them any claim to credibility; such an attitude is no longer possible to one who is acquainted with modern historical method. Still others have found it impossible to understand how religious belief could rest upon a "story." and they have detached the stories from what they call the "religious values" of the Old Testament. Others have thought it unworthy of God to tell, through human instruments, the story of the past; for God, who knows all things, would never tell a story, but would give us the complete and unvarnished factual account of the past. So He would, if He had not chosen to use human instruments in a human way. The men whom He used could tell a story, but they could not write a history; as we said above, if God wished to write a history, He would have to choose other instruments and, in this instance, other times and countries.

Why, we wonder, should the story be thought unworthy of God? Why should He refuse to stoop to that manner of narrating the past which is the universal human manner, and limit Himself austerely to the manner which is taught in the modern graduate school? The answer is no secret, and it is implicit in the unbelief of the skeptic and in the stout affirmation of the believer that the Old Testament is "historical fact"; we hesitate to attribute storytelling to God, because we fear that we shall charge Him with "historical error." Such a charge ignores the very nature of the story, as we all know it. "Historical fact" and "historical error" are modern concepts, formulated by modern historical science and defined in terms of that science and its methods; these concepts would have been unintelligible to the storyteller. The story, as we have been at pains to elaborate, is much more than a recounting of historical fact. It is the remembered past, remembered and told as it was significant, interesting; that the storyteller may narrate the past, he demands the right to be creative, and we grant him this right. The story has a function, and it fulfills that function without any reference to the modern concepts of "historical fact" and "historical error." To charge the storyteller with historical error is to make him a liar or a fool, and to render illegitimate the incalculable influence which the story has had in the history of human thought; it also denies to modern man the right to relate his own experiences and what he has heard of the experiences of others in the normal and accepted manner. No, the storyteller is, as he has always been, an essential actor in the human scene; let us permit him to do his work in his own way, and not think so meanly of him that we make him an unworthy instrument of God. There are some things which he cannot do, but there is much which he can do; and it is for what he can do that God employs him.

So much may be said to explain that the story of the Hebrews is not history as we understand the word. Now we must turn our attention to the singular character of the Hebrew story, the character which makes it unparalleled in the literature of the ancient Near East. The story, as such, is a detached item; the memory preserves incidents, and does not retain the past in a long consecutive account. The storyteller collects these incidents, but neither does the storyteller weave them into a consecutive account; he groups the incidents in "cycles," as they are called, revolving about an individual person, a particular group, a place. The stories thus assembled have no inner connection with each other, and they do not always fit neatly when they are put together; but this does not bother the storyteller. There are two incidents reported in which David met Saul for the first time, a story which must have been often told; but David can have met Saul for the first time only once. The Hebrew stories also are a collection of detached incidents; it is the higher unity into which they are woven that sets them off from other collections of oral traditions. In the

Old Testament we have, for the first time, the story of a people; and this story is continuous, moving toward a climax. The other Semitic peoples had no sense of history as an organic process; it was merely a series or, if the figure be preferred, a repetition of events revolving in the same orbit, with no term that could be foreseen. "The rivers run, but the sea is not filled." To the Hebrews the life of the race, the life of a people, was like the life of a man: unique, irreversible, moving toward a definite term. This they learned from no other ancient Semitic people.

To put it briefly and at once: the unifying principle of the Hebrew story is the action of God in the course of human events. Let us pause to recall the methods of the modern historian; for we must insist upon the difference between the Hebrew storyteller and the modern historian. To the modern historian, the action of God is not an "observable phenomenon"; he does not, as a historian, affirm or deny it, he simply cannot find it in strictly "historical" sources. In this he is quite correct; human deeds are recorded by human testimony, divine deeds by divine testimony. The Hebrew storyteller was also a prophet, in his own way; and the Jews, when they first arranged their sacred books in groups, called their storytellers "the early prophets," to distinguish them from the men of the word of the Lord, whom they called "the later prophets." The primary interest of the Hebrew storyteller is the action of God in human events, and not the events in themselves. We do not mean that the Hebrew story is not a record of human events. The writers of our biblical books collected stories, re-edited and rewrote the remembered past from their own God-centered point of view; but many of the stories which they used in composing the account were secular in origin and in character. These writers are the storytellers who have given the biblical story its peculiar form; and they were the men for whom the remembered past was the story of the action of God.

In the course of this book, we shall have to see what the story of God is; for it cannot be summed up in a single paragraph. But we ought to take a glance at the sort of material which the Hebrew storytellers wove into their account. There are stories of the origins of the world and of man, which were not written down until the beginning of historic times, at the earliest, and cannot preserve a proximate memory of the events recounted. There are family traditions of the Hebrew patriarchs, which were almost certainly preserved only by oral tradition for hundreds of years as detached stories. There are stories of Moses and his times, which preserve memories nearer the events; but we have little which we can be sure was written at the time of the events. The Hebrews lived in an age of writing, as we have noticed before, and it is no longer possible to say, as some once said, that Moses could not have written; in fact, it is impossible that he should not have written. But how are we to tell, in the mass of material which is "the books of Moses," what it is that he wrote? That the stories of the early age of man and of the patriarchs were put in writing in his time is a very good guess; beyond that, conjecture is less assured, and the stories of his own time which we read in the Old Testament are the work of later storytellers who used the existing memory of the past – partly in writing, no doubt, but largely in oral traditions. We have the stories of the years between Moses and David, which by their very form and traits exhibit themselves as the writing of popular stories which had been told by word of mouth. With Saul and David and Solomon we enter the period when the Hebrews, more securely settled in their own land, more conscious of their national unity, began, in all probability, to put together their remembered past in writing; and we meet stories which, again by their very external form and traits, show themselves as eyewitness accounts.

This is as it should be; a sense of history comes with civilization, a realization that the people and the nation have become a historical factor. A people which has advanced to this point makes a deliberate effort to preserve its own records; it is the same feeling which moves a man to keep a diary when he realizes that his daily life may have historical interest. The remarkable feature of the Hebrew story is not that this sense of history came late, but that it came early; there were other social and political groups like the Hebrews in the world of their time, but only the Hebrews exhibited this sense of history. The others are forgotten. Where is the history of the Philistines, the Edomites, the Moabites? The development of a sense of history, however, does not imply a change in the character of the record; the story still remains the form in which the past is remembered and reported. The Hebrew monarchies had their annals and their lists, like the monarchies of Egypt, Mesopotamia, and Syria; the Hebrew storytellers employed these written records, but they preferred the living story to the dead annals, because it was the living story which told of the action of God in the course of human events. The stories of the monarchy differ from the stories of earlier times because the memory of the past is nearer to the events; but the form and purpose of the story remain the same.

Now, when we look at these stories in detail and try to sift out the items which have been woven together, we see that they are generally stories which center upon persons; but these persons are not the kings and warriors who are the favorite heroes of popular tradition. The heroes are the men who were most concerned in the action of God in human events: kings and warriors, if they played a part in the story of God, but more frequently those in whom popular tradition, as a rule, has only an accessory interest. It may seem that much of what is told has little or no relation to what we have called the unifying principle of the Hebrew story. But the Hebrew storytellers, like all men of their trade, wanted a vivid and moving account, in which the persons thought and spoke and felt and acted; they could re-create the event in imagination, and they did so, for they knew that a bare statement of the thing which was their primary interest would have turned the story into a discourse, and into the most arid of all discourses, the sermon. So they wove their account out of human life as they knew it, and they preserved for us, with a realism all their own, the world and the men of their day: the scene in which the action of God was decisive.

It is easy to contrast the Hebrew view of the action of God in human events with the place of the gods in other ancient stories, especially in the stories of the Semitic kinsmen of the Hebrews. Certainly the gods are active in Homer; but no one will seriously compare the Homeric gods, who strive with each other over Troy and Hector, to the Lord of the Old Testament. In the pages of the literature of Mesopotamia one finds prosperity and victory attributed to the favor of the gods, adversity and defeat to their anger; such attributions arise from the conception of divinity which we sketched in the preceding chapter and, again, should not be compared with the Old Testament. The part which the Lord plays in the story of His people is like nothing ever related of the gods of any nation.

It is a commonplace in modern books on the Bible to say that "God reveals Himself in history." This commonplace admits a categorical denial: God does not reveal Himself in history. He does not reveal Himself in modern history, which is as profane a science as man has ever taught himself; the modern historian does his work without any reference to the celestial hypothesis. There are many things of which the modern historian cannot find the cause, but, as a historian, he would never think of invoking the Deity; it would be unscientific in the extreme. God did not reveal Himself in ancient history. The Greeks, when they reached intellectual maturity, knew how to estimate the place of the gods in the stories of Homer, in the myths and legends from which their tragedies were written; Euripides expressed the attitude toward "the gods of history" which was the attitude of the intelligent man of his time. God did not reveal Himself in the history of the ancient Semitic peoples. The Assyrian conqueror attributed his victories to Ashur, but Isaiah put his mind into words: "By the strength of my hand have I done it, and by my wisdom, for I have understanding." We have said that when the Assyrian worshiped Ashur, he worshiped himself. If "God reveals Himself in history," He did it only in the history of the Hebrews, and in the history of those who frankly admit that their religious beliefs are derived in part from Hebrew sources.

Must we appeal, then, to that peculiar religious insight which was the genius of the Hebrews? We have already tried to deal with this, and we have run up against a hard and ineradicable core of "otherness." If we say that the Hebrews saw God in history, do we mean that they saw Him as the thinker sees the conclusion in his premises? If so, then they were theologizing, rationalizing, they were interpreting history on the basis of beliefs already held and to be validated on other grounds. For the Hebrews, it may have been a brilliant intuition; but the modern man who is trained in historical method cannot follow this brilliant intuition, and he does not. If this be the Hebrew view of history, they did not "see" God in history, they projected Him into history, and we ought to call the process by its right name.

Before we go further, however, we ought to ask ourselves whether there is any reason why they should not project God into history: why they should not have deduced His present activity from what they observed, why they should not have "seen" this in one flash of brilliant intuition. There is nothing immoral in an interpretation of events; the most important historical work of recent years, that of Professor Toynbee, is such a projection, such a work of brilliant intuition. Nothing but such projections makes history intelligible, in the larger sense, and raises it above the level of the chronicle. If there is such a thing as religion, then there is such a thing as a religious interpretation of events; if not, then history has been secularized.

This would do, and we could accept the Hebrew theology of history as valid within its limitations, were it not that the basis of Hebrew belief would thus disappear. For in the hypothesis that "God reveals Himself in history," He did not reveal Himself elsewhere, and the Hebrews had nothing to project; and this is really what the commonplace means. What they "saw" in history was the reflection of their own minds; and their history ceases to be religious, in the proper sense of the term. The God of the Hebrews becomes one with Ashur and the gods of Homer, a figment of the creative imagination, more dignified and better behaved, but no more authentic. Let us not stultify our reason by such speculations. We can trace the origins of the gods of the Greeks and of the ancient Semitic peoples; they are the reflections of human experience, individual and collective, and they do not rise above the level of the men who created them. Where in human experience shall we find that tremendous, vital personality who dominates the pages of the Old Testament? Whose image and likeness does He represent? What manner of thinking has ever devised a god who runs so consistently counter to the universal beliefs, desires, and hopes of the race? There is nothing in Hebrew history to reveal any other kind of God than the kind which the history of every other people has revealed; the Hebrew writers could have projected God into history only if they knew Him by an extraordinary experience, the mystic awareness of which we spoke above.

Given this mystic awareness, this sense of a real personality, we can then speak of the Hebrew story as a projection of God into history. The Hebrew story is an interpretation of events, but an interpretation formed according to the knowledge of the God who asserts that He is the master of events. The Hebrews did not see their history and deduce His present activity; they knew Him, and were forced to admit His activity, for the God whom they knew was an active God, with an activity like that of no other god. The Hebrews did not see God in history; they saw history in God. It makes a difference which comes first.

This, we said, was the primary interest of the Hebrew storyteller, this was his story. Of this he can tell us, because he knows something we do not know. The mere reconstruction of the remembered past, the synthesis of "historical fact" and the exclusion of "historical error," is the work of any well-trained scholar, but the scholar cannot tell us the story of the activity of God in human events, because he does not know God. This was the peculiar gift of the Hebrew storyteller, and his story is of far more consequence than mere history.

Here is a point where biblical belief and modern thinking appear to diverge, and that rather hopelessly. Shall we call the Hebrew story revolutionary? Does it not threaten to destroy the nicely established patterns of modern thought? For we cannot submit the story of God to the ordinary methods of criticism. We may resent the intrusion of God into the story of mankind; and so we will prattle of history and criticism and theology and interpretation, always evading the basic issue: if these men knew God, their story imposes itself upon us with frightful necessity. If, enlightened by their knowledge of God, they interpreted the course of human events, then their knowledge will shatter any history and philosophy which fails to reckon with their interpretation of events. If God is active in human events, then we, for all our science and learning, risk failing to observe the greatest of all realities. And so it is easier to rationalize the Hebrew story into simple history as we understand the word, and to force it into the framework of our own preconceived ideas; if we make the Old Testament a mine of historical facts, then it will mean no less to us, and no more, than any other chapter in the human story. In this, as in so many things, the modern mind stumbles at the threshold of the Bible. Perhaps we must free ourselves from the constriction of our habitual patterns of thought if we are to look at this strange, obscure, revolutionary story which the ancient Hebrews told: the story of God and man.

COSMIC ORIGINS

UNTIL a century or two ago, the origins of the world in which we live were no problem. Men opened their Bibles to the first page, and there they read that God, in the beginning, created heaven and earth. The earth at first was void and empty, covered with darkness; but God spoke, and there was light. Then, during six days in succession, God spoke His creative Fiat each day; and there appeared land, seas, sun, moon and stars, vegetation, birds and fish, animals, and finally man, in the image and likeness of God. At the end of six days, God rested on His own Sabbath, and the universe, now established, began to run its secular course. In answer to the question of the origins of the universe, men made an act of faith.

How much the mind of modern civilization has changed can be seen by looking at almost any encyclopedia, any book of universal knowledge. There, in text and pictures, is presented vividly the growth of the visible universe from a cloud of gas and a blob of mud. In a few sweeping strokes, the reader is carried through billions of years, during which the forces inherent in material substance finally brought out the form of the world in which we live; and these forces, still active, are carrying the world yet further. For our world is not a finished product; the slow development which brought it to this point is still going on, and in more billions of years it will alter the face of nature beyond recognition. It is a majestic panorama.

At the moment, let us turn our attention to one point alone

which the confrontation of these two pictures suggests: the question of the origins of the world is no longer a religious question. The natural sciences have answered the question by their own methods, and the answer is not the answer which we read in the opening pages of the Bible. The formation of the visible world takes longer than the Bible allows. If one calculates the total number of years from the beginning, as the items may be gathered from various parts of the Old Testament, one reaches the sum of about 4000 years from the creation to the beginning of the Christian era, with variations according to some differences in calculation, and according to whether one reads one's Bible in Hebrew, Greek, or the Pentateuch of the Samaritans. But the variations are not significant; in no calculation is there any room for the eons postulated by geology. Light cannot have been created before luminous bodies, nor the earth before the celestial bodies. Botanical and zoological species did not appear all at once. Now the natural scientists, as such, are not interested in overthrowing traditional faith; they have reached their conclusions by thorough investigations and careful argument, tested and criticized over many years by a large number of competent men. In effect, they say: Here is what the earth itself tells us about its age and development. This is not what we read in our Bible. How the Bible is to be explained is not our problem; but the evidence from which we argue is such that we cannot honestly deny our conclusions.

Many people, overwhelmed by the solemn presentation of scientific data, have been convinced that the question of the origins of the world is a purely scientific question; the Bible and the Church, in which they find no investigation comparable to that carried on by the natural sciences, have, they believe, nothing to say on the matter. And so they have, regretfully, abandoned their faith in the religious explanation of the material world, and with it much of their faith in what the Bible says about anything which touches the fields of the natural sciences. Others have closed their eyes to the difference; they believe the biblical account, whatever it may mean, but their thinking is determined by the natural sciences. Some natural scientists, in the youthful flush of their enthusiasm, have thought that the Bible and revealed religion were finally unmasked as a fraud by the sciences; and some theologians, warmed by imputations of this sort, have unwisely attempted to meet the scientists on their own ground, with unfortunate results for the dignity of theology. The Bible cannot be defended by denying demonstrated scientific truth. On the other hand, neither can science be defended by the premature publication, on an often sensational level, of speculative scientific opinion. Many scientists have only themselves to blame if such scientific popularizations are called the contemporary form of the cosmogonic myth. In such presentations, quite assured conclusions and quite unfounded conjecture are mixed in a manner which makes them indistinguishable to anyone who is not a trained scientist; the popular reader gives a breathless assent to all that he reads when it is written with such pontifical assurance, especially if it be illustrated by three-color plates showing just what happened. The act of faith in the thesis of cosmic origins is still made, but it is offered to another source of authentic doctrine. Theologians who venture to mingle certain truths and unfounded conjecture on the popular level are rightly rebuked by their colleagues, and they may even feel the heavy hand of ecclesiastical authority; the scientist, of course, abominates such thought control, although one wonders whether the progress of science would really be impeded by some kind of board to screen popular publications.

Happily, we have survived into a day when science and theology no longer speak to each other in the language of fishmongers. Except for a few occasional outbursts of petulance on one side or the other, scientists and theologians have learned a healthy respect for each other and for the methods employed in each field. We have learned that the question of cosmic origins does not cease to be a religious question because it has become a scientific question. We know that earlier generations were wrong when they employed the Bible as a pseudo-scientific source; but let us not think too hardly of them, they could not have known better. We know that science can neither assert nor deny the answer to the religious question, because science cannot go beyond the level of the phenomena which it observes. Science must still begin with a void and empty waste over which darkness broods.

No matter how far back science pushes its investigations, no matter what it finds before that empty waste, it will never reach the level of the first chapter of Genesis. We are grateful to science for its gift of the knowledge of the world in which we live — while somewhat bemused by the gadgets it has given us — but it cannot answer the question which is answered in the first chapter of Genesis: an answer which is as relevant to human life as all the natural sciences put together.

We shall not catch the significance of the first chapter of Genesis unless we put this chapter against the background of the ideas of the time when it was written, and see the channels in which the author's thought moves. We must be clear, first of all, that the chapter is in no sense a scientific document. The author was as ignorant of the natural sciences as any man of his time, and it is idle to speak of a conflict between Genesis and science when Genesis says nothing about the objects of science. He sees the visible universe as the ancient Semitic peoples saw it: the earth is a disk, covered by the inverted bowl of the sky. The disk floats upon the limitless waters of "the lower abyss," which erupt at intervals into springs and fountains, and which are the source of the sea which surrounds the earth. In the sky are the heavenly bodies, revolving in their orbits, and above the sky are the storehouses of rain, snow, wind. Light and darkness are imagined as distinct entities, each with its proper place of repose, from which they go out to cover the earth in their regular turn. Above the sky is the heaven, the seat of divinity. This is the visible universe as it appears to the child or the savage, to anyone who is innocent of the explorations of geology, astronomy, and their sister sciences. This view goes no farther than the eye can see; without instruments of precision to observe and calculate, it is impossible to go farther. It is manifestly absurd to think that Genesis tells us anything about the structure of the visible universe, or exhibits the faintest notion of the processes of its development. It may be a little more difficult to understand that, for the answer to the religious question of the origins of the universe, it is not necessary to go any farther.

More than this, the account of Genesis shows some acquaintance with the Mesopotamian myth of creation; at the risk of boring the reader, we must say something about this myth. As in Genesis, the universe first appears in the Mesopotamian myth as a formless chaos; but this chaos is personified in two divine beings, male and female, the father and mother of all the gods. Through countless eons they beget their offspring, the famous deities of Mesopotamia. A quarrel breaks out between the progenitors and their children; the male deity is slain, and there is war between his spouse and the children. Now let us look more closely at this female warrior, the mother of all gods. She is a monster, described as unspeakably and terribly hideous, gigantic in size and awful in strength. She brings to her aid a host of demons as hideous as herself, whom she spawns from her unfailing womb. She is chaos personified; and the Mesopotamians saw chaos in the roaring waters of the restless sea, which, impelled by high winds, would attack the shore and wreck their cities and farms even far inland. They saw, much like the modern scientist, the sea as the mother of all living things; but the fertile sea is chaotic and hostile, she devours her offspring. Were she permitted, she would reclaim the land and the life which she has created. So here in the myth is the cosmic struggle between the sea, the mother of all and the enemy of all, and the forces of life and order.

The gods, the children of the monster, do not easily find a defender, for she is a dreadful enemy. There is no doubt that various gods played the role of the hero in the various forms of the myth; in the Babylonian form, which we possess almost completely, the hero is Marduk, the god of the great city of Babylon. It was not unfitting that Babylon, the "City of Light" of ancient Mesopotamia, should see her god as the creative deity, who makes order victorious over chaos. The combat is joined, and Marduk slays the monster. Now Marduk is manifested as the creative deity; for earth, sky, sun, moon, stars are fashioned from the gigantic carcass of the monster. Presumably, also, living creatures are fashioned; but this portion of the myth has not been preserved. Man is made of the blood of a god, an ally of the monster, who dies for his crime. The parts of the universe — earth, underworld, sea, upper air, heavenly bodies — are assigned to the various cosmic deities with whom they are traditionally associated; and the whole world becomes a palace of Marduk, the creative deity, the greatest of all the gods.

We mentioned earlier that the myth of creation was associated with the cultic myth of fertility in the ancient Semitic religions. The struggle between order and chaos, light and darkness was enacted annually in the cycle of the seasons, and represented in the cultic myth. While the myth is grotesque to the point of absurdity in many respects, it is a dramatic expression of some fundamental beliefs, and one of these beliefs is dualism: the thesis that reality is a conflict between two equal and opposing forces. One may call them good and evil, but it really makes no difference what name one gives them. In this myth, the struggle between order and chaos is constant in material reality; the cycle gives the victory to one, and then to the other. Neither ever emerges finally supreme, and reality remains this unstable equilibrium of conflicting forces. Man survives by adjusting himself, by submitting himself to the equilibrium. He does not worship the monster of chaos, because he expects nothing from the monster; he can only feel assured that the balance of forces which he sees, while it is not enough to give him a sense of perfect security, is enough to protect him from the maw of chaos, which would swallow him entirely if it were not restrained by the forces which he worships as his gods. But could he ever be sure that the forces of chaos, perpetually gnawing at the natural order which preserved him, might not break out of their bounds and make the earth once more a void and empty waste?

We say that the author of the first chapter of Genesis was acquainted with this myth: not merely because Genesis exhibits the same simple conception of the material universe, but rather because the myth was diffused throughout the ancient Near East, and the Hebrews could not have been ignorant of it unless they had lived under glass. Furthermore, there are more explicit allusions to the myth elsewhere in the Old Testament, as we shall have occasion to remark very shortly. Against this background, the Hebrew account of origins can scarcely be anything else but a counterstatement to the myth of creation. The similarity of the imaginative pattern is matched by a total dissimilarity of basic concepts. The Hebrew author puts the creative Deity, as clearly as he can, outside the cycles of natural forces. He is no one of them nor all of them. The Hebrew author enumerates all the natural forces in which deity was thought to reside, and of all of them he says simply that God made them. Consequently, he eliminates all elements of struggle on the cosmic level; the visible universe is not an uneasy balance of forces, but it is moderated by one supreme will, which imposes itself with effortless supremacy upon all that it has made. By preference the author speaks of the created work rather than of the creative act, because he wishes to emphasize the fact that the creative Deity, unlike Marduk, has not had to win his supremacy by combat with an equal.

Men have long wondered what the author of Genesis may have meant by his six days and his peculiar order of the works of creation, in which light and vegetation precede the sun. Did he mean merely to signify that the religious unit of time, the week with six days and the Sabbath rest, was as primeval as creation itself? If he did, he chose an involved way to express it, but we must accustom ourselves, when we read the Old Testament, to startling turns of expression. We may, perhaps, find the key in the myth of the struggle between order and chaos. The author certainly wished to remove the idea of struggle; may we not suppose that he wished to depict an orderly creation? The orderly activity of the workman who pursues his craft day after day and takes his Sabbath rest when the work is finished was, we may suppose, the best example of such orderly activity which he knew; and he did not think it unworthy to be attributed to the work of the creative Deity. It is a simple picture; but we have learned enough about Hebrew writing to know that the storyteller works through imaginative construction. Against the imaginative construction of the myth, with its cosmic deities locked in mortal combat, he presents his picture of the creative Deity working as calmly as the craftsman in his shop. There is no more danger that this creative Deity will fall before the monster of chaos than there is that the chair will devour the carpenter. It is imaginative, but it is far from pointless.

The picture of a calm Deity, presiding in majesty over an orderly universe, is not, of course, quite the same picture either as that which the ancient mythologers formed of the visible world, nor as that which historic man has formed of his struggle with the environment. This is an important feature of the picture: that, after each work and after the whole creative process, God sees that it is good. The first chapter of Genesis is an account of origins alone, not an exposition of the Hebrew mind on the visible universe in its entirety; we shall have to point out that the Hebrews were as well aware as any men of nature red in tooth and claw. But the great and the decisive difference in their view of origins is that the qualities of the visible universe which make men speak of it as disorderly or hostile are not primal. God made the world a home for man, which man was to rule as the viceroy of God; and He made it apt for human habitation, submissive to the will of the highest of his creatures. This it could not be if it were the dualistic world of the myth, in which the forces of order and of chaos had fought themselves to a standoff. In such a dualistic world, evil is inherent in the nature of the visible universe, as primal as good – indeed, in the ancient Semitic myth, evil came first, and good was evolved from it. The author of Genesis saw that this is an impossibility. If this be true, then the history of the world and of man is an endless revolution in the same orbit; good must finally fall before evil, even if it falls to rise again. But the creative deity, the agent of good and order, will never rule his universe, for in chaos he has an adversary as great as himself.

Let us not treat this view of things too casually; it is pessimism of the darkest hue, but it has a specious realism about it. It takes the world as it is, and refuses to be stampeded into hopeless dreams of altering it. If the gods themselves cannot break out of the cosmic struggle, much less can man. Let man take what pieces fall to his lot in this titanic combat, and seek no more. The hero Gilgamesh searched for the plant of life and found it, only to lose it by an unforeseen carelessness. A goddess consoled him with the admonition that the gods had apportioned life to themselves, death to man. Therefore let Gilgamesh anoint his head and enjoy himself, for this is the portion of mankind. There is a thorough concordance between the Mesopotamian view of cosmic origins and the philosophy which the myth and the cult express, as we have outlined it earlier.

The biblical writers, on the other hand, view evil as an intruder. Speculatively, perhaps, there may not at first appear to be much difference between the two; do the Hebrews escape in this manner the recurring dualism and its consequent despair? We touch here upon the riddle of the universe, and we cannot expect at this point to set forth the Hebrew answer to this riddle, for it is made of many beliefs. But let us note well now, and recall it at the proper time, that the Hebrew view of origins presents a creative deity who is supreme, who has no equal, no rival; if there is a combat, it is not a cyclic struggle between two equals. Evil is not a datum as primal as good, whatever be its source. The theory of origins which begins with cosmic order can visualize a return to cosmic order. The myth can visualize no such return, for cosmic order was not primary, and there is no supreme will with the power to effect it. The Hebrew view of origins is the foundation of hope.

We think that these ideas are of the highest importance in the first chapter of Genesis, and therefore it is not without surprise, nor even altogether without dismay, that we find a dozen allusions elsewhere in the Old Testament to the cosmic struggle between the creative deity and the monster of chaos. Let this one from the twenty-seventh chapter of Isaiah illustrate the type: "In that day, the Lord will smite with His sword, great and strong and hard, Leviathan the swift serpent, Leviathan the writhing serpent; and He will kill the dragon in the sea." Is it not something of a shock to find that the Hebrew prophet has quoted a poet of Ugarit almost word for word? For the poet of Ugarit wrote that Baal would smite "Lotan the swift serpent, Lotan the writhing serpent, Shalyat of the seven heads." There is no doubt that Leviathan or Lotan is a monster, a dragon, an embodiment of the wild forces of chaos. The poet of Job tells us, in Chapter 38, that by the power of God the sea was stilled, and that God enclosed the sea with doors, saying: Thus far shall you go, and no farther; and here the proud tossing of your billows must halt. It is through such allusions as these, which could not have been detected a hundred years ago, that we know that the Hebrews were acquainted with the myths of the ancient Semitic world; and we know by the same means that the first chapter of Genesis was not the only account of creation which circulated among the ancient Hebrews.

We can find in these mythological allusions the idea, vague but not without definition, that creation is a continuing process. God marshals the hosts of the heavens each day; He sends forth wind and rain from their storehouses; He breathes life into the animal world, as He did on the day of their creation. When we assemble all these allusions, we are inclined to wonder whether the Sabbath rest which the author of Genesis attributes to his creative deity is altogether in harmony with Hebrew thought patterns.

The question which thus arises in our mind will arise again before we finish with the beliefs of the Hebrews; and we must recall our earlier remarks about Hebrew thinking. We do not meet in the Old Testament systematic, logical constructions of thought; we meet ideas expressed through creative imagery. The educated Western mind resists what appears to be a lack of logic and consistency; when ideas collide, one must give way. Hence we are likely to say, quite often, that the Bible contradicts itself. The ancient Hebrew might answer: Of course it does; is it possible to speak about God and the world without contradicting oneself? For God is too great to be comprehended in any synthesis of thought, however logical it may be. In the Old Testament we meet what is frankly creative imagery; and the image does not pretend to make the reality perfectly intelligible. It presents what can be grasped in one glance from one point of view, and leaves room for other glances from other points.

We have discovered that the Hebrews looked at cosmic origins from more than one point of view. The point of view which appears in the first chapter of Genesis sees the world in its primal and original state, and it refuses, in virtue of its knowledge of the creative Deity, to admit the struggle of cosmic forces which the myth represents. The other point of view, never so formally expressed, but found in many more allusions, sees the world as it is, with the original cosmic order gone; this view is more conscious of the crosscurrents in nature which upset human designs. At the same time, it exhibits the basic belief in one supreme will; but it does not shun the imagery of the conquering creative deity. For it can speak of the cosmic order as something constantly achieved, and of the victory of the Lord over the forces of chaos as daily renewed. This second view seems to have been the more common Hebrew view, and probably the older.

But observe that this view does not exhibit the cyclic conflict, and it has no room for an uneasy balance of forces. It looks to an ultimate victory of the Lord of creation over the forces of chaos, and a restoration to the original cosmic order; this we shall have to consider later. At the moment, as we noticed earlier, we are not concerned here with the origins of cosmic disorder; be it enough to remark that, in the view of creation as a continuing process, as a constantly recurring victory of the creative Deity, Chaos and all that it represents are not primal. Hence we think it is clear that the two views are, by our standards of logic, complementary, not contradictory; but it probably would not annoy the Hebrew writers much if we called them contradictory.

In the Hebrew view of cosmic origins, the visible universe does not appear as a primary datum which either explains itself, or is inexplicable. The ancient mythologer and the modern scientist have this in common: neither can by observation and analysis go behind that vast and formless waste, full of gods in the ancient myth, of protoplasm in modern science. This is the end of the road, the bottomless abyss at which the mind stops. Christian philosophy thinks it can cross the gap, but we may wonder whether it would ever make the flight without the wings it borrows from revealed doctrine. For this flight is from creatures to God; neither mythology nor science can make it. Aristotle, the master of them that know, and the master of modern Christian philosophers, did not make it. For him, the visible universe was an eternal reality, the Prime Moved as opposed to the Prime Mover. The notion of an absolute beginning is a notion which the human mind finds very hard to swallow; St. Thomas Aquinas, not the dullest of men, did not think that the mind could form the idea by itself. Whether the biblical imagery contains the idea is not an irrelevant question. Do we suppose that the author gave any thought to the void and empty waste which first appears in his picture, which the creative Deity formed into the visible world?

The picture of the evolution of the visible universe from an unformed mass is one which the biblical writer shares both with mythology and with modern science; it is not this which makes his imagery distinctive. We have attempted to point out the gulf which separates him from the ideas of the cosmic myth, despite certain common basic assumptions. But it is not at all clear that he thought that the void and empty waste was the first term, so to speak, of the activity of the creative Deity. If he thought so, he was rather careful not to say so. "The heavens and the earth" which God created in the beginning are, everywhere in Hebrew speech, the heavens and the earth which we see, and not a formless waste; there is no reason to suppose that the words have any other meaning here than that which they have everywhere. The first scene in his picture is the "divine wind" soaring over the abyss: the wind, which we call the spirit, the breath of God, the principle of life, about to breathe the divine spark into this inert mass. Before that he says nothing, draws no picture. Does it not appear that his mind also met the blank which the human mind has always met at this point? Yet he could go farther, because the God whom he saw creating was not within this inert mass, nor anywhere within the visible universe; He was a living personality above and beyond it, surpassing it; He was in the beginning, and He was God. Since he wrote, much has been thought and said on the subject; and the Church now proposes, as an article of faith, that God created the world from nothing. Some think that the author of Genesis must have seen this article of faith; we think he did not, because he did not express it, but we are sure that the article reposes upon his vision of the creative Deity.

In a way, he does describe a creation from nothing; but he does it in his own way. The Catholic doctrine of creation presupposes a philosophy of nature of which this ancient writer had not the slightest idea. "Nothing" is an abstract conception which is not learned with the A B C's. To the ancient Hebrew, as we have remarked earlier, reality was apprehended as concrete, sensible, and thus with form, color, depth. For him a formless waste, a void and empty desolation was a denial of the reality which he knew. And he denied to this empty waste the reality which was foremost in his mind: the reality of divinity which it had in the myth. This formless waste is not the same thing as our abstract concept of nothing; chaos was not an imagined embodiment of "nothing," but an imaginary projection of the senseless wild force which man can see in the raging waves of the sea, beating against its shore like a monster charging at the bars of its cage. Here was chaos, restrained from devouring the earth only by the chains with which the good Lord had mercifully bound it. Let Him relax His control for an instant, and the monster would be upon us; were it to escape, it would be the destruction of all that is real, all that is good. The tossing billows of the abyss exhibit nothing of that form and color and depth, nothing of the life which the wind of God breathes. It is imagery once more, but it has its point. The important truth, to the Hebrew, was the elimination of the cosmic struggle, or, if its imagery be retained, the absolute supremacy of the creative Deity over the forces of chaos. This is as close as the concrete thinking of the Hebrews came to the statement of the absolute supremacy of God over the forces of nature which is contained in the doctrine of creation from nothing.

Whence came this peculiarly Hebrew view of the origins of the world? Some have called it a "purification" of the ancient Semitic cosmic myth: the myth, they say, is purged of a multitude of gods and their combat, and adapted to the monotheistic belief of the Hebrews. This might pass, were it not that the multitude of the gods and their combat are the essence of the myth; if the myth is "purged" of these, it is purged of content, and nothing remains except the external framework, the picture of the world as a disk under a globe, which is not mythological. We cannot find, in any known Semitic cosmic myth, anything which can be called a source of the first chapter of Genesis, and we are not likely to do so. We shall have to seek its source in the Hebrew mind.

In former times, many of the orthodox thought that the writer was granted a true vision of the cosmic process, or that he described what he had heard from the mouth of God Himself; and we cannot be sure that this understanding of the passage has disappeared entirely in our day. If this be true, then it is remarkable that God should adopt the imaginative view of the visible universe which is proper to the culture of the writer, and formulate His account on the basis of that view. It is, we think, sufficiently clear that the details of the account are the work of the creative imagination, not of divine revelation nor of scientific research. In these details the author did not rise above his own cultural level. Yet he rose far above his level in his conception of the creative Deity. His imagery we can trace in the literature of the ancient Near East; his God we cannot. We shall have to recall what we said earlier about the experiential knowledge of God which must be postulated to explain the element of "revelation" in the Old Testament. We think that this is well illustrated here. The chapter shows a realization of God as a distinct personality, who does not emerge from nature and is not a part of natural processes; this realization transforms the Hebrew view of cosmic origins. It enables the author to make the leap from the formless waste to the creative Deity, from science and philosophy to religion: a leap of faith. But this experiential knowledge of God contributes no scientific information; it does not alter the childish picture of the visible universe, but it essentially alters one's view of the relations between God and the visible universe, whatever theories one may entertain about the structure and development of the visible universe.

Some would call this mythologizing; after all, does not the author project the personal being in which he believes into the cosmic process? It would be myth of a much higher level, but of the same stuff; for it is not observation. In a way, it is perhaps unfortunate that the word "myth" is totally expelled by Catholics from the catalogue of biblical literary forms. Myth, in common usage, signifies the personalization of natural phenomena as divine beings; myth in this sense cannot be admitted in the Old Testament. But should we restrict the word "myth" to this common usage? If we mean by myth an imaginative representation of an abstract truth – and this is the sense in which Plato used myth – then the creation account could be designated as "myth," and perhaps more clearly by this name than by any other. Not a few modern writers have attempted to use "myth" in a wider and, they say, a more accurate sense than that which it has in common usage; after all, the Greek word from which "myth" is derived means simply "story." There is no reason why God cannot present an abstract truth by means of a story; the Lord Jesus did so, and it is a mere accident of language that we call His little stories "parables" and not "myths." But as long as the common idiom retains its force, it is better to abstain from the use of the words "myth" or "mythological thinking" to describe the first chapter of Genesis. For the name is, in the context of modern speech, misleading. The author does not project his personal God into the cosmic process. What distinguishes his cosmogony – and the whole Hebrew view of cosmic origins – from ancient Semitic myth is that this personal God completely transcends the cosmic process. The author really has no precise and philosophically elaborate concept of the relations between creator and creature; this he knows, that their being and their nature are separated by an impassable chasm. The God whom he knows cannot be a creator like Marduk; and imagery which fails to represent His absolute supremacy is false, and any view of the world which omits its utter dependence upon this absolute supremacy is so inadequate as to be false. Like the cosmic myth, such a view makes gods out of creatures.

Here precisely is the point of collision between the religious view of cosmic origins and the scientific view, a point upon which the faith of many has been shattered. Is it possible that the enlightened modern mind can learn of cosmic origins, which science has so brilliantly illuminated, from a religious document of such blatant scientific ignorance? If God were to tell us about the origins of the universe, does it not seem that He ought to tell us at least some of the many facts which are so essential to an intelligent view of these origins? Therefore many, thinking that God ought to do this, and misled by a false judgment about the significance of the external details of the biblical cosmogony, have concluded that we cannot look for knowledge in ignorance. Modern man has, for better or worse, wedded himself to the scientific method; a return to the biblical view of origins seems to involve an abandonment of that which makes our modern world what it is. They do not see how they can return to the Bible without casting themselves adrift intellectually, and deserting practically all that they know to be true; that way madness lies, and it is easier for them to treat Genesis as a noble refinement of the cosmic myth.

But we have to remember that we are men before we are scientists. When Laplace said that he had no need of the hypothesis of God, he said as clearly as he could that science as such is atheistic – or nontheistic, if one prefers. We mentioned earlier that God is said to reveal Himself in history, and we found that the remark is so misleading as to be false. Its companion adage is that "God reveals Himself in nature"; this adage also admits some explanation. God's existence can be known from nature; but the natural sciences, as they have been historically pursued, show that, the more closely and exactly nature is studied, the more it recommends itself as self-subsistent and self-explanatory, with no need of "that hypothesis." Now, as in Mesopotamia five thousand years ago, the creature wears the mask of the creator which the clever human mind has put upon it. Once science is given the datum of an existing universe, it seems able to examine the phenomena and explain them to its own satisfaction without once appealing to the celestial hypothesis. It is tempting to believe that the reality which does not disclose itself to the scientific method is no reality at all; and it must be more than coincidence that so many natural scientists have thought so.

In so thinking, they identify human thinking with the scientific method; and this is a fallacy, if we are men before we are scientists. Because science need take no attitude toward God, it does not follow that the scientist must not. If reality is larger than his observation, as a man he cannot afford to ignore it, even if that larger reality will not advance his science. Paradoxically, many men of modern science readily go along with the ancient Semitic myth of cosmic origins in accepting the universe as a datum which needs no explanation. They have, with the ancients, found the supreme reality within the system of nature. In their own way, they adore this system; they write about its processes with something of the mystic glow we find in St. Bernard when he writes about the love of God. And most of all they adore that being who is supreme in nature, the microcosmos who incorporates in himself all the divine attributes of nature: Man. The name of this religion is Humanism, and it frankly imposes man upon us as the supreme reality. "Man only shalt thou adore, and him only shalt thou serve" is a very close paraphrase of the first commandment of this religion. There is no middle course; if one does not rise above nature with the author of Genesis, one falls back into the cosmic myth.

Humanism is by no means a necessary product of the pursuit of the natural sciences; the Hebrew affirmation of the creative Deity neither advances scientific knowledge nor retards it. We have noticed that modern theology no longer treats the Bible as a source of pseudo-scientific knowledge. The line between reason and faith, between natural science and theology, can never be drawn with that precision which we would wish, but it can be drawn clearly enough to allow human reason to range at liberty within its proper field. Should man attempt to identify either theology or scientific knowledge with the whole of human thought and experience, a deplorable clash must result. This need not be; but, men being what they are, it seems vain to hope that this ideal harmony will ever be realized.

Hence the conflict between the Hebrew account of origins and the cosmogonic myth embodies a constant tension in the human mind. We are not, as we have already remarked, concerned with vindicating Hebrew beliefs, but merely with setting them forth; it is plain, however, that the Hebrew belief in the creative Deity cannot be compounded with any ideas of the self-sufficiency of man and of nature. Self-sufficiency keeps recurring, in one form or another, in religion, philosophy, and science; and there seems to be no convincing demonstration of its falseness except the hard facts of experience. As long as the cosmic myth realizes for us the goods of the material universe, we are not inclined to question the reality and the power of the gods of the cosmos. If they fail, then we either despair or submit ourselves to the God who was in the beginning, and who does not change or fail with the world which He created by His word.

HUMAN ORIGINS

IT IS surprising that the question of human origins is so lightly treated in the myths of the ancient Semitic peoples. In Mesopotamia, man was made of clay mixed with the blood of a god, a mingling of the terrestrial and the celestial; it was the Mesopotamian affirmation of the paradox of human nature. For man is a paradox in his biological community with the lower animals, while he is divided from them by an impassable psychic barrier. We have no trace of a Mesopotamian myth in which the creation of man appears as more than an allusion, almost casual. This offhand dismissal of the subject in Semitic myths brings the Hebrew account of human origins, by contrast, into sharp relief. For the Hebrew account is thoroughly Hebrew and, as far as we know, thoroughly original; and our experience with the cosmic myths of the ancient Semitic peoples does not lead us to think that the Hebrew account will ever lose its originality, whatever may be discovered.

The account of human origins is found in the second and third chapters of Genesis, and it forms a story which is independent of the cosmic story in the first chapter; the literary seam between the two accounts occurs in the middle of the fourth verse of the second chapter. The second chapter is often called the "second creation account," but it is manifestly no such thing. Here the creation of the visible universe is mentioned only by allusion; the interest of the chapter is in the origin not of the world, but of man. And the interest is less in the origin of man as a species than in the origin of the two sexes; the creation of the woman and the statement of the relationship between man and woman are the climax to which the whole second chapter leads. In the third chapter, these two primal human beings, dwelling happily in their innocent nakedness in a garden which God has planted, disobey the rules of the garden and are ejected from it; the transition from happy innocence to the world of human experience which we know is obvious. The third chapter tells why the world is in its present condition, and not the "paradise of delight" in which God first established man.

It is remarkable that this account of human origins is not certainly mentioned again in the Old Testament before Ecclesiasticus and the Wisdom of Solomon, written in the last two centuries before the beginning of the Christian era. One would think that the Hebrews shared what appears to be the indifference of the ancient Semitic world to the origins of the race; God made it, and what else is there to say? But it is more peculiar that the biblical view of evil – of which we shall have much more to say – never appeals to this account. We do not mean to suggest that there is any opposition; indeed, we hope to show that this story is entirely in harmony with the biblical view as expressed elsewhere. But we cannot help wondering why it is not mentioned, and we cannot find a reason.

There is one allusion which we cannot let pass without notice. In the twenty-eighth chapter of the book of Ezekiel the prophet, we read of a marvelous being who dwelt in Eden, the garden of God, "full of wisdom, complete in beauty, perfect in your ways, dwelling among the cherubim." When some unspecified guilt was found in this being, he was expelled from Eden. The similarity between the two stories is striking; more striking are the differences in detail. For Ezekiel clothes his being with precious stones and places him on a holy hill of God; but there are no trees in his story, and no woman. It is really impossible to suppose that Ezekiel is rewriting the story of Genesis, although some interpreters have insisted that this is true; for we ought to be able to find some reason why Ezekiel should have modified the story, and we can find no reason. The conclusion recommends itself that the prophet has preserved another account of primitive man and his fall from grace; and thus we may conjecture that the story of human origins was told in more than one form among the Hebrews, with variations in detail. This should not surprise us; after all, both the author of Genesis and Ezekiel lived a long time after the first appearance of the race, and after the first appearance of the Hebrew account of human origins. But Ezekiel uses the story as a parable of the king of Tyre, not for its own sake; and thus he illustrates the apparent indifference to the question which we observe elsewhere.

The first chapter of Genesis also lists man among the works of God, and says little more. But this little is of great significance; for man appears as the supreme work of God, in the divine image and likeness. We may guess – for we cannot do much more – that the divine image and likeness meant, to the author, those qualities which enable man, under God, to assume the rule of the lower creatures: qualities which we call intelligence and free choice. The Hebrews, who did not distinguish the psychic powers of man in this way, saw the difference between man and the lower animals in this, that man rules the lower animals: he tames them, directs their vitality to his own purposes. A similar idea is expressed in the second chapter, where man is shown, by a parade of the lower animals, that there is not among them "a helper meet for him"; but the idea of the divine image and likeness is not here expressed. The Mesopotamian blood of the gods also expresses the community of man with the gods, although the Hebrew mind rejected this too gross conception of divinity. But man comes to life, in the second chapter of Genesis, when God breathes into him the breath of life. The author may have meant to indicate here also the superiority of man over the lower animals, for he does not speak of God inspiring life into them; but the poet of Psalm 103 (104) did not scruple to speak of God communicating His spirit to the animals also. This detail does not alter the common biblical conception of man as the lord of creation. It is very late in Hebrew thought when Ecclesiastes, who is in many ways a special case, wonders whether there is one spirit in man and in beasts.

The condition of man at his creation is described vaguely, but the description is obviously intended to indicate a state of primitive peace and security. Man dominates the world of the animals; he lives in a garden, such as was attached to the palaces of the kings and the wealthy in the ancient world. He is free from toil and mortality, for these do not appear until after his crime. Most significant of all is the intimacy with God which he enjoys; God walks in the garden in the cool of the evening as the lord of the manor strolls over his acres to refresh himself after the heat of the day. This simple intimacy was lost once and for all when man was expelled from "the garden of God," the place where one finds God, so to speak, at home. It is imagery, but it is brilliant; it gives color and form to the simple statement of the first chapter that what God made was good, and applies the statement with special force to man.

Here is a vast difference between the Hebrews and their neighbors. In no Semitic myth or legend is man represented as living in a state different from that known by experience, especially as living on such terms of intimacy with the gods. One may, indeed, adduce the widely diffused belief in a "Golden Age" at the beginning of the story of man, and affirm that it is a human tendency to believe that things used to be better than they are now. One may think that the Hebrew story of primitive man is simply another expression of the belief in the Golden Age; but the Hebrew story remains distinctive, because it is shot through with the Hebrew idea of God. And it is still more sharply defined by the story which follows, in which is related the end of primitive innocence.

We said that the second chapter of Genesis is a story of the origin of sex rather than of the origin of man. We shall have to say more about the origin of man as a species, for modern discussion of this problem can scarcely be ignored; but let us, for the moment, notice that we have nowhere else, in the Bible or in ancient Semitic myth, such a circumstantial account of the origin of woman. We have already noticed that in the Mesopotamian myths sex was as primeval as nature itself. The Hebrews could not accept this view, for there was no sex in the God whom they worshiped. God is, of course, masculine, but not in the sense of sexual distinction; and the Hebrew found it necessary to state expressly, in the form of a story, that sex was introduced into the world by the creative Deity, who is above sex as He is above all the things which He made. We are safe in believing that this feature of the Hebrew story of origins is best understood against the background of the mythology which it rejects.

There is not, however, merely a question of the origin of sex, but also of the relationship between the sexes. Here we must recall a paradox of the ancient Semitic world. The female principle was deified in the goddess of fertility, who was at once a virgin and a mother; she was the ideal woman. But in the ancient world the real woman was a depressed class. Studies of Mesopotamian law and of the thousands of legal and business documents which have come down to us have led modern scholars to affirm that the position of woman in Mesopotamia was higher than it was in the rest of the ancient Semitic world; and, to be precise, we should distinguish differences of time as well as differences of place. Furthermore, the position of woman, the relationship of the sexes, is determined by the intangible factors of personality, which cannot be measured by law and custom. With these reservations, our generalization will stand. We call woman a depressed class in a society in which a man may take several wives (or one wife and several women); where the wife may be divorced for slight cause, or even at will; where the husband does not offend the rights of his wife by philandering, while the unfaithful wife is punished by death or mutilation; where the primitive idea of woman as the property of man survives in such institutions as the purchase price of the bride; where hard physical work, as hard as that of a man, is imposed upon woman. Such, with some of the reservations noted, was the position of woman in the ancient Semitic world; it was a man's world.

Now, it is the paradox of her sex that this property of man is capable of giving her lord and owner the highest animal pleasure; and she is the very embodiment of the source of life, which comes from the gods. She is deified in her grossly sexual aspects, but depressed as a living human being. And because she was a goddess of delight in ideal and an inferior species in reality, no true personal dignity was granted to her; she existed to minister to the pleasure and the convenience of the man, and by so doing to bear him children. There was and there could be no sexual morality, no solid basis of family life, in such an evaluation of woman. The more austere morality of the desert nomads was some protection against the disintegration of sexual morality; for the woman, while still a drudge, was too important for the survival of the family and of the clan to be degraded. In the teeming cities of the rich valley of Mesopotamia, where woman was less a drudge and more generously endowed with legal rights, the highest eminence which woman could attain was that of temple prostitute.

We regret the necessity of dredging up these repulsive elements of life in the ancient Semitic world; but the significance of the second and third chapters of Genesis has often escaped their readers because the readers were unacquainted with the world in which the Hebrew story was told, and they have missed the importance of the contrast which the story points between woman as God made her and woman as she existed. In Hebrew society also woman was a depressed class; the storyteller was not attempting a feminist reform, but he wished to state that in the beginning it was not so.

We may see in the Hebrew attitude toward woman a reflection of the attitude which prevailed throughout the Semitic world, even though it had not among the Hebrews the same basis in mythological thinking. Nevertheless, as we shall have to notice later, the Hebrews were much inclined to adopt the cultic myths and all they stood for; and it was with these facts in mind that the storyteller of Genesis has described the true nature of woman, and her true relationship to the man. In contrast to the goddess of fertility, that Ideal Woman who was the very embodiment of sexual attraction, the Hebrew story describes the "helper meet for man": his partner and, in the context of the story, his equal. She is made to share his life and not merely his sexual experience; it is not good for the man to be alone. What could be more directly contrasted to the image of the goddess than the description of this couple as "naked and unashamed"? In human life, as it first proceeded from God, the fiery appetite of sex did not even appear. Woman did not find her fulfillment in becoming a goddess of pleasure. It is a strong and noble rejection of the frightful overemphasis upon sex and sexual pleasure which cursed the ancient world. For the only secure foundation of sexual and family morality is monogamy, the perpetual and exclusive union in marriage of one man and one woman until death do them part. It is for this, as the story shows, that God made man and woman of one bone and one flesh; and from the beginning, as Jesus was later to point out, God wished that a man should leave father and mother and adhere to his wife, and they should be two in one flesh. In this institution, with all its restrictions, and in this only, is sex an intelligible part of human life.

When we read the second chapter of Genesis against the background of ancient religious practices and social customs, the implications which we have just proposed must, we believe, have been instantly evident to the Hebrews. Shall we suppose that the third chapter has no reference to the second? We do not imply that the chapters were composed as a literary unity in their very origins, for, as we have seen, the Hebrew writers knew how to weave into one strand anecdotes which once stood independently; but, as the two chapters come to us in the book of Genesis, the stories are joined in a unity not only of plot, but of mood and of atmosphere. In any case, let us see whether we can re-create the impression which the third chapter would make upon its first hearers.

The new elements in the third chapter are the serpent and the tree of "knowledge of good and evil"; we can call the tree a new element, for, while it is mentioned in the second chapter, it has no significance in the narrative of that chapter. Even from pre-Christian times interpreters have scoured their brains to find out what is meant by the sin of eating the forbidden fruit; they realized centuries ago that the fruit must be an imaginative feature of the story, and that it must have a meaning which does not appear on the surface. Both ancient and modern interpreters have been quick to see in the "forbidden fruit" the meaning which it has acquired in popular speech – the pleasures of sex –

and some have thought that the man and the woman sinned by some form of illicit sexual pleasure. The most obvious and a very common interpretation has been that the prohibition of the fruit signifies a prohibition of sexual relations, and that the sin was a violation of this command. Against the background of the second chapter, there seems to be no room for such an interpretation of the third chapter; for the second chapter, as we have understood it, is an elaborate statement of the normal place of sex in human life. Nor is there anything in the Hebrew attitude toward sex, as we see it expressed elsewhere, which would suggest that they believed that God placed man and woman in a puritanical world. Such a view runs so contrary to the general Hebrew attitude that we could not accept it unless it were demonstrated beyond all doubt.

In spite of this, what Joseph Coppens has called the "sexual milieu" of the story remains apparent; and this "sexual milieu" has been confirmed in modern times by our knowledge of the religion of the ancient Semitic world. Upon these modern discoveries we venture a hypothesis of interpretation which is novel but, we think, plausible. A sufficient number of statues and plaques have survived to permit the statement that the serpent was a sexual symbol. We cannot affirm that the serpent in art had no other symbolism, nor can we deny that it had sexual symbolism; when it is found in an artistic context where sexual symbolism is appropriate, its meaning is inescapable. Should we not say the same thing of a literary context? When the serpent is introduced immediately after the conclusion of an account of the origins of sex, it is difficult to see how this symbolism would not have entered the mind of the Hebrew listeners. When, as a result of the seduction of the serpent, the couple discover their nakedness, this symbolism would be manifested anew; and the designation of the serpent as the perpetual foe of the woman would make it more evident. When the woman is cursed in her sexual role – in childbearing, in her submission to man, in her unfailing desire for man – the ancient Hebrew would have no doubt of what the serpent meant.

Yet we cannot suppose that the storyteller meant to characterize the sexual appetite itself as the serpent in the garden. He meant the sexual appetite unbridled. Now, the Hebrew did not need to speak of the unbridled sexual appetite in the abstract, as a modern pulpit orator does. For the Hebrew, the unbridled sexual appetite was personalized in the deities of fertility, sanctified in the myth and ritual of fertility. We know that the Hebrews thought of this cultic myth as a perversion of sex and of the ideal of sex relations, of the position of woman, who becomes both a goddess of pleasure and a degraded being, and of divinity itself, which is identified with an animal function. Can we, therefore, make the long leap to the conclusion that this idea is implicit in the third chapter of Genesis?

We can do no more than examine the story itself, and its possible relationships with ancient religion and mythology. We have been at pains to show how the Hebrews presented their beliefs in pictures and stories, not in abstract propositions; few, if any, would deny this in modern times. Where we have details which appear to be the creative imagery through which the idea is embodied, we can look for their significance only through known literary and ideological forms. If we do this to the third chapter of Genesis, then the serpent suggests itself as the sexual appetite; and the sexual appetite emerges not only as an ungoverned passion, but as an ungoverned passion which superstition and idolatry have made a god. Once we are acquainted with the myth and ritual of fertility, we can read the third chapter of Genesis as a polemic against this vicious superstition. There is a similarity between this account and the account of cosmic origins. Just as the first chapter of Genesis does not approach the problem of cosmic origins against a background of modern philosophical and scientific inquiry, so the second and third chapters do not approach the question of human origins against a background of modern philosophical and theological inquiry. For the Hebrews, the question took a form determined by the background of ancient beliefs; and it is this form which we endeavor to re-create here.

The cultic myth is also suggested by the "likeness to gods" which the serpent promises, and which recurs a second time in the chapter after the crime. We must recall that sexual intercourse under sacral auspices with sacred personnel was a communion with the deity of fertility; the same goddess of pleasure revealed herself each time the action was performed. Again, we look for what the phrase "likeness to God" would have suggested, in this context, to the ancient Hebrew. It is sharply ironical that they who seek to be like the gods discover, when they have performed the forbidden act, that they are naked; striving for the level of the divine, they discover only themselves in their brute animality. Not until the man and the woman make a god of the human body does it become an object of shame, for man was truly made in the image and likeness of God. Not until the appetite of sex is embodied in a female deity and put in the place of God Himself is it accompanied by a sense of shame. By this the story suggests, we think, that the communion with the deity which the ancients sought in the cult of fertility did not divinize them, it debased them.

The woman also is cursed in her sexual role. The Hebrew would agree that unbridled lust, hallowed in the cultic myth, was the greatest enemy of the female sex. While deifying sex, the cult demeaned the human person. It had rendered her the slave of the man, and turned the function of motherhood, which the Hebrew esteemed as the crowning glory of woman, into pain. And it had made her the curse of the man. The Old Testament is not entirely free of misogyny. Here, as elsewhere, one can find reflected the widespread ancient belief in the moral instability of the female sex. It is the weakness of the male that he is attracted by a being that is weak.

The curse of the man, as it is phrased in the third chapter of Genesis, does not appear immediately to belong to the same background. But is it merely coincidental that his curse also is concerned with fertility, the fertility of the soil? In the cultic myth, man would insure the fertility of the soil, the earth-mother, by the performance of the ritual; let him learn that the earth is not his mother, but his enemy, and that it will yield its fruits begrudgingly to the sweat of his brow and the toil of his hands. For, by deifying the processes of fertility and refusing to recognize their creator, man has perverted also the cosmic relation between nature and himself; the world which God saw as good has been rendered inept for human habitation and use. We shall have occasion to remark how the idea of the curse which has corrupted the relation between man and his environment finds expression elsewhere in the Old Testament.

When we consider the chapter in this way, as we have good reason for thinking the ancient Hebrews considered it, we see that it gives a reason for the change from the ideal cosmos of the first chapter to the real cosmos at the end of the third chapter. Evil, personalized in chaos, is not a primal fact; it is introduced by the human will. The Hebrews, apparently, never followed the subtleties of modern thinkers, who try to explain to themselves how God could permit that which we cannot conceive of Him as creating. For the Hebrews, it was enough to say that the demented will of man had upset the divine order of things. And it is a great deal to say; for it escapes the cosmic dualism of the ancients, and the cyclic revolutions of a hopeless universe. Why God should permit evil was, to them, much less important than the fact that He can overcome it.

Do we find in this chapter an extraterrestrial personal principle of evil, which Christian belief calls diabolical? Catholic faith believes that the cosmic forces of evil antedate the human forces; we do not question this belief when we ask whether it had taken form in the days of Moses or of David. To us, it appears that it had not; such an extraterrestrial principle would have been very close, in their minds, to the dualism which was expressed in the myth of the combat between the creative Deity and chaos. We cannot see that they were capable of the metaphysics which is involved in the formulation of this doctrine. On the other hand, the monster of chaos was serpentine in form; and we cannot be sure that this was not implied in the serpent of Genesis. But there can be no possibility that they thought of the monster of chaos as a real extraterrestrial being.

The Hebrew story, then, makes the sin of deifying nature – in particular, the cult of the forces of fertility – the primeval fault. In doing this, the story presents what we would call a theology rather than a history. Actually, the storyteller had no historical information whatever about the moral species of the sin by which man first severed himself from God; and neither have we. The fault which he described is primeval in another sense, that it is radically corruptive of religion and morality; and this we must grant him. The whole of Hebrew tradition reflects this conviction that "idolatry," the sin of deifying nature, is essentially opposed to all that the God of Israel was, and all that He taught was good in human life; and the history of Hebrew religion can be summed up as a combat against this "idolatry." And it was all the more insidious because it was a hidden rather than an open denial of God. From a literary point of view, the description of the psychology of temptation in the third chapter of Genesis has often been admired; it is one of those priceless pieces of realism which the ancient Hebrew storytellers have left us. We may be sure that it was carefully and deliberately constructed; for the worshipers of the Baal pleaded that they intended not treason, but "likeness to God." The fruit was indeed pleasing to the eye and good to look upon; and it was the naked goddess of fertility who handed it to man, promising him that thereby he would become a god. Could he not then reach the tree of life, and live forever?

The man and the woman in the story were, to the Hebrews, less significant as individuals than as representatives of humanity. We do not mean to imply that the story is a kind of ancient morality play, featuring Everyman and Everywoman; for this kind of performance was unknown to the Hebrews. But — as we shall have occasion to remark elsewhere — they liked to tell the stories of their ancestors in such a way that the character and the career of their descendants would appear in the progenitors. It is rather gratuitous to suppose that the story of the Man and the Woman has to be entirely free of such typologizing. It was told as a story, but as a story in which each one could look and see himself.

Hitherto we have tried to expose the significance which we think the story had in its original composition and diffusion. We cannot state too emphatically that this exposition will have to be regarded as an educated guess. Nevertheless, such guesses have their place in the study of the Bible, as in the study of any body of literature; and they proceed more securely the more accurately they place the story against its own cultural, religious, literary, ideological background and appraise the influence of this background. This statement is more necessary here than elsewhere because of the tremendous place these chapters have had in the formation of Catholic faith and Catholic theology; and of this we must speak, if only by way of summary, for we have nothing to add or to take away from the standard theological treatment of these chapters.

It is evident, of course, that theological interest in these chapters has run in other directions than that which our study has indicated. This is not hard to understand. The theological treatment of these chapters began with St. Paul. They were very near the center of the whole Pelagian quarrel, when learned men intended, by closely reasoned argument, to reduce the works of God's grace to the innate powers of man; and they loom large in the counterarguments of Augustine. They occur again in the disputes of the sixteenth century, when the question of the primitive constitution of humanity was once more raised by the Protestant Reformers; and they came into attention again in the nineteenth century, when the scientific account of human origins and of primitive man began to take form. Theological interest has concerned itself entirely with other features of the narrative than those which we have outlined; for in none of these theological discussions was the conflict between the God of Israel and the gods of Canaan a live issue. The question of human origins has been broadened and deepened since the Hebrew storyteller composed his account, and the emphasis has fallen where he did not lay it, and could not have laid it. The theological discussion of these chapters has fixed itself upon such questions as those of mortality and immortality, the presence of concupiscence in man, and, most of all, the effect of this primeval sin upon the race as a whole: what is called in Catholic doctrine original sin. These are all legitimate questions, and we may ask the biblical writers what they have to tell us about them; but we ought not to be surprised if we find that these questions were not primary in their minds, or that some of these questions never occurred to them. But if we seek in the Old Testament "the words of eternal life," we must suppose that what it says can be reinterpreted to answer our own theological questions.

There can be no doubt that the story describes man as free from what we think are the normal ills of human life, in particular from death; the storyteller could not imagine that God would create a world in which evil would be inherent. There is no doubt also that he attributes the deterioration of man and of nature to human guilt. Let us recall, for a moment, the collection of stories which follow the story of the man and of the woman. In a few pages, we have the story of the first murder, of the invention of the arts of civilization, including the invention of arms, of a universal corruption which moves God to return the world to chaos and to destroy man, "because the inclinations of his heart are evil," and because "man has entirely corrupted his way," of the building of a city and a tower by which men think to reach the heavens. Here again is imagery, but brilliant imagery; for the growth of evil in man is steady and irreversible. Indeed, the stories seem to imply that civilization itself is a doubtful blessing; was not the first murderer the builder of the first city? Do not the arts — domestication of animals, music, metalwork — come from the men of his line? Is not Babel — the same word as Babylon — and its temple tower another effort of man to reach the heavens, the level of the divine, and so to make himself "like the gods"? We shall see elsewhere in the Old Testament that the Hebrews looked at civilization as they knew it, and observed that progress in its arts was, it seemed, inevitably connected with a loss of religion and morality; they realized, vaguely, that this progress too was a cult of false gods, an effort to wrest from nature what it would not give as long as the primitive rebellion against God endured. So they felt that civilization was bound to fall of its own weight, of its own inner rottenness: "unless the Lord build the city, they labor in vain who build it." No, there is no doubt of the universality of human guilt. We cannot see that the hereditary transmission of guilt, which St. Paul saw in the story of primitive man, occurred to the mind of the ancient Hebrews; but the doctrine is thoroughly in accord with their beliefs.

Theological interest in recent years has centered even more on that verse of this passage which is called "the beginning of the Gospel": "I will place enmity between you (the serpent) and the woman, between your seed and her seed; it shall wound (?) your head, and you shall wound (?) its heel." The figure of the serpent is maintained; the man kicks at the serpent's head as the serpent strikes at his foot. In the context, the line is less a promise of victory than of perpetual strife; but it is a strife, at least, in which the man is not foredoomed to defeat. We are not even certain of the meaning of the key word. But the line is not always read in the context. Did the Hebrew storyteller see in vision the figure of the Man who was to overcome sin and death on behalf of the race? We must measure the clarity of his vision by the clarity of his enunciation, because we have no other measure; and the enunciation is most obscure. Still less can we detect in his mind any awareness of the mother of Jesus; she who was to be truly the Ideal Woman, and who was to raise her sex to a dignity undreamed, was too great a figure for the comprehension of those times. Let us leave to the Incarnation some of its novelty. We do not wish to depreciate those writings in which these lines are applied to the Redeemer and His mother; such studies have their value. But they contribute nothing to a discussion of the religious beliefs of the Hebrews; and it is in such a discussion that we are now engaged.

Finally, we approach the relations between these chapters and the contemporary scientific account of human origins. We were at some pains, in treating cosmic origins, to discuss the relations between the Bible and the natural sciences at length; for the principles there involved are valid whenever the question recurs. Even the illiterate are nowadays aware that scientific thinking about human origins is dominated by the idea of evolution, even though they have a very vague idea about what evolution is. It does not mean in modern science what it meant to Darwin and Wallace, to Huxley and Haeckel and Spencer. One need not be advanced in years to remember the Scopes case of 1925, when a Tennessee schoolteacher could be charged with attacking religion because he taught evolution. In that case the forces of orthodoxy were routed in a defeat from which they have never recovered; and many of those who followed the case only in general thought that the biblical account of human origins was once and forever shown to be ridiculous. In 1925 and now, the principle of evolution is an accepted conclusion of the natural sciences; as we have remarked, one cannot simply reject such generally accepted conclusions of the natural sciences, or of any other sciences, without stultifying the mind.

But what was this orthodoxy which was so grievously routed in 1925? It was not the orthodoxy of Catholic theologians, although their attitude toward evolution affords the opportunity for some interesting study. Seventy-five to one hundred years ago, when the theory was first launched, theologians almost immediately, and with no apparent lack of assurance, labeled it heretical. A number of theological efforts to reach a compromise with the theory were failures. Yet theology could not continue to stand against what came to be an accepted conclusion of the sciences; finally, and begrudgingly, theology accorded evolution the freedom of the city of scholarship, while insisting that its hypothetical character be emphasized. This is quite a change from leading it to the stake. What was routed was the orthodoxy called "Fundamentalism": the crass literal interpretation of the Bible without regard for literary forms and literary background. Fundamentalism has been losing ground in Catholic interpretation of the Bible for the past fifty years.

This is not the place, and we are not competent to outline the modern theory of evolution. But it seems that modern evolution rests upon two affirmations, the second of which is really a particularization of the first. The first affirmation is the continuity of the vital principle, which possesses the vital energy that enables it to grow not only in the individual, but also in the species, and to develop, in response to the challenge of environment, new forms which permit it to survive. Not, indeed, that this inner force, this drive to the development of its potentialities, is a result of the environment, for life tends to grow in any environment; for the species, as for the individual, rigidity means death. But the environment affects the direction of the growth.

The second affirmation is the continuity of man with lower forms of life. In man the vital principle has reached its peak; he is the most effective response of vital energy to the environment. Evolution does not mean that the monkey became the man, but that monkey and man and all forms of life go back to a common ancestor. The biological continuity of man with the lower animals, in the opinion of the natural sciences, is as securely established as it ever will be; the structural similarities between man and the lower animals, which are especially apparent in the remains of primitive man, leave the scientist no room for doubt. In this respect, theology is now willing to admit that modern science has a well-founded hypothesis.

It is evident that the author of Genesis 2–3 knew nothing of any such theory of development; and we can extend this denial to the stories of primitive man in Genesis 4–11. There is not, and there ought not to be any question of a "conflict." Genesis does not contain the fruits of scientific research, but a collection of ancient stories, without roots in space and time; it has no geography (except in Genesis 10) and no chronology. The external world of the garden of Eden is the world which the author knew. His man is not the "primitive man" of Java or Peking, but the man of his own day. It is fallacious to treat him as a source of scientific information. On the other hand, what he has to say about human origins does not fall under scientific observation. Natural science has not pushed its investigations back to the very beginning of the race; it would be foolish to say that it will not, but its relations with the biblical account will not be altered. For the science of human origins also has a threshold beyond which it cannot go; and it cannot remove the creative Deity from reality because He is not an object of scientific observation.

Theology insists that the question of the biological continuity of man with the lower animals be kept distinct from the question of psychic continuity. But it does not appear that the question can be settled on purely biblical grounds. The Hebrew story, like the cosmic account of Genesis 1, accepts the belief that man is not continuous with the lower animals; the difference is certainly on the psychic level, and the question of the biological level never entered the mind of the Hebrew, as it never entered the mind of anyone in the ancient Semitic world. Not until certain modern scientists came along did man find a way in which, by a single brilliant piece of reasoning, he could identify himself both with the Deity and with the lower animals. Not only the biblical account of human origins, but the whole of biblical religion, and the whole of Christian belief, which has incorporated biblical beliefs, rest on the truth that man has a nature and a destiny which he shares with no other living creature. Evolution, as we know it, probably cannot incorporate this belief into its system; for this nature and this destiny do not spring from vital energy, and we do not see how it is possible to think of them as doing so. The faith of the ancient Hebrew lies very close, again, to the basis of our own faith. The dignity of the human person and the values of human life rest on a belief in the inner worth of the human person, a worth which consists in this, that there is a kinship – if we may use the word – between man and God that is not shared by the lower animals. Otherwise, man is trapped in the organic cycle of birth, nutrition, and decay, and there is no hope more foolish than the hope that he can escape from this cycle. For there is nothing except God outside this cycle.

The key to the meaning of human life which the Hebrew story puts into our hand is the belief that human life is distorted and crippled; one does not see what it is until one measures it against what is straight. This is to measure it against God, and against a God-impregnated view of human life as it was originally constituted. But the distortion has not destroyed its essential goodness, has not altered the nature and destiny of man. He is still lord of the world, although he has weakened his dominion over the world by losing his dominion over himself. He is still a being with the divine likeness, although he has defaced it. And he will straighten out the distortion only by restoring his life to its original measurements. For this, the Hebrew story sees the need of another intervention of the creative Deity, as He intervened to create man; and the story of the Hebrew people begins the story of this intervention. Man can escape the organic cycle to God, because God enters the cycle to reach man.

When we spoke of cosmic origins, we asked ourselves whence came the peculiarly Hebrew view of these origins. The same question is even more relevant here, because the biblical account of human origins is, in its whole conception and detail, unparalleled. It cannot be derived from any known source, and we do not believe that any such source will appear. Neither can we treat it as mechanically handed down from Adam himself; the gaps in the account, the imaginative background, the Hebrew thought patterns forbid us to treat it as that type of tradition. Nor can we suppose that it is entirely the creative composition of the Hebrew storyteller; some details suggest that he employed existing accounts of the origins of the race. What gives the story its unity and its impact is, again, the mystic awareness of God and of what man is, understood against the vision of God. It is less a story of how man came to be than of what man is. It is important to see that man is like God, but is not God; it is important also to see that man is like lower forms of life, but is not one of them. This the Hebrew story tells us, and no account of human origins which alters these distinctions can be assimilated to the biblical story.

NATIONAL ORIGINS

NATIONAL origins generally lie beneath the surface of history. It is not often that we have so definite an event in the rise of nations as a group assembled to declare that "these United States are and of right ought to be free and independent." But shall we say that the United States began to exist as a nation on that glorious day of 1776, or in the Constitutional Convention which really determined what the nation should be? Shall we begin the history of modern England with 1066 and all that? Shall France celebrate her birthday with the baptism of Clovis, or Philip the Fair, or the fall of the Bastille? A nation never emerges full-panoplied from the brow of history; we have to go behind William the Conqueror and Romulus and Remus and Washington and other founders. The Greeks satisfied their curiosity by the legends of eponymous ancestors; the Ionians were the descendants of Ion, the Hellenes the descendants of Hellen, and so forth. We do not find that the ancient Semitic peoples spoke of eponymous ancestors, with the exception of the Hebrews.

What name shall we give the community of Israel? They called themselves by the word which we translate "people," and they meant much the same as we mean: a group united by common ancestry and common language. But a people is not of itself a "nation," a word for which we find no equivalent in Hebrew, until it is united by a centralized government, a "state." As we shall see, to the Hebrews the nation was a "kingdom," and the state was the "king"; for it was the king who made the people an "organized body politic." Because the unity of ancestry and language lies deeper than the unity of centralized government, Israel remained one "people" even after it had become two "kingdoms," two "nations." Furthermore, a people becomes a nation when the centralized government extends over a continuous geographical area; the United States is a nation without community of ancestry, and Switzerland is a nation without community of ancestry or community of language. It is possible to create a nation artificially at one stroke, as the statesmen did after World War I; such nations have not shown themselves durable. But a people is of slow growth, and proportionately more tenacious of its life, surviving the rise and fall of nations and states. Israel was a people before and after it was a nation.

Indeed, we should not transfer the modern idea of "nation" to the ancient Semitic world in which the Hebrews lived. The great valley of Mesopotamia, despite its geographic unity and the ethnic and linguistic community of its inhabitants (for there is little trace of a fission between Semites and Sumerians after the third millennium B.C.), was organized in independent city-states, not in larger political units. Against this diversity there was an active centripetal tendency; but this tendency did not create a true political community, a "nation" as we know it. Political unity in the great valley took the form of empire of one city-state over its fellows. The same type of city-state appeared in Syria and Canaan, without the unifying tendency; for the geographic diversity of these lands was favorable to political diversity. Egypt, which is, geographically, the long ribbon-thin valley of the Nile, appears from prehistoric times as an ethnic and political unity; historians think its own peculiar social necessities early overcame the politically divisive tendencies which arose from the geographical differences between the Delta and Upper Egypt. Assyria, on the upper Tigris, was welded into a political unity over a wider and undefined geographical area by the pressure of hostile neighbors; there, it seems, the sense of ethnic community was more profound than elsewhere in Mesopotamia, and who is to say why this should have been? The Hebrews were surrounded by little states – Moab, Ammon, Edom – which, like the Hebrews, exhibited political, linguistic, ethnic community over a continuous area. These peoples have left almost no written records; and we may ask where the line is to be drawn between the loose organization of the tribe, which is an enlarged family, and the "body politic." The inscription of Mesha, a king of Moab of the eighth century B.C., is the sole written record from these peoples; one finds there an expression of political consciousness which is not inferior to that of the Hebrews or the Assyrians. Whatever one calls them, these peoples present a type of political organization and social structure which is like that of the Hebrews, at least in the large outline; they had all responded to the environment in the same way.

Political unity, in the ancient Semitic world, was outwardly expressed in the person of the king. Thus the system of satellite or subject kings employed by the Assyrians was essentially unstable, and it was deliberately so; the Assyrians did not intend to make all their subjects Assyrians. But the political unity of the conquering empire demanded that one king and one only, the Assyrian, "the great king, the king of kings," be recognized as supreme. Where he ruled his subjects directly, there was his own state: Assyria. We have already spoken of the religious significance of the king as the representative of the gods and the visible incarnation of the state itself. In theory, the king did all things; he made all laws, judged all cases, maintained public order, was the high priest, led his armies — indeed, the account of battles sometimes reads as if the king fought in solitary grandeur, although, in fact, he may not have been personally present at the engagement. In all this there was no trace of personal aggrandizement; the king was the state, and he could not become too great. When we see the king as he appears in ancient records and in ancient art, it is hard to understand how there was any room left for such realistic politics as conspiracy and assassination; but these things occurred, because the theory of the divinity of kings is contrary to reality, which will have its way sooner or later.

We have already mentioned that a sense of history comes to a people with the self-consciousness of civilization; the history of an ancient people is the history of its monarchy, for a "people" which has not become a "nation" is not interested enough in its past to keep records. We have remarked that the Hebrews were an exception; their traditions begin with the origins of the "people" long before it became a "kingdom," with the departure of Abraham from Mesopotamia to Canaan. We think that we can now place this movement of Abraham against a larger background of disturbances and upheavals in the early part of the second millennium B.C., but Hebrew tradition is silent about these things. For the story of the Hebrew people is not the story of a kingdom, but the story of the intercourse of the Lord with men, and of His interposition in human affairs; here is the ancestor of the Hebrew people who first heard the word of the Lord, and felt His hand.

In Abraham, Isaac, and Jacob we see those figures which we call sheiks: the head of the patriarchal society of the clan or the tribe, an enlarged family. They were nomadic (more strictly, seminomadic): they did not settle in towns or villages and till the soil, but lived off their flocks and herds, which they pastured over an ill-defined region to which they laid claim. We have not yet a people, for a people is more than a large family, but we have the name which the people gave themselves. They called themselves "the sons of Israel," or "Israel," after the surname of Jacob, the grandson of Abraham. "Sons of Israel" is a typical tribal designation; pride of blood and race runs no less high in the tribes of the desert than in ducal palaces and Mayflower families. Not every Israelite was a son of Israel by blood; the connection could be made by adoption, and the man was reckoned in the genealogies as the son of X, a true Israelite. The tribes of Israel, named after the twelve sons of the patriarch, persisted as social entities long after they had ceased to have any political or geographic meaning; one thinks of the dismal but blessed failure of the Revolution to wipe Aquitaine, Normandy, Picardy, Gascony off the map of France and replace them by departments. The tribal names recalled their fathers, to whom the Lord had uttered the promises upon which the hopes and the destiny of Israel rested. Their descendants were the heirs of the promises; the tie of blood, real or fictitious, was the link between the Israelite and the God of his fathers.

It is a trait of Old Testament tradition that the ancestors and the heroes of the people often appear as the ideal representatives of the group. To recognize this trait is in no way a denial of the historical reality of these ancestors and heroes, or of the events related of them; it means only that tradition, by preference, dwells upon those lineaments of character and those incidents which best reflect the character and the adventures of the group, both as it is and as it likes to think that it is. With the exception of Isaac, who is colorless, the patriarchal traditions tell us much about the ideal Israel and the ideal Israelite. Abraham appears as "the friend of God," as the Arabs call him: he deals with God on familiar terms, is assisted by God in all his undertakings. His religion is the simple faith and worship of the desert, but faith and submission to the will of God raised to an eminent degree. He is the ideal head of the family: kindly, successful and prosperous, hospitable. That he is not entirely the lord and master of his froward wife is a human trait which keeps the ideal from turning to plaster. He is a peace-loving man, not described as a warrior-hero outside of one isolated story; the Hebrew warrior-heroes arose in a later day and in later traditions than these. As a man of integrity, God blesses him and spares him from tribulation, although his life was not untroubled. He is something less than noble, and therefore an ideal which is not out of touch with reality.

Jacob, on the other hand, is an ideal in his cleverness; his religion, substantially identical with that of Abraham, does not rise to an eminent degree. But the cunning and skill which Jacob exhibits is a quality which the Hebrews thought they possessed; it is related of others also that they possessed it, and it is viewed with admiration. Jacob may be called, in one way, the first "wise man" of the Old Testament. His cleverness appears to particular advantage in his bargain with his short-witted elder brother and in his duel with his unscrupulous foreign kinsman; could not the "sons of Israel" see themselves in similar conditions, and hope for similar success? But Hebrew tradition also told that such cleverness was not without its toll; Jacob, in spite of his prosperity, endured much evil which arose from his very success. He is an ideal, but not wholly admirable.

Joseph, in turn, is the ideal Hebrew in high place: skilled in the management of men and affairs, who preserves his integrity amid the temptations of office, incorruptible, just, respected by high and low. As Abraham and Jacob, God protects him because of the rectitude of his life. In high office he provides for his own family; this was a family obligation which was taken for granted. He is the ideal Hebrew in the highest and finest way because he shows love and forgiveness within the family itself. Such quarrels as those of Joseph and his brothers must have been common enough. Unless there be magnanimity like that of Joseph, the family will destroy itself, just as it will perish in adverse circumstances unless it be saved by wisdom like that of Joseph.

Because the selection of patriarchal stories is so largely determined by these ideal traits, there is much about the story of the clan of Abraham which we would like to know, much about the conditions of the Canaan in which they lived which we are not told. But tradition pruned off what was not essential to the story. We know, however, that it was still a patriarchal group which went, in whole or in part, to Egypt from Canaan during a famine and thence, led once more by a man to whom the Lord had spoken, returned to the land of Canaan, whither Abraham had come from Mesopotamia. The Egypt which they left was the richest and the most powerful state of the Near East at the time; and Hebrew tradition never forgot how the Lord had delivered them by His strong right hand and His outstretched arm. It was in this passage from Egypt to Canaan that the relations between the Lord and Israel took the form which they retained.

We spoke of the sons of Israel as the heirs of the promises made to the fathers; and we shall have to see what these promises were. The relationship between the Lord and Israel is formulated as a "covenant." This term needs some explanation for modern readers. In our days, a solemn agreement between men is expressed by a written instrument, signed, witnessed, sealed, and placed in the records; the act of the mutable human will is thus given an artificial stability, and men are secured against their own treachery and mendacity. In ancient Mesopotamia also such records existed; we have recovered thousands of them. But the Hebrews came more freshly from the desert, where the written instrument was less common; for the nomadic life lacked the settled stability which makes records practical. Hence the agreement was made by the spoken word, but the spoken word was invested with a ritual solemnity which gave it a living reality of its own. The agreement was concluded not only before human witnesses, who are mortal and corruptible, but also before the gods; and the parties bound themselves by terrible imprecations, ritually enacted, to stand by the agreement. These curses took on the same reality as the words of the agreement, and followed it like avenging furies, waiting to fall upon the unfaithful party. In a society which writes little, the spoken word has a dignity and a solemnity which it loses in civilization; call it superstition if you will, but it is not an altogether unhealthy attitude which thinks of the spoken word as a vital entity which, once it is brought into being, cannot be annulled or retracted. In such communities, veracity and fidelity are of the essence of society. So the covenant was the most solemn form of the spoken word, the most binding of obligations, sacred because the gods themselves witnessed it. Israel regarded itself as covenanted to the Lord.

Covenant stories were told of the patriarchs; indeed, it was related that in one mysterious theophany the Lord Himself passed through the covenant ritual, as one man would do with another. It is as realistic as the story of the Lord dining with Abraham. These stories are preludes to the great covenant scene of Sinai, described with no less realism. The object of these covenants is stated most simply: "You are my people, and I am your God." May we see in this statement an echo of the Hebrew marriage covenant, as it is preserved for us in some documents a thousand years younger? "She is my wife and I her husband from this day forever." If so, we may more easily understand how the prophets spoke of the wedding of the Lord and Israel, which we shall have to consider in its proper place. There is more involved than this, of course, but all that is involved flows from this central idea of the bond which united the Lord and Israel. A covenant between men established a kind of artificial kinship; in the ancient society of the desert, where life outside one's kin was impossible and inconceivable, the kinsman was bound to protect the life, the goods, the name of his kin at any personal cost, for the survival of the group itself depended upon the covenant fidelity of the kinsmen. And the word which is most frequently used in connection with "covenant" designates this peculiar bond of affection and loyalty which holds the kinsmen together; it is the blood of their social life. We misunderstand the ancient covenant if we think of it as merely a contract.

The covenant is a human way of thinking of the relations of God with the people Israel; like all such human modes of thinking, it is an imperfect expression of the contact between the divine and the human. The covenant cannot, of course, be a truly bilateral agreement; God cannot submit Himself to obligations after the manner of men. Nevertheless, the covenant permitted the Israelites to appeal to His fidelity and to the bond of covenant affection which arose as its consequences; by making Israel His own people, God had undertaken "to act as a kinsman" toward them, and this word also is frequently used.

It is of the essence of a covenant that the contracting parties be present; and so Hebrew tradition described the Lord as manifesting Himself in "smoke and flame" at Sinai. The Old Testament contains a number of allusions to such theophanies; one may read, for instance, Psalm 17 (18), or the third chapter of Habacuc, or the opening lines of the fifth chapter of the book of Judges. We have already mentioned the Hebrew attitude toward natural phenomena; it is in accord with this attitude that they should recognize the presence of the Lord in the thunderstorm, the earthquake, and other natural convulsions which strike terror into the human heart and place man in the presence of forces which he knows he cannot control. But we cannot believe, as some writers would have us think, that the Hebrews at Sinai made a covenant with a thunderstorm or an earthquake or a volcanic eruption. Were this true, the God whom they worshiped would not show the attributes which He does show. We have not yet ascertained beyond all doubt the kind of natural convulsion which is described in the book of Exodus; that there is some kind of natural convulsion involved admits no doubt. But the imagination rebels at the idea that the patriarchal traditions found their fulfillment merely because a violent storm happened to blow up. To see God in nature is one thing, and to form a covenant with Him is another. The terms of the covenant, as we shall see, are not derived from the perception of God in natural phenomena. The covenant rests on the belief that the Hebrews at Sinai perceived the present reality of God in a manner which surpasses the normal capacity of man; that God broke through the veil which hides Him from view and was perceived, however briefly and dimly, for what He is. The covenant was not a theological conclusion, but an experience which rent the soul and uprooted human wisdom as the storm rends rocks and uproots trees.

It is a striking feature of the covenant promises that there appears from the very beginning an affinity to the land: the land called Canaan, of which we suppose Abraham had hardly heard. There he settled, and there his sons after him lived the pastoral nomadic life; the land was not yet given them as a "possession." "Possession," in this instance, means the ownership of the landholder, the settled inhabitant who tills the soil and builds cities. Throughout the ancient Near East, as even in modern times, there persisted the antithesis between the Desert and the Sown, between the pastoral nomad and the peasant. Between the two there is an immemorial and an irreconcilable feud; they are two opposing ideals, two contrasting ways of life. The life of the nomad is poor compared to that of the peasant, but it is, he thinks, free; it involves none of the mean and exhausting labor of the soil. He owes no obedience except that which he freely gives to his sheik; he is a fighter, a freebooter, tied down to no patch of soil. The peasant has accepted the discipline of communal life as a better way; he thinks the nomad a starveling bandit, a parasite on the borders of civilization. We find this antithesis running through much of the Old Testament, and we shall have to refer to it again.

What we wish to notice now is the perpetual attraction which the Sown exercises upon the Desert. For all his prating of freedom and nobility, the nomad looks with envy upon the abundant food and the comfort and the security of the settled life; and he drifts to the villages and the cities, as he has drifted since the first cities were built. The Israelite, when he offered his annual sacrifice, was to recall that his father was a "vagabond Aramaean," and thank the Lord who had brought him into the goodly land. The patriarchs also felt the pull of the land, and the promise of the land recurs throughout those portions of the Old Testament which tell the stories of the patriarchs and of the Hebrews in Egypt and in the desert.

There is more here than the attraction of the Sown for the nomad. A people is not truly a people, a nation, until it takes root in the soil. Until that time, it is a tribe, one of the innumerable tribes which flit across the deserts of the east, as nomad tribes once flitted across the prairies of North America, leaving nothing but their names in rivers, creeks, mountains, and the cities of the men who wiped them off the map. For the nomad cannot survive against the sturdy peasant; nor can he survive even in his own proper element, the inhospitable desert, for the tribes lack any defense against nature and against each other. They vanish, and other tribes rise to take their place; they have no history, and they contribute nothing to the sum of human experience. Such was the clan of Abraham, "the sons of Israel," and they yearned for the land because the Lord had marked them as His own; until He gave it to them, they remained rootless wanderers, without the stability they needed to meet the destiny which they believed awaited them.

This will help us to understand the Hebrew conquest of Canaan, even if it does not excuse it. The Hebrews were children of their time, and they practiced the art of war as it was practiced in the ancient world. Such episodes as the sack of Jericho and of Ai can be duplicated dozens of times from ancient records; and it is not seemly for a world which has evolved the concept of total war to point the finger at Joshua and his Hebrews. But sound moral instincts are revolted by the Hebrew conquest of Canaan, as they are revolted by total war, which spares not aged nor infirm nor women nor children – in fact, it is against the helpless that its most scientific weapons are most effective. What makes the wars of Joshua especially repulsive, however, is the righteousness with which they were conducted. Ancient peoples always marched behind their gods; but we feel a particular loathing in this, that the future home of God on earth should have been taken by fire and sword in His name, and that the Hebrews should have slaughtered hundreds near the spot which Jesus chose as the scene of the parable which eminently shows that every man is the neighbor of every other. How had God revealed Himself, we wonder, to a people who could offer this slaughter to Him as a sacrifice, and cover these acts of mass murder with the mantle of religious devotion? We shall have to notice again that the covenant of God with Israel was not an immediately transforming and ennobling agent; and we should not have to learn that God deals with human beings in a manner which befits their humanity. The Hebrews were the scourge of God for the Canaanites, as the Assyrians would be His scourge for the Hebrews; in each case the mysterious divine justice permits the sins of man to be punished by the sins of man. But of this law of history we shall have to speak again and at greater length.

To sum up: we find in the covenant the center of the unity of Israel: not community of blood nor community of land nor community of language nor a centralized government, although all these things were present or to come, but the unity of the people of the Lord. The Israelites were His people because He had chosen them; He had even chosen them in their fathers before they were yet a people. We have spoken earlier of the national deities of the ancient Semitic world, and designated them as personalizations of the nation itself. We cannot speak of the God of Israel as the personalization of the nation; for we meet again that overpowering sense of otherness. Furthermore, as our subsequent consideration of Israel and its God will show, the God of Israel, far from embodying the genius of the people, runs directly counter to the national genius in any sense that we choose to understand the word. He is not devoted to its national welfare before all else, and He does not promise to defend it against its enemies. Even the normal function of the state and its gods, the promotion of peace and security, He does not guarantee. His will is that His people become something different from other peoples, as He is different from other gods. Except as His people, with the character which He imposes upon them, there is no reason why they should exist at all. This is their destiny, vague and unformed as it may be, and it looks to some thing other and greater; but, in its beginnings, Israel saw itself as the people of the Lord. This it was that made them a people in any sense at all.

Hebrew tradition told how the Lord had established His people beyond all human hope by delivering them from Egypt. The story of the exodus from Egypt left its mark as deeply on the national consciousness as did the story of Sinai – perhaps more deeply, for it was a more spectacular story. Modern historians have come to realize that they should not treat the story of the exodus as if it were entirely the creation of ancient ballad singers, any more than they should expunge Lexington and Concord and Bunker Hill from the history of American origins. The Hebrew idea of God was determined, to no small extent, by the stories of how He had bent the forces of nature to liberate His helpless people from bondage in the most powerful country in the world. Modern historians are somewhat perplexed by the fact that the episode has not left even a ripple upon the surface of Egyptian history; but we should not be surprised that the Hebrews were much more interested in their own story than were the Egyptians. But modern historians have also asked the question whether the Hebrew faith, as far as it rested upon the power exhibited in the exodus, did not rest upon a false foundation; for they believe that the wonders of the story can be proved to be entirely the work of the normal course of nature – proceeding, perhaps, in an unusual manner, but not in a manner which exceeds its own resources. And in order to avoid this, many theologians have supposed that "God reveals Himself in nature," that the Hebrews saw the hand of God in disease, in the movement of cloud and wind and tide. They think the concept of a "God who works wonders" is a child's view of God, and scarcely to be reconciled with a modern scientific view of nature. This modern scientific view seems to run smack against the traditional Catholic and Christian faith that God is a God who works wonders.

Now, a philosophic judgment that God cannot or does not work wonders is neither scientific nor defensible. We can leave the philosophic question there; for the belief that the Lord is a God who works wonders is fundamental to Hebrew faith and the Hebrew conception of God, and from this the Catholic and Christian faith is derived. But we have to remember that the Hebrew belief took its form in a world of different thought patterns. The modern question arises only because of modern philosophy of nature and modern natural science, which view the world of nature as a closed system. In this system, observation leaves no room for a transcendent power to work, and scientific reasoning does not require such a transcendent power. The Hebrews, as the men of the ancient Semitic world generally, did not form the conception of nature as a unity, nor did they depersonalize its forces. The operations of nature were the expressions of a personality: a personality within nature in ancient Semitic religions, a personality above and outside nature in Hebrew belief. We have already noticed the singular Hebrew concept of the creative Deity. This is the concept which governed their view of nature as an existent reality; they neither observed nor were interested in the interplay of natural forces, but only in the action of God, which could be seen in every natural phenomenon. This is unscientific, and perhaps a child's view; but one has to be an atheist to say it is false. In this view, the "God who works wonders" is understood in a quite different sense from the understanding of modern man. We, so to speak, have a certain minimum standard of wonder, and we do not credit God with performing wonders unless He surpasses this standard; the Hebrews never took for granted what we call the ordinary operations of nature, the course of nature, but found each day a wonder in itself.

Hence the Hebrews, in telling the story of their deliverance from Egypt, did not submit the events they related to the measurement of instruments of precision; the story was a story of wonder because the Lord had been faithful to His promises and had rescued His people from a hopeless situation. It is doubtful whether the modern curiosity to examine the intimate nature of the phenomena would have had any significance for them; the significant fact was that they were no longer in Egypt, that they had left Egypt aided by the Lord when they could not aid themselves. Some writers have remarked that we ought not be surprised if the miraculous should occur in such a crisis of history; but there is no crisis in which the miraculous can be expected, for it is by definition unexpected. The examination of the phenomena is an accessory question; the main point is the faith of the Hebrews in a God who is the Lord of nature, and who can bend it to His will. One could hardly seek a more convincing vindication of this faith than the very survival of this people, in the crisis of their origins, who had nothing but their God to help them. To such a God nothing is impossible. Because we are less aware than the Hebrews of the pervasive reality of God in the world around us, it is difficult for us to enter into their view of this part of their story.

Let us return to what we said was the will of God, that the people of the Lord should be different from other peoples, as He is different from other gods. When we read over the stories of the patriarchs, we are intrigued by how little is demanded of them. We should not minimize the renunciation of Abraham, which makes him the proverbial hero of faith; but his stature, and that of Isaac and Jacob and Joseph, is something less than heroic. What is demanded of them is that they believe in a God who can do what He promises to do. It involves no revolution in their manner of life; they do not rise notably above the mores and folkways of their time. They marry several women, they lie and deceive, they abandon those who are dependent upon them, they quarrel, they live in an atmosphere of nomad morality in which theft and murder are accepted as normal means of achieving one's ends. We cannot but marvel at what has been called the divine economy; it is really an authentication of the faith of the patriarchs, that its revolutionary possibilities are hidden in these early days. For God approaches men in their own way, not blinding them with the brilliance of His holiness, but adapting Himself to their ignorance, their meanness, their narrowness. No article of the Hebrew faith is bigger with consequences than faith in the divine condescension; it is the inability of men to grasp this which makes them keep God remote and distant. God will change them, or rather He will make them change themselves. The change is so slow that it appears almost imperceptible, but it is sure. One needs a godlike view of humanity as a whole in space and time to grasp the divine patience and condescension; this view the Hebrews possessed. And it is a view which must be taken by anyone who would read either the Old or New Testament with intelligence and sympathy. God does not do everything at once.

It is not in the stories of the patriarchs, but in the story of Sinai that the implications of Israel's acceptance of the Lord begin to appear with all their urgency. We say they begin to appear, for Israel never grasped them fully. We spoke earlier of the origin and growth of Hebrew law, and we do not want to think of the Sinai adventure as no more than the promulgation of a code of law; for Israel, it was a terrifying meeting with the Lord. And there they met Him as a God whose will governs the whole of human life, a God who loves good and hates evil. There are moral instincts in man, and they can remain human; they usually do remain human, and consequently man adjusts them to what he conceives to be his needs. The moral will of the Lord is independent of human needs and circumstance, and stands inflexibly behind an ideal of human life in which moral goodness is the primary good, the truly human good. To this good the power which the Lord displayed in the deliverance of Israel is directed, and, should they fail to attain this goodness which He demands, He will do to them as He did to the Egyptians.

This ideal of a society governed entirely by the moral will of the Lord is the true legacy of Moses to his people, and it makes little difference what might be, in detail, the laws through which it finds expression. These laws may not differ from the pedestrian morality of the ancient world, and the Hebrews may have been blind to the finer possibilities of the moral judgment. God revealed not a code of laws, but Himself as the moral force of the universe. With this faith at the base of Hebrew life, moral growth is possible; without it, there is nothing to halt the moral degeneration which has brought down all the nations of history, as it will bring down the nations of the modern world. And we say this because of the Hebrew faith in the moral will of the Lord. Men may view moral wrong as unprofitable or antisocial or ill-mannered or in any of the many ways in which they view it; but unless they see moral wrong as something which the Lord abominates, they have no abiding reason for not doing it. A purely human or civic or democratic or liberal morality is not an ignoble ideal; it is a false morality. The Hebrew faith could have found such a morality, for it was the morality of their world; they did not accept it because the Lord would not let them accept it. So the Hebrew ideal of a society governed by the will of the Lord in all things has passed into the Christian ideal of the kingdom of God. This society is the true fulfillment of human life here upon earth, and this was the destiny which the Lord gave the Hebrew people.

Religion is more than morality, and the society governed by the will of the Lord had formalized modes of expressing its submission to Him: priesthood and sacrifice and ritual prayer. One notes that in these things the Hebrews adopted the manners of the ancient world, and knew nothing of the worship which was purely "in spirit and in truth" which some modern Christians think they have. It is easy to forget that this ritual corresponds to an inner need of man to express his most profound sentiments through some external form of words and ceremony. This need for expression is most acute when the sentiments are not merely those of the individual person, but those which he shares with a group. Much of ritual is vain, archaic, unintelligible; but it cannot be eradicated from human behavior. And it had its place in the religion of the Hebrews, because the Hebrews, in common with most of the ancient world, exhibited a deeper group consciousness than does modern civilized man. We have already pointed out that the individual meant nothing to them except as a member of a group. They could not have made any sense out of modern gibes at "institutionalized religion." Religion, like all human activities, could be carried on only within the community; it could never be entirely interior, a religion of the heart, a religion of the spirit, because men do not live in such solitude, and neither could they approach God in solitude. God came to them through the people Israel, and it was as the people Israel that they responded to Him. It was a religious attitude which was suitable to the social scene of the ancient world, and it has its place in religion as long as men are conscious that the individual person cannot live as a man outside the social group.

Let us not be too quick to sneer at the crudity of animal sacrifices; after all, the Hebrew prophets called them superstitious long before our time. But sacrifice in itself symbolizes man's belief in a community of exchange between himself and the deity. He believes that it is possible to reach God through an attestation of the divine supremacy, of his own submission to that supremacy, and of his utter dependence on the Deity for life and the things that sustain life. He believes that the Deity will dispense the goods which man needs in exchange for such submission; for he cannot think of the Deity as a blind mechanical force. He thinks the Deity is a person, who cannot be indifferent to the personal attitude of man. He fears and reverences the near presence of the Deity, the sphere of the holy; and therefore he surrounds this sphere with barriers which cut it off from the profane and the human. He guards his sense of the difference between the divine and the human by committing the holy to authorized persons, by setting aside certain places and select implements of worship; these things he hallows, for what is near to the Deity should not be employed for profane purposes. In our sophistication, we see that the idea of a banquet for the gods is an intolerable anthropomorphism. But the banquet expressed, in its own childish way, the community of exchange between man and the divine, and men intended to acknowledge the giver when they offered him some of his own gifts. Modern ways of thinking permit man to live without any expression of such dependence, which he probably does not feel anyway; or, if he thanks God in his heart and his spirit for the gift of life, he feels it is beneath the dignity of civilized man to assemble with his fellows to profess their common submission to the Maker of all things. One questions the sincerity of a sentiment which never finds expression.

This ritual was, for the ancient Hebrews, the concrete way in which the divine personality was made real for them. We must remember that we are dealing with a people who were not "intellectual," who lived before the days of creeds and dogmas and articles of faith. For them the law of worship was the law of belief in a sense more profound than we know. The cult is the framework which protects the form and substance of belief, not yet stated in precise formulae. The Lord was different from other gods, and the difference was emphasized by the special nature of the worship shown Him. The worship which was paid Him could be paid to no other god, for no other god could claim the divinity which is His. We have already spoken of some of the practices of ancient Semitic religions; when we view the Hebrew cult against this background, we see that it was comparatively a worship "in spirit and in truth." And we shall have a better insight into the religion of the Hebrews if we give some thought to one or two of the features of its cult. We have already spoken of the nonmythological character of the Hebrew cult and its implications in their belief; let us here recall the fact that the cult of the Hebrews was imageless.

The significance of this singular fact does not appear until we consider the practices of other ancient Semitic religions. In these religions, the image was extremely important. The meaning of the image is hard for us to define, for the image was more than merely representational; it was identified with the god in a way which escapes rational analysis, it was sacred with a nearly absolute holiness. The image was the god, and the temple his palace: an earthly counterpart of the heavenly reality. The god was represented, in Semitic lands, in human form; there were none of the hybrid forms which were so numerous — and so unaccountable — in Egypt. The Hebrew law prohibited the worship of images with unusual emphasis. Images of the Lord are not prohibited; the point of the law is that they need not be prohibited. There could not be an image of the Lord which would not be the image of some creature "in the heavens above, on the earth beneath, or in the waters under the earth." None of these things were like the Lord, and so there could be no image which the Hebrews could adore, even with the intention of directing their adoration to the Lord through the image—although perhaps we credit them with more refinement of thought than we should when we introduce this distinction.

The Hebrews did observe this law; this is the conclusion of more than one distinguished Palestinian archaeologist. The conclusion is not, of course, rigorous; but a large number of ancient Hebrew sites have been excavated, some of them extensively, and there has been nothing that could even remotely be identified as an image of the Lord. This absence is all the more striking when we learn that the same Israelite levels of occupation contain a large number of divine images, easily identified as Canaanite deities; the same Hebrews who adopted the worship of the fertility gods did not abandon the Hebrew belief that the Lord could not be represented by an image. We feel that, were images of the Lord in use among the Hebrews, one would have turned up by this time. One thinks, of course, of the famous golden calf; but modern studies have shown—rather conclusively, we think—that the calf was the pedestal upon which the divine image stood; for gods in this posture have been found in the remains of ancient Canaan. On the golden calf stood—nothing; even in this reprobated image, the Lord remained invisible. Furthermore, it is a commonplace of Hebrew belief that no one could see the face of the Lord and live; such a countenance admitted no iconic representation, for mortal eyes could not look upon it.

This absence of images is in contrast with the innumerable instances of what is called "anthropomorphism": speaking of the Lord in human terms. Was not man himself made in the image and likeness of God? The Hebrews could not have thought of a purely spiritual likeness, because they did not think of any purely spiritual reality. They speak of God's eye, ear, lip, hand, arm; God walks, talks, listens, answers, is angry, and His bowels are moved with compassion. We spoke earlier of the convincing realism with which the Hebrews talked about the Lord, how they were aware of a living personality. It is this human language which gives the God of the Old Testament His vivid personal traits. Yet we know that they are merely human terms, which suggest rather than describe the divine reality.

The imageless worship of the Lord shows that the Israelites also knew this, although they could not find a philosophical formulation for it. Their faith revealed to them this living divine personality, and they could think and speak of Him only in language which applied to Him the traits of human personality; but, as a counterpoise, there was the revelation through the same faith that this living God lived in a manner utterly different from the life known to human experience. There is nothing within the universe of visible creatures which can be likened to the Lord. He is above and beyond human experience and human knowledge, and it is a falsification of divinity to represent it by the image of a creature. So the paradox of anthropomorphism joined to imageless worship keeps the divine reality vividly in the awareness of the Israelites, while the absence of the divine image removes the danger of reducing the divine to the level of the created.

In a similar way, the name of the God of the Israelites was an explanation of what He is. We have to recall that, in the ancient world, the name was regarded not as a mere designation to distinguish several individuals of a species from one another, but, in a manner, as identical with the thing named. The name was the person, and it not only designated him, it described him. Thus, in biblical idiom, we often meet "the name of the Lord" where we should speak simply of the Lord; His name is Himself. We speak of "God," and need no further qualification; but the Hebrews thought of "god" as a common name. While they did speak of the Deity as "the god," they felt that not to know His name was not to know Him at all; for "the god" must have a name, if He is to be a real person.

So God revealed to the Hebrews His name; Hebrew tradition wavered concerning the point of time at which the divine name came into use, but the weight of the tradition identified the revelation of the divine name with the story of Moses and the burning bush. This divine name is represented in our modern English Bibles by "the *Lord*." This represents the Hebrew word *Yahweh;*

we avoid the use of the Hebrew word here, because readers of vernacular versions of the Bible are not accustomed to what appears to be an uncouth and barbarous word. Yet, if one will notice how many times "the *Lord*" appears in the English Bible, one sees that it was the name by which the Hebrews normally mentioned the Deity or addressed Him; it is more common than all the other appellatives put together. This is as it ought to be, for the name is the person.

This identity of name and person gave the divine name something of the sacredness of divinity itself; and it was the exaggerated reverence of the Judaism of later centuries for this divine name that has interfered with its preservation. Only since medieval times has it been established that *Yahweh,* and not the "Jehovah" which the King James Bible adopted, is the correct pronunciation. Like all Hebrew names, the divine name has meaning; but it is like the names of Mesopotamian and Canaanite gods in this, that its meaning has been lost. Most Hebrew names are a sentence, usually a prayer, such as Isaiah, "salvation of Yahweh." But the divine name is only a fragment of a sentence, although some sense can, by conjecture, be derived from its present form. Unfortunately, the meaning is so general that it cannot be certainly defined; of the possibilities suggested, "He brings into being" is as likely as any other. This is even more probable if the name is, with W. F. Albright, reconstructed as the sentence, "He brings into being whatever comes into being." The name, so understood, defines the difference between the Lord and the creatures of His hand; this is a dominant idea in the beliefs of the Hebrews, and it may well find expression in the divine name. The "I am who am" of the Latin and English Bibles has little justification in etymology.

We said above that the ideal of a society governed by the will of God was the true legacy of Moses to his people. Let us remember that this legacy rests upon the knowledge of God as a real personality, whose will has a genuinely personal impact upon men. We see the reality of God in His name, in the language in which the Hebrews spoke of Him, in the imageless worship which they paid Him. Surely we shall not find elsewhere a people in whom the idea of God is so real, so vital, so pervasive. The mystic awareness of the divine reality was diffused through the people of Israel as a whole from those men who possessed it, so that Israel, even in its sins, could still think and speak of the Lord as near to them, in their very midst. So it is evident that Israel was "the people of the Lord," that it was their knowledge and their worship of this one Lord that made them a people.

We touch here upon the mystery of divine election, which becomes an urgent question in the New Testament and in the history of theology. Why should God choose one people as His own? And, by so choosing, does He reject other peoples as His own? The Old Testament knew no other reason for the choice than that which St. Paul knew: because He so wished it. The Old Testament finds in this no problem arising from what appears to be an arbitrary choice; with St. Paul, it sees the divine election of Israel as an act of divine love. With St. Paul, it feels that it is not the part of man to probe the motives of the divine will. Modern theology, less humble before the fact of the divine choice, must still accept the Hebrew belief that God's election is not motivated by anything in the object of election which makes it worthy. The divine election confers worthiness, it does not presuppose it. Israel, in the utterances of those men who were its true voice, was aware of its unworthiness; but we are all acquainted with the self-righteousness which so easily follows from an awareness of election, and this self-righteousness was not absent from ancient Israel. The Gentile nations were not the people of God, and as such they were, for many Hebrews, beneath contempt. We must admit that the Hebrews rarely rose to the height of spiritual vision which appears in the book of Jonah and a few other passages to see that all men are the people of the Lord, and that the Lord, by choosing Israel, had not rejected others. To such men as Amos it was plain that election meant responsibility rather than privilege; they knew the meaning of the words of Jesus: "To whom much is given, of him much shall be required." Israel, as the people of God, ought to live as the people of God; if it failed to do so, it would feel the visitation of divine justice more severely than others. But the divine election is not really a mystery to the men of the Old Testament; the subtleties of modern theology, which has created this intricate problem, were beyond them. Were the problem proposed to them, they would probably find it fatuous; the mystery, they might say, lies not in the election of Israel, but in this, that God should choose any people as His own. But if He wished to come to men, as He did, He had to choose a point of contact, and no one point is better than any other. The marvel is that He wished to come at all.

VIII

KING AND PROPHET

A NATION, we said, is an "organized body politic," constituted by a centralized government of a population which occupies a continuous territory. Israel, "the people of the Lord," in its earliest years exhibits neither a centralized government nor possession of a continuous territory; for Israel, as we have tried to see for ourselves, was unified around the Lord its God. And thus it preserved its unity through the difficult years in Canaan which followed its settlement in the land which the Lord had sworn to give to its fathers.

In earlier interpretation, it was easily assumed that Israel in its early days was a theocracy: a community living in close discipline under the Law, ruled by God through His vicar, the high priest. Older interpreters liked to see in Israel the foreshadowing of the ideal state, which they conceived as the union of the Holy Roman Empire and the Holy Catholic Church. The high priest – Eli, for instance – corresponded to the Roman Pontiff; to the Emperor there corresponded no ruler by dynastic succession, for Hebrew tradition denied any such ruler in the early days of Israel. Instead, a man called a "Judge" arose, inspired by the Lord, to deliver Israel from a particular danger, and "judged" Israel for the rest of his life. This happy state did not endure without interruption, for the Israelites regularly fell into idolatry from which the Lord regularly rescued them through punishment and delivery from punishment; but the older interpreters thought of the theocracy as the normal state from the settlement of Israel in

Canaan until the rise of the monarchy of Saul. Such a tidy state of affairs can be conjectured from a superficial reading of the Hebrew stories; in modern times we know that it is fanciful.

We are not attempting to write the history of the Hebrews, but to sketch some of their religious beliefs; and so it might appear that the discussion which we now begin is not altogether in place. But we have to remind ourselves of what we have found verified in a number of instances: that Hebrew beliefs appear not in abstract propositions, but in the concrete, in nature and life and history. The impact of the divine upon human life in Israel cannot be seen except in the history of Israel, and this means the history of the nation; for much of Hebrew belief, as it is set forth in the Old Testament, has to do with the response of the nation to the voice of God, with the function of the state toward its members and toward other states. So we must enter upon the question of the government of the Hebrew people, and of the unwonted struggle for power which we shall find throughout most of the history of the Hebrew people.

As elsewhere, we shall see Hebrew institutions in clearer focus if we look at similar institutions in the ancient Semitic world. We have already noticed that kingship was a power, and that, like all forms of power, it came to earth from the divine level. The power to govern was almost universally incorporated in a king in civilized peoples. We do not find in Mesopotamia or Canaan that the king was a god as he was in Egypt: Horus the son of Re. Rarely in the history of mankind has the deification of the state been so frankly declared as it was in Egypt. Yet, in striking contrast with other absolute monarchies, the Egyptian monarchy seems, as a rule, to have given its people stability, peace, and prosperity; unsettled conditions were the exception. Other factors, such as the comparative isolation of Egypt from the rest of the world, have been alleged to explain this; but the fact remains that the divinity of the king did not infallibly involve the vices which we associate with absolute rule. The Pharaoh, like the sun-god with whom he was identified, shed his rays of light and warmth upon all his subjects alike; under his beneficent glow the classes of Egyptian society were integrated into a harmonious unity, which afforded so pleasant a life that the Egyptian asked no more in the next world than a continuation of life under the sun of Egypt. The Pharaoh was the source of this life.

In the more stormy politics of Mesopotamia and Canaan, kingship never achieved the serene divinity of the Pharaoh. The king was not a god; there were few rulers who claimed the divine title, and we have no satisfactory explanation of these exceptions. The king was the greatest of men, the representative of the gods, who had placed him on his throne and maintained him there. In the earliest period of which we have record, the god himself was the king of the city; the human ruler shunned the title of king, and called himself viceroy, the vicar of the god. This ancient scruple disappears early in recorded history, but the principle upon which it was based did not disappear. For the king was a visible incarnation of the divine rule and of the state itself; each year he received anew his kingship from the gods, who thus showed their favor and continued to accept him as their representative. The gods marched before him to battle, they gave him wisdom to make laws and judge his subjects, and their authority gave sanction to his will. There was no other who shared in this divine authority, not even the priests; for the king was the high priest, the representative of his people before the gods. Nor did this divine king disappear from the historical scene with the states which he ruled. The divine royalty of the ancient kings of Mesopotamia passed in succession to the conquerors of Mesopotamia: the Persian kings, Alexander and his successors, the emperors of Rome.

Let us turn to the Hebrew people and observe the contrast it affords. During the early years after the settlement in Canaan, the Hebrew polity appears as a loose confederation of tribes grouped around the shrine of the Lord: the ark of the covenant, the sacred vessel where the Lord resided among His people and in which He had led them through the desert. The rule of the Hebrew people was patriarchal, vested in the "elders" of the clan, the tribe, the city. The absolute rule of the cities of Mesopotamia and Canaan was foreign to the freedom of the desert. The sheik and the elders ruled by a kind of common consent; there was no divinity about them, and nothing sacred about their authority. We need not think, of course, that the absolute rule of the Semitic king was not tempered to some extent by the popular will, for we are sure that it was; but in theory it was not, and it is sometimes important what theory lies at the base of action. Here we are confronted by two opposing theories. We may suppose that the Hebrews would look upon a human representative of the divine power to rule much as they would look upon any image of the divine; no human being could represent the Lord, just as no image could represent Him. And the question did not become urgent in their early years, for they were able to maintain themselves by the resources of tribal organization.

We have to consider what Max Weber called the "charismatic leader," for this type of leadership shows itself early in Hebrew story and remains essentially throughout its course, although the leadership is externalized in different forms. The most obvious type of charismatic leader is the "judge" of Hebrew story, and so we may take him as a laboratory sample. Men like Ehud, Gideon, Jephthah, Samson were not community leaders; in fact, they first appear as undistinguished, or even as inept to "judge" Israel — "judge," in these contexts, meaning to defend Israel and to give it victory over its enemies. These men rise to the occasion not in virtue of their own personal qualities and attainments, but in virtue of a divine impulse, which the Hebrews called "the spirit of the Lord." This is the *charisma,* the divine impulse which enables a man to speak and to act in a manner beyond his own habits and powers; he becomes a channel through which the divine power flows to reach the people of the Lord. The charisma comes for a certain occasion, and does not establish the man in a different condition; once its work is accomplished, it leaves him much what he was before. The stories of the judges are not without a tragic element. Gideon makes an "ephod" — here probably a divine image — and "makes Israel to sin"; his sin is visited upon his sons, and his whole house perishes. Jephthah sacrifices his only child when the Lord gives the victory he asked through his rash vow. Samson, a brutal, wenching lout with astonishing strength, dies amid the ruins of the temple which he has pulled down with his own hands. So the charisma was a perilous gift to its receiver, although it was deliverance for the people of the Lord.

This elementary polity broke down in a crisis which arose a century or two after the Hebrews entered Canaan. The Canaanite city-states, while more civilized and prosperous than the Hebrews, were politically disunited and, it seems, decadent; in any case, they could not effectively prevent the Hebrews from settling in their land, even though they preserved some areas for themselves. After the initial wars, the two peoples entered into a gradual amalgamation, in which the Hebrews finally absorbed the Canaanite population and most of their civilization. But then the Hebrews met the Philistines. This people, possibly connected with Homer's Pelasgi, appears in ancient art with the helmets and plumes of Homeric warriors, and with some of the prowess of Achilles and Agamemnon. Unlike either Hebrew or Canaanite, the Philistines burst upon the scene as a closely knit social and military organization, and they were armed with iron, the terrible new metal to which the Hebrews were still strangers. Before these professional warriors the Hebrew peasants wilted; and stories such as those of Samson did not alter the fact that the Philistines became masters of the Hebrew country. Unless the Lord arose to help His people, He would have no people. Neither tribal organization, charismatic heroes, nor prophecy showed a way of survival. The people called for a king "like all the nations," who would unite the people of the Lord and lead them to victory.

Now let us notice a strange ambivalence in the books of the Old Testament toward this kingship. There is an attitude of disapproval; kingship is seen in its most unpleasant features — oppressive and extortionate, militaristic, subject to the influence of foreign religion and foreign culture, leading the people away from the Lord after wealth, after power, after other gods. The expression of this attitude, as we read it in the Old Testament, is probably determined in part by the unhappy history of the Hebrew monarchy, but there is no reason to suppose that it does not go back to Samuel and those who felt like him. To these circles, human kingship was an infringement upon the kingship of the

Lord. It must have seemed, also, a denial of faith in the Lord who had delivered their fathers from Egypt and brought them into the land of promise; could not the same Lord deliver them from these Philistines without the foreign institution of kingship? To many, the Hebrew faith in the Lord seemed tied in with a peculiar way of life. Canaanite culture they repudiated, for the pursuit of wealth and luxury was a pursuit of the goods which the gods of Canaan promised to their worshipers. Faith in the Lord could, they thought, be preserved only in the simple pastoral and agricultural life which the Hebrews had adopted in Canaan. We have already taken notice of an opposition to civilization and culture which appears in the pages of the Old Testament; this opposition crystallized against the monarchy.

When we consider these things, it is strange not only that a contrasting attitude appeared at all, but that this contrasting attitude finally prevailed. We find it most fully and very early expressed in the oracle which Nathan delivered to David, promising him an eternal dynasty. The kingship was accepted as the form of society in which the people of the Lord should find peace, stability, order; more than this, it was accepted as the framework in which the will of the Lord should have its final realization, as we shall have to consider later. The old charismatic judges had arisen in response to a particular need; in the king, the Lord gave His people a charismatic ruler who held a permanent office. He, too, was endowed with "the spirit of the Lord" for the works of a king.

If we ask how the Hebrews thought of the ideal king, the answer is David. We wonder how this could be, when we see how Hebrew tradition has preserved the story of his sins and their punishment without any effort to conceal them. We have little information from the Old Testament about his military conquests, although we know that he finished what Saul had begun and destroyed the Philistine threat; in this respect, the monarchy had justified itself by meeting the need which had been the occasion of its creation. We have few stories of the attributes of David as a ruler; we read something about his piety, which appears to have been quite elementary. The picture of his piety has long been drawn from the Psalms, many of which he did not write. We do have the story of his life as a bandit; he was a fugitive from Saul, it is true, but no less a bandit for that, and a bandit who served the Philistines, the bitter enemies of his own people, as a professional soldier. We have, at some length, the story of his adultery and murder, a classic of Old Testament narrative, and of the rebellion of his son Absalom; what kind of ideal king was this, we wonder, against whom his people could be so easily incited?

Scarcely less ideal was his son Solomon, who enjoyed the fruits of his father's conquests and, in the wistful exaggeration of popular story, made gold as cheap as silver in Jerusalem; who built the temple which the prophet had not allowed his father to build because David was a man of blood. The temple was modest enough even by ancient standards, but the Hebrews, who had long forgotten the great structures of Egypt and Mesopotamia, saw in it a magnificent house of the Lord – too magnificent, indeed, for most of them continued to worship Him on "the high places." We have also the story of Solomon's defection from the worship of the Lord; and Hebrew tradition tells us frankly that the exactions of his taxgatherers were largely responsible for the rebellion which split Israel into two kingdoms almost immediately after the accession of his son.

David and Solomon were certainly ideal in this sense, that the Lord blessed them in all their undertakings up to the point of moral crisis in the life of each. Both reigned during a period when there was no strength either in Egypt or in Mesopotamia, and Hebrew territory and trade had their greatest expansion. Well might later generations look back on those glorious days. These two kings ruled over a united Israel for the first and the last time in its history. Ideal they certainly were in contrast to the stupid and predatory murderers who followed them upon the throne. But the two, and David first, best exhibited the Hebrew ideal of kingship in this, that they were men devoted to the Lord, as best they knew how. Their devotion, not always enlightened, was sincere. As long as such men reigned – despite David's crime and Solomon's defection – the Hebrews could feel that the Lord was still in their midst. But even in the ideal king those traits appeared which were the symptoms of death in the Hebrew monarchy.

Was the demand for a king, and its fulfillment in Saul, David, and Solomon an outbreak of secular ambition in the popular will? The later prophets knew and taught, as we shall see, that military defeat was not the supreme disaster for the people of the Lord. Samuel and Nathan and the men of their day did not seem to understand this, and we should not blame them; it is not a truth which is easy to understand at any time. David was great as a conqueror, and Solomon as a merchant; was this the will of the Lord for His people, that they should subdue other peoples by force of arms and bring the wealth of nations into Jerusalem? Was it for this that He had spoken to the patriarchs and to Moses? Of such secular ambitions the ancient Semitic king was the visible embodiment, and his personal pomp was the testimonial of the glory of his nation. Those Hebrews who lived long enough could see the contrast between the austere palace of Saul, which has been uncovered by the excavator's spade, and the magnificence of Solomon, with his gold plate and his thousand ladies of the harem – another wistful exaggeration of popular story. And the aged Hebrew would wonder whether the Lord was really with the king. It was an urgent question, and it could not be answered at once. For the people of the Lord were to be a society governed by the will of the Lord, and it was not yet plain what the will of the Lord might be. Events, it would seem, showed a not obscure indication; Solomon's gold was plundered by an Egyptian king during the reign of his son, and Solomon's kingdom was rent in two by a dissatisfied citizenry. The ideal monarchy was badly tarnished and cracked; yet the ideal itself endured.

But the older and more conservative circles were right to some extent; the demand for a monarchy, which had arisen from the need for survival itself, had turned into secular ambition, and this secular ambition was never so well satisfied as under those two ideal kings, David and Solomon. On the other hand, the way of the Lord could not be identified with a particular way of life; pastoral-agricultural economy could not be canonized as an infallibly sure fulfillment of the will of the Lord. For the will of the Lord went much further than this, and was directed to more than a prosperous commercial state or a simple economy of the soil. But it is so easy for men to identify the will of the Lord with their own will. So when the monarchy came, it came to stay; it was born from the merging of irresistible forces of change within both Hebrew society and the world around it, which no political and social conservatism could halt.

As the Hebrew monarchy took form, without any deliberate planning, it was, in its own way, an externalization of the will of the Lord governing the Hebrew community. Many men contributed to give it the peculiar stamp of the Hebrew faith, and events themselves further determined it. The Hebrew king could not be the visible representative of divinity. The Lord remained above and beyond Hebrew society and Hebrew politics, just as He remained above and beyond the world of nature; He actively intervened in the course of events, but He did not become a part of it. To identify Him with the kingship would be, in its own order, like identifying Him with the forces of nature. The Hebrew king was a charismatic leader, an instrument through which the Lord worked, and as such he possessed a sacred character; he was "the anointed of the Lord." But he could not rise above the subjection to the Lord which was the proper position of every human being. Not the will of the king, but the will of the Lord, was the supreme law of the land; and of the divine will the king was not the only organ.

Against him stood the prophet, the man of the word of the Lord; and the history of the Hebrew monarchy shows a series of efforts to reach a balance between these two charismatic figures. These efforts are worth our attention, for in them appears the growth of the biblical understanding of the social life of man.

Samuel believed he could establish a theocracy, in which the king would be the pliant tool of the prophet, the executor of the will of the Lord as declared by the prophet. The plan of Samuel failed, as we would expect, because power cannot be dissociated from responsibility. The crime of Saul was disobedience to the prophet, though we cannot say exactly what the concrete fault was, because Hebrew tradition preserved two accounts of Saul's deposition. Some modern scholars think Saul attempted to exercise sacral kingship, a Mesopotamian and Canaanite and entirely un-Hebrew institution. This is a good guess which cannot be demonstrated. Was the crime of Saul more heinous than the crime of David, who flouted the fundamental principles of morality? Perhaps it was. Despite the fact that Samuel arrogated to himself a power which did not belong to prophecy, Saul seems to have rejected the very idea of the sovereign will of the Lord as the governing principle of Hebrew society, and to have identified the will of the king with the will of the Lord. This, as we can see, overturned the idea upon which the Hebrew polity was founded. But when Samuel tried to depose him, the popular will refused to ratify his decision; the king had proved himself by defeating the Philistines, and the people were not in a mood to dismiss the first winning leader they had known. It was Samuel who had to retire, discredited, powerless to do more than anoint the successor of Saul, who could not take the throne until Saul's death. It was not the office of prophecy to administer the affairs of state; Samuel learned this the hard way, and we find no other prophet attempting the impossible.

In Hebrew story, it was not unimportant that this episode was the tragic turning point in the career of Saul. He retained the throne, but the Lord was no longer with him. His initial victories over the Philistines had not been decisive, and the foe reorganized to smite Israel more severely than before. The king now gives evidence of a mental breakdown, which popular belief attributed to "an evil spirit." He becomes moody and suspicious, liable to sudden and unpredictable fits of murderous anger. He alienates his faithful followers, even his own children. He dissipates the military strength of Israel in a futile pursuit of David, while the Philistines mass for a final blow. In the closing scenes of his life, he stoops to the superstition of witchcraft, and dies by his own hand on the field of battle amid the ruins of the Israelite armies which had once followed him to victory. Such, the story tells us, is the end of the man who would not be king according to the will of the Lord. Prophecy and monarchy had failed to reach an understanding as to how the monarchy should head a society governed by the will of the Lord; both suffered in their tragic failure, and Israel suffered with them.

But if prophecy could not administer the affairs of state, it could make use of the popular will to restrain the monarch. In the kingdom of Israel, when Jezebel, Ahab's queen, introduced the cult of the Baal of Tyre, a serious crisis arose for the religion of the Lord. The issue was clear, and Elijah stated it clearly: "How long will you limp between two opinions? If the Lord is the god, follow Him; if the Baal, follow him." They were strange men, Elijah and Elisha, who fought for the Lord in those days; but, like Samuel, they were deeply concerned that Israel should remain the people of the Lord, that the will of the Lord should remain the supreme law, and that the king, the anointed of the Lord, should not become His enemy. We admire the boldness with which Elijah defied the power and pomp of royalty; and we can share the despair which he felt when his words appeared to have no effect, not even when they were accented by the rain which the Lord sent at the challenge of His prophet. There is no more vivid account of the meeting of God with man in the Old Testament than that in which Elijah learned that the Lord was not in the storm, not in the earthquake, not in the lightning, but in "the still, small voice" of the breeze. The work of the Lord was not to be accomplished by spectacular and violent means.

The prophet and his followers were desperate, and we should not be too sanctimonious in pointing out that Elijah and Elisha misunderstood the nature of the quiet workings of the Lord. If the religious aberrations of Israel could not be halted in any other way, then, they felt, the infamous dynasty must be removed. Samuel had attempted to remove a king by a prophetic oracle, and he had failed; these prophets turned to the weapons of conspiracy and assassination. Elisha did not anoint a shepherd lad, but the commander of an army in the field; the dynasty of Omri was drowned in blood, and Hebrew storytellers liked to recount how Jezebel was devoured by scavenging dogs in the very field of Naboth, whose judicial murder she had engineered. The dynasty was removed; the evil was not removed, and in a hundred years another generation was deploring the bloodshed of Jezreel and excoriating the same vices under the dynasty of Jehu, which had inaugurated its course in a devout blood bath of its predecessors. Not in this way was the will of the Lord accomplished. Not by conspiracy and assassination and mass slaughter was the integrity of the religion of Israel to be maintained. The prophets had been true to the Lord, but false to His principles.

Prophets were active also in the schism of the kingdom of Solomon under Rehoboam, the son of Solomon; but Hebrew tradition tells us nothing of any activities similar to those of Elijah and Elisha. It is altogether in accord with prophetic principles that they should have been appalled by the religious degeneration which set in under Solomon; but the story does not make religious degeneration a leading motive of the division of the kingdom. The division was rather a reaction to the heavy taxes and the forced labor upon which the glory of Solomon was founded, and to the favoritism which he showed toward Judah at the expense of the proud tribes of the north. Later prophets would take scandal at the wealth of the upper classes and the social evils which came with it, but prophecy of the tenth century appears to have had no voice on these subjects; it uttered rather an inarticulate cry of protest at what the glory of Solomon did to ancient Hebrew customs. The division of the kingdom cannot be called a reasonable reaction to the reign of Solomon in any respect, for the division fostered rather than removed the very evils which had evoked it. In this instance also the prophets had attempted to employ impossible means, and they made the last state of the kingdom worse than the first.

Prophecy was more effective in imposing restraints upon the monarchy when it operated within its own sphere and with its own weapon, the word of the Lord. When Nathan rebuked David for his adultery and murder, he stood up before the most powerful and successful ruler of his day. The issue was not a question of disobedience to the prophet, as it had been with Samuel and Saul, but of fundamental Hebrew and human morality; but it was the same question of the nature of the monarchy and the society governed by the will of the Lord. If David could do a thing like this, then the Hebrew king was no different from the kings of the nations; he had become an absolute ruler, a very god upon earth, and the moral will of the Lord was no longer the supreme law of the land. The prophet spoke, and the king submitted himself; here, more than elsewhere, David appears as the ideal king, who bent himself to the will of the Lord at the cost of his own personal dignity.

But more was demanded of him than a single act of submission. The storyteller knew that he told the story of a crisis, a definitive turn in the life of David and the history of Israel. The story of David's life from this point onward is the story of how the moral will of the Lord imposes itself upon human life when it is challenged. Up to his crime, David had been the darling of the Lord and of Israel, a conqueror who had not only made his people secure, but had made their name fearful far beyond their own borders. After his crime, he is a broken and discredited man. His own sons murder each other, and his eldest raises the cry of rebellion; and David, no longer the darling of Israel, dares not remain in the city which he had taken from the Jebusites to make it the most Hebrew of all cities, the city of David. The rebellion is quenched, but at the cost of many lives, including that of his son. From the time that he sinned his great sin, the light of happiness in David's life was put out; and we see him in his last days, prematurely aged while his contemporaries are still vigorous. Those who told this story knew that there was a power above that of the king, and that the king challenged this power at the peril of all that he was and possessed. Even the ideal king could not escape the law of the Lord that governs the actions of men. The collapse of an ideal and the wreck of a life are implied in the remark of the Hebrew storyteller: "This thing which David did was displeasing to the Lord."

The duel between prophet and king continued through the subsequent history of the kingdoms, although not in the acute forms which we have sketched above. After the days of Elijah and Elisha – and perhaps because of the dismal results of their practical operations – prophecy met royalty on the high level which Nathan had reached in rebuking David. We shall have to consider some of these clashes in more detail in a later chapter; but because they involve broader issues than the development of the Hebrew monarchy and the Hebrew state, we can omit them here. They are further expressions of the principle that the king lies under the will of the Lord, and that the prophet is the accredited spokesman for the divine will. But there is one more instance of an attempt at external restraint which is so extraordinary that it must be mentioned.

The reign of Manasseh in the seventh century was such an unhappy period that Hebrew story has told us little about it. The kingdom of Judah, which had survived the whirlwind which swept away Israel in the eighth century, was a vassal of Assyria; and, as was common in such vassal states, the conquered king imposed Assyrian religion and culture upon his subjects. Tradition stated that he made the blood of the servants of the Lord run in the streets of Jerusalem. Shortly after the end of his long reign, it became evident that Assyria was losing its grip upon western Asia; there was a resurgence of national feeling and of the national religion, which came to a head in the reign of Josiah, the grandson of Manasseh. Josiah was but a child at his accession, and those who wished to see the worship of the Lord restored apparently took care that he should be well schooled in that worship. In his eighteenth year – while he was still a young man – there was discovered in the temple, during its repair, a "book of the law of the Lord." Modern scholars have long agreed that this book contained part of the present book of Deuteronomy; and they generally agree also that it was a new codification of ancient Hebrew law and custom. But how new? This is not easy to answer, but a date in the seventh century is probable. There are few now who would maintain the older theory that it was put in the temple in order that it might be "discovered"; at the same time, its discovery seems to involve more than pure coincidence. Its origin was, directly, from priestly circles, although some modern scholars like to see in it a "fusion" of priestly and prophetic elements. Whether coincidental or not, it came at the right moment to be used as a guide of policy for the monarch in instituting a reform of the religion of Judah. Josiah accepted this guidance.

According to the prescriptions of the new book, foreign cults were rooted out of the land by violence, and the pure worship of the Lord was restored. The monarchy was once more submitted to the will of the Lord, this time expressed in a codified form. Unfortunately, the reform did not outlive the king himself. Jeremiah, contemporary of the period before the discovery of the book and after the death of Josiah, is a witness of the total religious and moral corruption of Judah. It was the last attempt to govern the king by religious authority, and it was no more successful than the earlier efforts. Twenty years after the death of Josiah, the kingdom of Judah was in its death agony.

We have run over – in a sketchy and disorderly manner, I fear – the story of the Hebrew kingship; and we have not yet finished it, for it will meet us again in the chapters which follow. For Hebrew kingship was an expression of the Hebrew state, within the limitations which we have tried to point out. The peculiarity of Hebrew kingship lay in this, that the Hebrew state was an ideal expression of the will of the Lord; it was this that created the tensions which we have seen, and elicited the restraints upon the Hebrew monarchy which we do not find in other states.

Viewed in the short perspective which we have adopted, the Hebrew monarchy appears to be a magnificent failure – if, indeed, one is willing to grant the word "magnificent." It fulfilled the immediate purpose for which it was established, and secured the national identity of the Hebrews against the danger which threatened it in the eleventh century. Once the monarchy was created, however, it began to run its own course, and we have seen that it could not do otherwise; for neither priest nor prophet was qualified either by nature or by office to do the work of the king. Running its own course, it followed the line of kingship, despite the restraints imposed upon it by Hebrew religion, until it finally brought the nation down to ruin with itself. It is a pathetic series of shortsighted little men whom we meet in the rolls of the kings of Israel and Judah. Rarely does a man appear who rises above the dreary level of the series to show vision and imagination, courage and execution. And some of the most successful rulers are dismissed by the Hebrew writers with a few words, such as Omri and the second Jeroboam. Was this all that could be expected of the charismatic leader?

What was expected of the charismatic leader? In the people of the Lord, in a society governed by the will of the Lord, the charismatic leader had not the same functions as the Mesopotamian and the Canaanite king. In these communities, the state, the integrity of society, was an absolute good, for human life was inconceivable outside the state. Therefore the king, the embodiment of the state, provided those goods which men expected of the state; if he and the state failed to do this, they perished. If they succeeded, they had done all that was required of them. And the king was thus an expression of the popular will, despite his absolute character; he represented what the people wanted. The Hebrew king, on the other hand, was to represent what the Lord wanted, and the popular will was of consequence only as far as it was identical with the will of the Lord. The sin of the Hebrew monarchs was that they represented the will of the people rather than the will of the Lord; and in doing this, they failed to give the popular will even those goods which it desired, those goods which it was the function of the Semitic king to give. Hence the Hebrew monarchy could not live.

But the will of the Lord is higher than the popular will, higher than the goods which the king and the state can confer. We have said that the charisma of the word of the Lord was not given to manage the affairs of state, and we can repeat it, for it is important. Samuel was willing to risk anarchy to depose a disobedient king; he failed, and his methods could not possibly have succeeded, but the principle behind his actions was a principle of Hebrew belief, that anarchy is better than disobedience to the will of the Lord. The prophets of the time of Rehoboam, as well as Elijah and Elisha, stooped to the methods of anarchy. We cannot approve their methods, and we can see how these methods must fail; but again the principle involved is that it is better for Israel to have no king than a king who does not embody the will of the Lord. The compilers of the stories of the kings paid little attention to the conquests of David, which are barely recorded, and to those of Omri and the second Jeroboam, because they knew that the

Hebrew king could not be measured by the standards of the kings of the nations. Not, indeed, that Hebrew story was indifferent to its external glories, for the Hebrew storytellers were human; but the prevailing tone of the story of the kings is one and the same. It is the story of the failure of the Hebrew kings to realize the will of the Lord, of the secularization of the Hebrew monarchy and of its consequent fall.

Shall we say that it could not have maintained itself? Samuel and Saul, Nathan and David, Elijah and Elisha and Jehu all seem to have had the same implicit purpose and assumptions, which we can thus formulate: the society governed by the will of the Lord is possible if we can submit human institutions to the will of the Lord, especially as that will is expressed by his prophets. By so doing, we shall establish the ideal society, the kingdom of God on earth; by legitimate rule, by prophecy, by law, we shall remove evils and create a community in which good prevails. But the ideal was not realized in Israel. The "theocracy" was not a society governed by the will of the Lord. Institutionalization would not accomplish the will of the Lord upon earth. The king failed because he represented the popular will rather than the will of the Lord, but this was not the only reason why he failed; he failed also because it was not the function of monarchy or of any civil government to create a perfect religious society. In legitimacy, prophecy, law, there is no interior regeneration of society, no revolutionary element; the existing framework is left unchanged, and changing its direction does not change its nature. It is still the kingdom of this world.

Such thoughts may seem to lead to despair; is the society governed by the will of God, then, a dreamworld, an impossible ideal? If so, has the impact of the divine activity upon the world no relevance for human society? We should not like to say that it is only a dream; and even if it should be, perhaps it is an ideal for which men must strive even if it is impossible. Sometimes the possible is reached only by aiming at the impossible. But the Hebrews were unable to attain this ideal by political means; and this may be the lasting significance of the story of the Hebrew kings. And this may be the lasting fruit of their experience: that there is no system, no device, no organization which will assure the realization of the will of God in society. If the kingdom of God were to be identified with any purely earthly society, any human government or human law, it would not be the kingdom of God. The words of the great prophets of the eighth and seventh centuries can be read more intelligently against this background of the story of prophet and king of the tenth and ninth centuries; it is to the words and the events of this later period that we must now turn our attention.

IX

THE NATIONAL WELFARE

MODERN philosophers define the function of the state as the procurement of the common good. The common good, they go on to tell us, is not the sum of the personal good of the members of the state, but that good which no single member, or single group of members, can procure; it is the good of the whole as opposed to the good of the parts, just as the life of the body is more than the sum of the health of the members of the body. This common good is the supreme temporal good; the state is not concerned with any other good and, indeed, has no competence to procure any other good. The common good is the enjoyment of all those goods which are offered within the structure of the material universe, and which are attained by the means available within the same structure. It is not a material temporal good; in the concrete, it means such things as peace and civil order, law and its enforcement, the protection of the members of the state from evils which they cannot ward off as individuals. In sum and substance, it means the creation of those conditions in which the individual members of the state are enabled to lead a peaceful life and reach that degree of prosperity which is within the grasp of the normal man.

All this philosophy was unknown to the ancient Semitic world; men lived it without thinking it out. They knew the function of the state in the concrete, not in the abstract, and they judged the success of civil government by its procurement of the common good That civil government which failed in its essential purpose would soon be overthrown, either by external enemies or by the uprising of the popular will. The sacred character of the king did not protect him against human nature.

As we have already noticed, this common good, like all temporal goods, came to the ancient Semitic world from the gods. And so the common good was dependent not only upon the effectiveness of civil government, but also upon the good will of the gods, which could be capricious. Hence it was a function of the state, which was also a religious society, to secure the good will of the gods by appropriate cultic ritual; and we have already taken notice of the character of this ritual. But it is of some importance to understand, when we come to the Hebrew idea of the state and the common good, that the Hebrews were like their neighbors in thinking that the attainment of the common good was a divine gift; the Hebrew belief differed from the belief of their neighbors not in the fact of the divine good will, but in the character of the divine will.

Now, it is a recurrent phenomenon in the history of religions that the performance of ritual petitions soon degenerates into something very close to superstition. Roman religion, in particular, exhibited this in a very high degree, so that Roman religion is without warmth, enthusiasm; the Roman sacrificed to his gods in the same spirit in which he closed a business deal. He had done his duty; now let the gods do theirs. He had paid the gods his debt; now let them perform the promised services. Then, as men began to think about these things more critically, and to notice that the gods help those who help themselves, they began to think that the efficacy of the ritual is really determined by the wit and the will of the men who perform the ritual; and they continued to perform the ritual out of rote, or a superstitious fear of some unknown danger which might strike them it if were omitted. But they aimed at the procurement of temporal good by purely secular means; and thus rationalism is born, because religion was thought to be a means of procuring temporal good from on high.

Israel, as we have repeated perhaps too often, was a society governed by the will of the Lord. Israel as a state could not be indifferent to the common good, for otherwise it would cease to be a civil society; but it had to think out what was primary in its own existence. If Israel was not a society governed by the will of the Lord, then it ceased to be the people of the Lord; it had no reason for existence other than the reasons which bring any civil society into existence, and it was subject to the same laws of history which govern the rise and fall of any civil society. The common good, for the Israelite state, was still the supreme temporal welfare of the community; but this could not be attained except in subordination to the will of the Lord. For Israel, like all ancient Oriental states, expected the common good from the Deity; but the good will of the Deity of Israel could not be ensured by the cultic ritual alone. The entire character of Hebrew society was determined by the will of the Lord.

If we open at random some of the pages of Leviticus or Deuteronomy, we meet what appears to be a rather crass statement of the relationship between the common good and the law of the Lord. Stated in summary fashion, these lines seem to say: If you are good, I will reward you with prosperity; if you are bad, I will punish you by adversity. The same thought may be seen in the book of Judges, where the editors have framed the stories in a cycle of sin, repentance, and divine deliverance. The scheme seems to us rather mechanical, and not in harmony with the facts of experience. When was Israel so morally upright that its prosperity was assured? And when it was most prosperous, do we not hear the prophets telling us of its moral corruption? They threaten future disaster, it is true; and their threats are valid, as we shall have to explain more at length. We are not concerned with the delay in the execution of the threats; where we deal with a nation as such, our perspective is larger than a single generation. Our question arises because the prosperity is derived from those very vices of which the prophets speak.

Furthermore, we ought to recall what we said earlier; the word of the Lord is not given to administer the affairs of state. Should we not go on to say that the power of the Lord is not devoted to secure temporal good, material prosperity? Is it not putting too cheap a price upon the will and the law of the Lord to reward their fulfillment with national prosperity? This way of thinking has now become associated with the word "Calvinistic"; if it is Calvinistic, we do not care to have it identified as biblical, even as a half-truth. Yet there is a paradox here; the devout Hebrew, like the devout Christian, was taught to expect material blessings from the hand of the Lord – even if a narrow reading of some Old Testament passages would lead us to think that they believed that the Lord rained only upon the just. The question, we might suppose, is: how much material blessings should we expect? The Christian is taught in the prayer of Jesus Himself to ask for his daily bread; perhaps no one but Jesus could teach us this, for no one else has.

Let us keep in mind this apparently mechanical view of the observance of the law and the common good, for we shall have to return to it. But, at the moment, let us glance at the history of the Hebrew state as an agent of the common good. We shall notice first of all that the Hebrews never lived by this simple mechanical view. They accepted the principle that God helps those who help themselves. Their most glorious days were the days of David and Solomon. These were the days of conquest, when tribute from subject peoples swelled the revenues of Israel. They were the days when the Hebrews began to profit by commerce. Palestine is not rich in natural resources, but neither is it destitute; by good management, it was possible to exchange the goods of Israel for the goods of other peoples at a tidy profit. In those glorious days the Hebrews first became aware of their cultural barbarism; they looked at the houses, the temples, the household furnishings, the art of their neighbors, and they blushed when they saw that they were culturally naked. By commerce with these peoples, by squeezing the good land until it cried to heaven, they could expand their own production to meet the prices of the current market. Solomon developed the mineral resources of Israel by slave labor in mining operations which must have been a living hell. So the Hebrews could buy these fine goods from afar, and ape the ways of the nations; they could dress in purple and fine linen, and dine sumptuously each day. This high living never lost its fascination for the Hebrews; each succeeding king had the ideal of Solomon before him, and his duty as the monarch, as the visible incarnation of the state, was to re-create the golden age, or to approach it as nearly as possible. So war and commerce and such things were the proper work of the Hebrew king, for by such things the national welfare was secured.

At the same time, the religious means of securing the national welfare were not neglected. From earliest times the Hebrews had asked the Lord for fruitfulness in their flocks and herds, in their fields and vineyards, and thanked Him annually for His bounty in the great harvest festivals. But early in the sojourn of the Hebrews in Canaan some of them began to believe that this was not enough. Why this doubt arose we cannot say; perhaps it had its origin in a drought, a failure of the crops, or some such hazard, for agriculture in Palestine was marginal and subject to many unfavorable factors. Perhaps it was their acquaintance with the Canaanites. In agriculture, as in other things, the Hebrews had to learn from the Canaanites; and they would certainly have heard that the Canaanites expected nothing from the soil unless the rites of fertility were faithfully enacted. Perhaps, also, it was the timidity of men in a strange land and a new atmosphere; they felt that the gods of the land which they had entered should not be neglected. And we may conjecture a more fundamental reason: it may have been an unvoiced consciousness that the Lord was not a God who promised material blessings, and that these had better be asked from gods who, frankly, promised their worshipers nothing more and asked of them nothing except the performance of the rites of fertility. For one or for all of these reasons, we find the Hebrews adopting the beliefs and the cults of the Canaanites.

The prophets and the Hebrew storytellers were not historians of religion, and they have not told us of these things with the precision which we expect in a modern monograph on the subject, but we can be reasonably sure of some aspects of the change. In the first place, the Hebrews did not abandon the Lord, or did not think they were abandoning Him; they rather added to His worship the cult of the gods of the land, seeking from them the things which they were not quite sure the Lord was interested in giving. In some instances — though some modern scholars do not think so — the Hebrews may have transferred the rites of fertility to the Lord Himself, believing, in their malicious simplicity, that this sort of blessing should be asked of Him in the manner proper to the blessing itself. And so they thought they had provided for the welfare of the community by all the religious and secular means available.

What else, we may pause to ask, should they have done? They learned the arts and crafts from the best masters they could find; they strengthened their economy by all the means at their disposal, and set up channels of trade through which goods were regularly exchanged. Even from the religious point of view they had left nothing undone, as long as one believes that one religion is as good as another. Committing themselves to these policies, they cast themselves upon the resources of worldly prudence and accepted the chances which such a course involves. Under proper administration, there appears to be no reason why such policies should not succeed over a long period of time — subject, of course, to the inevitable and unpredictable hazards of political realities. The policies did not succeed, of course, and many modern writers say they did not because they were poorly administered. What else can modern writers say, since they can offer no other policy for the national welfare of any state than that which the Hebrews adopted? But when they write in this strain about the Bible, they should know that they diverge here from the Hebrew prophets, who said that these policies could not succeed in any hypothesis, no matter how wisely they might be administered, because the national welfare of the Hebrew state had been divorced from the will of the Lord.

Let us return to what we have called the crass and mechanical view of the observance of the law and the national welfare. These passages of Leviticus and Deuteronomy are companion pieces to the books of the prophets, who express, in better defined concepts and clearer language, the same fundamental belief. We can formulate this belief for ourselves and in our own modern modes of utterance in this manner: The national welfare and the very order of nature itself are integrated with the moral order. The Lord does not have one will for the course of nature, another for the course of political and economic events, another for the moral life of man. His will is directed to a universe which is a harmonious unity, in which all its members co-operate under the single direction of His will. In this harmonious unity, the governing force, under the will of the Lord, is the will of man; by submission to the divine will, man communicates to the rest of the world the harmony which is established by the divine government. This is what the writer of the first chapter of Genesis means when he represents God making man His viceroy over the visible creation. This is the meaning also of the writer of the second and third chapters, when he represents the combat between man and nature as issuing from the combat of man against God. That is what the writers of the codes of law and of the prophets mean when they speak of national sin. Sin, to them, is not merely a moral disorder, a breach of a statute; it is a cosmic disorder, with repercussions that go far beyond the moral order and affect the entire life of man – his biological, social, political, economic welfare. For all these things depend upon the maintenance of the cosmic harmony of man submitted to the will of the Lord; once this harmony is disturbed, the harmony of the whole is lost. This is the Hebrew belief.

On the basis of this belief, nature becomes in Hebrew prophecy the weapon of the wrath of God. If the crops fail, if storm or blight or locusts wreck the careful works of man, it is not an unfortunate concatenation of natural forces, but the will of an angry God, who will not permit men to enjoy His gifts when they are unsubmissive to His will. For God works in nature as He does in man, and it is inconceivable to the Hebrew that there should be no correlation between His will governing nature and His will governing man. And so the national welfare cannot be secured unless it be the will of the Lord to grant those things which make for the national welfare. His good will cannot be secured by rebellion. Shall we call this too human a conception of the Almighty, that He is angered by disobedience and withdraws His favors in punishment? Perhaps; it is no more human than the conception of a fatuously benevolent Deity who knows or cares little about the conduct of His creatures. In this, the Hebrew saw the Lord as immediately present and active in the world.

It is the glory of the Hebrew prophets that they never looked at sin in the abstract and in theory. The vividness with which one is aware of the evil of sin derives directly from the vividness with which one apprehends the goodness of God; if one does not care much whether men do wrong or not, one does not care much about God, nor does one take seriously His moral will. We shall do well, if we wish to penetrate the profundity of the Hebrew faith, to read and consider the incandescent words of the prophets about the supreme menace to the national welfare, to human welfare. Taken by themselves, their words might give us a one-sided view both of Hebrew belief and of human life; but the danger is nearer, and always has been, that the words of the prophets will go unread, or that they will be unconsidered, or rationalized into "ethical teaching" and "social reform."

In Hebrew, as in Greek, to "sin" means to miss the mark; linguistically, there is no difference between sin and error. The distinction comes from the flaming passion with which the prophets have invested the word. The fundamental reality which they see in sin is, we think, that it is a personal offense. Let us pause and reflect upon what this means. A crime, a felony, a breach of a statute are legal offenses, offenses against the law, against society. They may be offenses against a person – such crimes as murder and theft certainly are – but they are not personal offenses against authority, because authority is impersonal, collective. Or one may take a superstitious view of wrongdoing, fearing that it will release some impersonal evil force of retribution. Or one may feel that he sins against the integrity of man, against the autonomous conscience. The Hebrews sinned against a person. They could not have thought of sin in this way were it not for that mystic awareness of the personal reality of God which we have, more than once, pointed out as pervading the whole people. A personal offense exhibits a malice which we do not see present in crimes against society or humanity; for the person elicits from us a response of love or hatred which we cannot give to an institution or a collectivity. Is it not relevant to recall that in modern social and humanitarian and impersonal morality the evil will of man comes, finally, to be denied altogether? Sin, in such morality, is not malice, but ignorance, psychic imbalance; sin is a disease to be cured by education and psychiatry, not a basic corruption of the person to be removed by repentance and a revolutionary change in one's life.

The prophets describe the response of the Lord to sin as personal, and they describe it in fully human language. Sin arouses the Lord's anger, His hot and burning anger. He is jealous of His glory, which is impugned by sin, and of His people, which is snatched from Him by sin. He hates evil and evildoers, He loathes and abominates them. He smites the wicked to sore destruction, and rejoices at their downfall. Our modern theology does not permit us to attribute human sentiments to the Deity; we use the language of the Bible, but we rationalize it away. This we think we must do; but the Hebrew prophets did not feel the necessity. They were aware that the Lord is God and not man, spirit and not flesh; but they were afraid that the irreconcilable and deadly opposition between God and sin would vanish if one looked at sin as a merely human failure. This was a greater danger than the danger that the Deity might be demeaned to the human level. One must risk some distortion in speaking of the ineffable, and this is the risk they chose to run; they feel that above all else men must believe that sin is a personal offense, an act of personal hostility to God. When we look at modern morality, in which the malice of sin has been enveloped in a cloud of metaphysics, shall we say that they took a childish view of sin?

To the prophets, sin was "evil," with that peculiar force which the Hebrews attached to the word: the corruption of all that is good. It was rebellion, treachery, ingratitude, not against an impersonal force, but against the God whom they called their father, their kinsman. It was injustice against a God who was scrupulously just and fair. It was hatred of a God whose most frequent appellation is "loving-kindness"; the word catches the spirit of the Hebrew, even if it is not an exact translation. Sin was "twisted," "crooked," a distortion. It is "falsehood"; it is what Plato called "the lie in the soul," the refusal not merely to speak the truth, but to think the truth. It is all these things and more, because human language is incapable of finding words to tell what it is.

And it is the work of man doing what he pleases. Sin arises from pride, which the Hebrews called "loftiness"; the attempt of man to raise himself above his proper level, "to become like God, knowing good and evil." The Hebrews knew nothing of heredity and environment and compulsions as explanations and excuses for what men do; a man does this thing because he wants to do it, because he loves evil and not good, darkness and not light. He is a responsible agent, and he will have to be treated as such; having it in his power to do good, he chooses to do evil. And it is the height of futility; the Hebrews called it "folly," and they have no word for the sinner more harsh than "fool." It achieves nothing of what the sinner hopes to attain through it, but rather destroys the present good while it renders the future good impossible. It is death: not death in the ordinary biological sense, but death as the negation of all those values which we put in the word "life." Were it to run its course unchecked, it would reduce the world back to the primitive chaos, which Jeremiah in prophetic vision saw in the land of Judah:

> "I looked at the earth, and it was chaos –
> at the heavens, and their light was gone.
> I looked at the mountains – they were quaking;
> and the hills swayed back and forth.
> I looked – and no man could be seen;
> even the birds had disappeared.
> I looked at the cultivated land – it had become a desert,
> and its cities were desolate before the Lord,
> before His burning anger."

Such a catastrophe is not merely the result of social maladjustment.

This is sin in the concrete, but not in the particular; to give their words body the prophets must go on and speak of sin in its specific varieties and its individual manifestations. This they do, with a frankness which no modern pulpit orator dares imitate unless he is willing to risk what the prophets risked. Can we find, in the prophetic discourses, some radical vice which underlies all the moral evil which they find in the people of the Lord? It would be interesting if we could; but the prophets are not moralists nor psychoanalysts. To them, moral evil appears as a single unholy entity. The distinction between religious and moral evil would have no sense for the prophets, for they were unconscious of any such distinction. In our own language, however, we do make the distinction; and we would say that the prophets appear to view the religious corruption of their people as basic, from which moral corruption flows of necessity. Morality was "to know God"; if one does not know God, then one does not know good.

The religious corruption of which they speak we have already indicated more than once. It was what is called, in the history of religions, syncretism: the introduction of Canaanite beliefs and practices into their own religion, the worship of the Lord. This meant either that the Lord shared His supremacy with the Canaanite Baal, the lord of fertility, or that the Lord took on the traits of the Canaanite Baal: that is, that the Lord became a god within the forces of nature, not the invisible Deity who stood above and beyond the things which He had created. The Hebrews did not have enough natural theology to see that this destroyed their God. Worse than the obscene rites of fertility was the debasing of the idea of God in the minds of men, the reduction of the divine to "nature," the annihilation of the divine person whom their fathers had known. A god whose primary interest to his worshipers was the national welfare was no true god. A god who promised nothing except material blessings – wealth, pleasure, victory over enemies – was nothing but a hallowing of the concupiscence of the eyes and the concupiscence of the flesh. A religion in which the security of the nation and its citizens was foremost in faith and in worship was not a religion. This we can see in the prophets' discourses; for if the religion of the Lord was nothing different from the religion of Canaan, then it had perished, whether the name remained or not.

But the cults of Canaan were not the only superstitions which the prophets attacked. Sometimes they speak of the sacrificial worship of the Lord Himself, conducted, as far as we can see, with due liturgical protocol, and they call this worship superstitious, irreligious. From such language many have concluded that the prophets repudiated the whole idea of external worship. We have tried to point out earlier that the Hebrew genius accepted the principle of cult, and we cannot easily suppose that the prophets abandoned it. The "religion of the spirit," the "religion of the heart," is a modern invention, devised to meet the need for religion and at the same time to escape submission to the restraints which necessarily follow from organized religion. To the prophets, as to all Hebrews, men met God as members of a group, and the group as such, not merely as a collection of individuals, owed God the social expression of that which was a social reality.

Nor is it necessary to read the religion of the spirit into the words of the Prophets; for the cult which they attacked was superstitious, even when it was directed to the Lord, the God of Israel. Into the sacrificial worship of the Lord also the corruption of Canaanite ideas had entered; sacrifice had become an automatic means of securing the divine good will, an adequate symbol of submission to the will of the Lord. What the Lord demanded was not merely the offering of victims, but the reality which was thereby symbolized: the execution of His moral will, the will which governed the whole of human life. Without this total surrender, sacrifice became a symbol with no reality behind it; it was pure superstition, in which magical efficacy is attached to words and actions in themselves. By such things, and by other forms in which the religion of the Lord was "Canaanized," His moral will was effectively obscured. "The Lord does not know, He does not care"; these were the words of the benighted Israelites who preferred to think of the Lord as an amiable Baal who had no moral will, who gave His worshipers the worldly goods which they sought if they went through the proper motions.

It is a vice of all organizations and institutions that the structure itself tends, with the passing of time, to become sacred. Theologians have seriously discussed whether the Church must of necessity have the seat of its supreme authority in Rome, as if God were nearer in Rome than elsewhere in the world which He created. There are reasons for this attitude. These material associations with ideal and spiritual realities give a local habitation and a name to these realities, and are a boon to mankind at large, which can see these realities better if they have some such material association. But the symbol can be confused with the reality. The Hebrews had their sacrifices, their temple, their ark of the covenant, on which the God of victories was enthroned. They had their priesthood and their king, sacred functionaries who embodied the presence and the power of the Lord. They had Jerusalem, which the Lord had chosen as the place where His name should dwell. They were not ready to hear that the Lord was greater than all these material symbols, and dependent upon none of them. They rebelled against the prophet who told them that the Lord would remain when all these material symbols were wiped out. And wiped out they would be, because they had no sacredness of their own. The Lord dwelt among His people in their submission to His will, not in any material symbol; when they destroyed the bond which linked them with the Lord, the symbol became an object of superstition. And the Hebrews naturally regarded the prophet who attacked these symbols as a traitor, because they knew that when the symbols perished, they also would perish.

When this religious perversion was very near its peak, there appears in Hebrew prophecy the image of the Lord which is at once most personally intimate, and most terrifying when seen in contrast to sin. Hosea, in the eighth century, was the first to see the Lord as the spouse of Israel. This parable of espousal has had a long history in biblical writing, and in the compositions of the mystics, for it appeals to the most tender human affections. It would be false to say that Israel never heard of the love of God before Hosea; but it would be very near the truth, at least, to say that they had not thought of the love of God with the depth of feeling which is suggested by the parable of conjugal love. One may, if one wishes to be captious, point out that ancient marriage was not a romantic union after the modern manner; but such pedantry takes away none of the warmth of the words of Hosea, nor of Jeremiah, who also adopted the image. These men knew the profundity of this mysteriously unique sentiment which unites man and woman in one flesh; it was their vision of the divine personality which led them to apply it to Him. It is not only His will which the Lord imposes upon Israel, it is His love; and as a man can pay a woman no greater compliment than to ask her to marry him, so the Lord could offer Israel nothing more than His love, which is Himself.

It is quite possible that the image arose in the prophet's mind as a reaction to the gross hedonism of the fertility rites; we have suggested that a similar reaction lies behind the story of Genesis 2–3. Against this obscene background, the pure love of the Lord for His people shows His true character at the same time as it dignifies that sexual relation which the fertility cult profaned. And so the prophet charges Israel with the supreme human infidelity: the faithlessness of one who has pledged love, has known love, and has withdrawn from love. We said that human language lacks the resources to tell what sin is; if it has reached the limit of its resources, it reaches it here. Not until the Gospels can one go beyond this. The picture of God as the rejected lover pursuing His faithless beloved is too bold for any man to draw; only God can disclose it.

Because the moral will of the Lord was obscured, because His love had been concealed by the adulterous affection of the Hebrews for the gods of Canaan and their blandishments, the whole structure of Hebrew law and of basic human morality was imperiled. We adverted earlier to the expansion of Hebrew production and commerce which occurred under the monarchy. Such expansion is the aim of any enlightened government; thereby the standard of living is raised, prosperity is more widely diffused and more solidly founded. It cannot be emphasized too much that the prophets entirely repudiated this policy. It is not a question of purifying it, of reforming it, of putting it upon sound principles; Isaiah spoke for the whole line of prophets when he said that trading is whoring. We may not like this feature of Old Testament prophecy, but let us not therefore deny that prophecy said it; let us rather try to understand it. As we have remarked earlier, we are not concerned with defending Hebrew belief; but we are very much concerned that it be proposed in its integrity. In the prophets, we have not yet reached the point where the poor will be called blessed, a more revolutionary formula than anything in the prophets; but we have a well-defined attitude toward what happened in the Hebrew state under the monarchy, and toward the measures which the state adopted to secure its national welfare.

There is not in the whole canon of prophetic literature one word of praise for the measures which were calculated to secure the welfare of the state. There is never a word of rejoicing because the nation has been made richer by trade and commerce. We, of course, studying the history of the Hebrews from our own point of view, can see the essential vice in the growth of Hebrew wealth; it was not widely diffused. Solomon's wisdom simply created a wealthy class and left the mass of the population as poor as it had been before. In the course of time, they became even poorer; for the peasant was not at home in an economy of hard metal. He became a habitual debtor, and ultimately a slave. Ownership of land, once widely scattered, became concentrated in the hands of a few wealthy families. Labor could not compete with the growing number of slaves, who came in by purchase or by conquest. The contrast between the riches of the cities and the poverty of the villages and the countryside was sharp. The resources of the nation, since they were not widely possessed, were squandered on luxuries and not on the necessities of life.

Now we ought to notice that this state of affairs, which we would call an unsound economic situation, was not limited to the Hebrew community; it was normal in the ancient world, in the medieval world, as it is normal in most of the modern world. In most societies, historically, there has been no middle class. Nations grow wealthy, but the wealth is not diffused; their wealth weakens their national stamina, and they fall a prey to some hungry horde of barbarians, in which every man is poor. But the barbarians in their turn learn to love the sweets of possession, become civilized, and fall before the next hungry horde. It is interesting and discouraging. The Hebrew prophets were not philosophers, and they did not generalize; they spoke only of their own people Israel, and they declared with all their conviction that this sort of thing is not the will of the Lord.

We may grant that the ancient world knew little of carrying on its economic activities in an ethical way. With the pursuit of wealth, certain vices seemed to follow with inevitable necessity. Dishonesty was a prerequisite for success, dishonesty in word and in deed. There was no room for compassion; in a highly competitive world, the devil takes the hindmost. Where human beings are handled as chattels, there is little respect for human life, and even less for the dignity of the human person. The prophets speak of their community as one in which mutual confidence, the cement of human relations, has perished. The poor are oppressed by the rich, and of nothing do the prophets speak with more heat; they are the spokesmen of the Lord for the helpless. Can we, then, accept the designation of "social reformers" which has been laid upon the prophets? A social reformer, in modern language, means a person with a program of reform. The reformer accepts the existing institution in principle, but not in practice; he would modify it, change its operations, correct it, but he would not destroy it or change its nature. We do not see how the prophets can be called reformers in this or any other sense. It is the very pursuit of wealth, they say, which brings these things with it; they have no program for pursuing wealth in an orderly manner. They have only threats that the wealth of the nation is eating it up, and will finally consume it. The measures which the Hebrews took to secure the national welfare are destroying the national welfare; for they are not according to the will of the Lord.

Are the prophets, then, revolutionaries? Do they envisage a new socioeconomic order rising from the ruins of the old? Again, we find no such thing – unless we are to call a society submitted to the will of the Lord "a new socioeconomic order." It would be that, indeed, but that hardly describes it. The prophets are revolutionaries, and they do envisage a new order; this vision is so important that we shall have to treat it subsequently at length. But it goes beyond the national welfare, and this is our concern at present. They are certainly revolutionaries in this, that they announce the destruction of the existing order; it cannot survive, because it has created the seeds of its own destruction, it perishes by its own activity. It is we, of course, who speak in this manner;

the prophets say that the Lord will bring it to an end. And so the Hebrews seem caught in an economic cycle which infallibly returns to its beginning; the pursuit of wealth issues in the loss of wealth.

Can we not find in the prophets, however, some kind of social and economic platform? Can we not baptize the economic life of man? Do they not tell us some way in which the pursuit of the national welfare can be surely submitted to the will of the Lord? We should be pleased if they did, but they do not. They have no program in which man, by the employment of his reason and his good will, can surely submit his activity to the will of the Lord. They have no system which will deliver man from the necessity of facing, each day, the decisions which will bend his life to the will of the Lord or make him a rebel.

Nor do the prophets mean that the national welfare is secured, that the common good is attained, when the pursuit of material goods is conducted in an ethical manner. Their idea of the common good is different. The common good was the subjection of society to the will of the Lord. Wealth and its appurtenances were the goods which the gods of the heathen promised their worshipers; one did not do the will of the Lord in order to secure these things, for such a motive made it impossible to do the will of the Lord, who is served for His own sake or not at all. Jesus put the thought of the prophets in a single sentence, as only He could do, when He said, "Seek first the kingdom of God and His justice, and these other things will come to you." But neither the prophets nor Jesus meant that doing the will of the Lord would bring men the goods of this world; they meant that one who does the will of the Lord will always have enough, for one will not want more than one has. The perfect enjoyment of material security is not possible until the cosmic disorder of sin is removed; a mode of life which compromises with that cosmic disorder in order to promote material security fosters the very agent which destroys material security.

Is there not, perhaps, something fatally unrealistic in the attitude of the prophets toward this question? Perhaps, but we ought to ask whether there is not something fatally realistic in any other attitude. A political society which accepts righteousness as the common good and undertakes to realize it by political means has never existed; we have considered some reasons why it cannot exist, and ought not. The mind of the prophets is nothing so blatantly absurd as this. Nor can we suppose that they were so simple as to believe that a community of the righteous could create for itself a little island of security in a godless world—security, that is, in the sense of temporal security; the thought of the prophets, as we shall see, goes far beyond this, although it does not reach its fullness in the prophetic books. Their "unrealism" consists in this, that they refuse to accept sin as a normal part of human life, and they will not listen to any other explanation of the ills of society. And that realism is fatal which surrenders to the fact of the human will for evil, and believes that an evil will can produce good, even material good. No, the prophets have no social or economic or political program.

One might say: then this is despair of human institutions. And one would speak the truth. There is no element of hope in the prophets which is based upon the human will, whether institutional or individual. But in a world in which God is present and active, man can learn nothing more important for his welfare than the fact that there are some things beyond his power which only the Lord can achieve. When Israel believed that deliverance is from the Lord, they did not mean that it was possible for man to save himself from some things.

National guilt, as the prophets describe it, is a chilling thought. Such pictures as the wounded man of Isaiah, beaten and bruised from head to foot until there is no place left to strike him, or the painted harlot, shrieking as she is murdered, whom Jeremiah gave to his people for their thoughtful consideration, are not intended to cheer. This, they say, is you; this is your nation, the people of the Lord, and there is no soundness, no goodness in you. There is nothing in you that is worth saving. One thinks of Abraham asking whether there were not ten just men in Sodom, of Ezekiel assuring himself that the just man would at least save himself, although he did not know how the just man would do it. This, again, is a problem which does not come to a solution in the writings of the prophets. For them, the operative fact was that the malice of the citizens had corrupted the national life, so that the nation as such could no longer endure. A national regeneration might save it, at least in the sense that it would survive; and this the prophets preached, although it is plain that they had no hope that it would happen. But even a belated return to the will of the Lord would not reverse the forces of evil which their wickedness had set in motion. These forces must come, because there was no human power which could halt them, and it was folly to expect the Lord to avert the course of the moral law of history; for this law is His justice in action. The state had failed in its primary purpose to secure the common good; and it had to experience the terrible results of its failure.

"Unless the Lord build the city, they labor in vain that build it." The Old Testament does give a basis for human society, even if it does not delineate the form and structure of the ideal society. It is not the Republic of Plato nor the Utopia of More. But it is a basis which modern society calls impractical: it is the knowledge of God. If the fundamental defect of the Hebrew state was a failure to know God, then its fundamental stability must rest upon the truth about God; and, for the Hebrews, men learned this truth only from what God tells them. From the truth about God flows the truth about human relations: social, political, economic, every activity which men carry on. The complex organization of modern society would have bewildered the Hebrews; but, once recovered from their astonishment, they would say: complexity does not change the nature of the thing. It still rests upon the knowledge of God, or it rests upon nothing. It worships the gods of Canaan, if it believes that its common good, its welfare and security lie in the maximum enjoyment of material goods. How men are to regulate this complex machine they have made so that the monster does not destroy them is something which they must answer by their intelligence and good will; but they will never answer it if they treat the problem as purely secular.

This, we said, the modern world treats as impractical. So did the men of the Hebrew monarchy. The prophets told them what would happen because they did so.

ISRAEL AND THE NATIONS

THE reader of the Old Testament is never allowed to forget that he is in a strange and unfamiliar world; and he is never more aware of this alien atmosphere than when he meets the exotic names of the peoples of the ancient Semitic Near East. Canaanites, Moabites, Ammonites, Edomites, Aramaeans, Assyrians, Babylonians, Chaldeans, Persians — who were all these? We have mentioned already that scholars knew no more about these peoples than the casual Bible reader did up to the nineteenth century. Until the ancient Near East had been revealed in the ruins of its cities, until its literature had been discovered and the riddle of its languages solved, even learned men knew no more of these peoples than they could gather from sifting the pages of the Old Testament. Now these peoples are better known to us; we know more of Babylonia and Assyria, for instance, than we do of the Gauls whom Caesar conquered. They have a history of their own, and it can be studied for its own sake. Until the modern discovery of these peoples, their story had interest only as it touched the story of the Hebrews. For students of the Bible, this is still the primary interest of their story. We cannot expect here to dissipate the fog which conceals these peoples from the knowledge of those who are not professional historians; excellent books have been written which do that for those who wish to learn. We are concerned with them for their impact upon the religious beliefs of the Hebrews; this impact was profound, scarcely to be ignored by anyone who wishes to apprehend the meaning of the Hebrew faith.

No people, tribe, or nation ever existed which determined its destiny all by itself. The social group cannot live its own life any more than the individual person can. The conditions in which it comes to be and develops its own ethos are created by others. The give and take of political and commercial intercourse keep it constantly unsettled, undetermined; its ideas, its use of material goods, its religion, everything that it is are bombarded by the influence of external agents. Before the history of the ancient Near East was known, it could be thought that the Hebrews lived in a kind of cultural and religious desert island; in preceding chapters we have seen how much they were affected in their thinking and their religious beliefs by their neighbors, and the same is to be said of the other departments of human activity. Now, in addition to these facts of Hebrew internal history, we have to consider what we call international relations: the external politics of the Hebrew state.

International relations, in the history of the Hebrews, begin with the monarchy; we have already seen that it was the pressure of the Philistines which impelled the Hebrews to establish the monarchy. There could have been no international relations before the Hebrews had a strong central government. Once the monarchy had been established, it became a focus for the latent national energy of Israel, which burst out in conquest under David, in commerce under Solomon. The conquests of David were not really extensive; but they subjected the states on Israel's immediate borders. These conquests would have been impossible if either Egypt or Mesopotamia had been, at the moment, the seat of a great power, as they normally were; but both regions were plagued by internal weakness and division, and could exercise no effective influence upon events in Syria and Palestine. This state of affairs did not outlive Solomon; under his successors the divided kingdoms of Israel and Judah, now themselves the victims of their own internal weakness, lost their hold on the territories which David had conquered.

Hebrew religion seemed to have no voice about the external politics of David and Solomon. There are traces, not very strong, of the ancient Hebrew conservatism which frowned upon this expansion as an imitation of foreign ways. It might have been better for the Hebrews if this conservatism had found articulate expression; but nothing succeeds like success, and there was no visible blot upon the success of David and Solomon. A keen observer might have seen on the horizon a cloud no bigger than a man's hand; but this is second guessing. The dreamworld of the early monarchy should have been shattered when the Pharaoh of Egypt, not long after the death of Solomon, marched across the whole of Israel, and exacted tribute even from the city of David and the holy temple of the Lord. The Hebrews might have learned from this that, in the world of international politics, they were boys playing with men; and who can tell what turn this might have given to their history? They did not learn it. The kingdom of Judah was too small to play a part in the game of politics; but Israel, in the ninth and eighth centuries, was a powerful member of the group of Syrian states. The revolution of Elisha and Jehu which overturned the dynasty of Omri was a religious revolution, as far as we can tell; but the prophets were sympathetic, to some extent, with the Aramaean kingdom of Damascus, the chief political and commercial rival of Israel, because it was a check on the dynasty which they hated and wished to overthrow. But the revolution of Elijah and Elisha exhibits no development of ideas about international relations. The time was not too far off when Israel and all the states of Syria together would find that they were too small for power politics; here also a keen observer might have noticed the signs of the future, but no such observer is mentioned at this point in the Hebrew story.

From a purely secular and political point of view, the small kingdoms of Syria and Palestine were devouring each other during the ninth and eighth centuries. Local autonomy is a beautiful ideal, no doubt, and much blood was spilled in Syria, as it was in Greece, for the defense of local liberty; in either case, local liberty generally meant the liberty of each state to enjoy its own domestic tyranny and misrule. In Syria, as in Greece, the chronic folly of these military displays, with their squandering of material and human resources, cleared the road for a monolithic empire which had the merit of establishing a single centralized tyranny in place of a multitude of petty tyrannies. One watches the sweep of these events with the fascination with which one would watch the approaching funnel of a tornado. There are moral forces, human forces, at work, not the inflexible forces of nature. These are men — for the social entity is a collection of individual persons — doing things with almost the same fearful necessity which we see in nature; for the policy which they adopted could have had no other issue than that which it had. Yet, at every step, there was a point where vision and courage could have diverted the stream of events in a different direction. It is a pattern which has recurred so frequently in history that it almost bores us to give it our attention. Yet to understand the history of Israel it is important to place the Hebrew monarchy and the Hebrew prophet against this background of quarreling petty states of the Syrian littoral, a political world of incredible self-interest, shortness of vision, narrowness of sympathy. So far can the ideal of the common good, the national welfare, take men down the path to their own annihilation. This, we said, is the story viewed from a secular and political point of vantage; but we want to see it from the point of Hebrew belief.

Into this political and moral vacuum marched Assyria, the first real world power in recorded history. To read the history of the Hebrews without Assyria would be to ignore the supreme political factor which crushed all others; Assyria bulked more largely on the horizon of ancient Near Eastern politics than any nation has in modern Europe. The world empire of Assyria at its peak, in the middle of the seventh century, extended from the mountains east of Mesopotamia to the Mediterranean and the mountains which divide Asia Minor from Syria, and from the mountains of Armenia into the Arabian desert and up to the cataracts of the Nile. Some modern scholars see in this world empire the realization of an ideal which first appears, they think, in the much smaller Akkadian Empire of the latter part of the third millennium B.C., and which was the ideal of every strong government which subsequently appeared in Mesopotamia. The Assyrian king took the traditional titles of the Mesopotamian rulers: "great king," "king of kings," "king of all," "king of the four quarters." These scholars would see the Assyrian world empire as the final realization of the drive to unite this vast territory into a single civilization and culture under a single government which was "the world"; the outer barbarians were not counted. And they think that the Assyrians were impelled by a religious drive to fulfill the will of their god to subdue the world to himself.

Other scholars, less mystical, see the empire as a response to the geographical fact that the original territory of Assyria had no natural frontiers and was subject to attack from all directions; in resisting enemies and seeking a natural line of defense, the Assyrians found no halting point until the limits of "the world" had been reached. This, however, is true: Assyria realized the idea of the world empire, whether it created the idea or not. The empire remained substantially integral for three hundred years after the Assyrians disappeared; it passed into the hands of the Babylonians, then to the Persians, and then was assumed into the larger empire of Alexander, whose world state was broader than that of Assyria; and the old Assyrian empire came apart only under the successors of Alexander. The counterpoise had been set up, the principle of unity opposed to the disunity of the ninth and eighth centuries: the world state, what we call "one world." The imperial idea has never disappeared from the Near East; from the conquerors of Islam to modern Pan-Arabism, there have always been those who believed that these regions attain their maximum of order and security under a single government. Some scholars would say that the idea of a world state came to the Mediterranean through Alexander from Mesopotamia. It is a tremendous legacy which the men of Assyria have left to the world.

These conquerors from the banks of the Tigris are no longer strangers to us; we can read their records and look at the pictures they have left us – pictures largely devoted to war and the chase, for the Assyrian king hunted lions as he hunted his foes. We can view the closely joined columns of sturdy bearded warriors, each with the same expressionless countenance, watch them as they ford streams, climb mountains, assault city walls, all with the same imperturbable calm: "Speedily, swiftly he comes, none weary, none stumbling in his ranks. His arrows are sharpened, his bows are bent; the hooves of his horses are like flint, his wheels like the whirlwind. His roar is like the roar of a lion. He will seize the prey and carry it off, and none shall deliver." Thus did Isaiah describe the advance of the Assyrian armies into the land of Israel. We can read their own accounts of their conquests: cold statistical reports, behind which we can see the smoke of burning cities, the impalement stakes about the walls, the piles of heads by the ruined gates, the long lines of prisoners shuffling off to slavery in some far country. Modern scholars, as we have seen, think they have discovered what was the insatiable drive this people possessed, what genius it was that pushed them to create the greatest military machine, the most massive political structure which the world had yet seen. But we know that the hour was ripe for such a power, for the world into which the Assyrians moved was rotten. And in this world was Israel, the people of the Lord. Here was something new, something for which their past had not prepared them; how were they to meet it?

Israel is first mentioned in the Assyrian records by Shalmaneser III. In 853 or 852 "Ahabbu of Sirla," Ahab of Israel, was one of the allies who fought Shalmaneser to a standoff at Karkar in upper Syria. The check to Assyrian arms was only temporary; the "Black Obelisk" of the same Shalmaneser, which enumerates his conquests up to 826, the thirty-first year of his reign, shows us a relief illustrating the tribute of "Iaua the son of Humri," the Jehu who had overthrown the dynasty of Omri. But the course of Assyrian empire was slowed for the next seventy-five years by the weakness of its kings, and the Israelites forgot their fear of the Assyrians. The alliance of the Syrian states, formed against the Assyrian threat, was joyfully dissipated, and the kingdoms resumed their habitual wars. But the significance of events was not lost on the generation of prophets who began to speak the word of the Lord about the middle of the eighth century. These were Amos and Hosea in Israel, Isaiah and Micah in Judah, in whom prophecy rises to a new height. It is common to speak of the "political insight" of these men, of their historical intuition of the true nature of the Assyrian threat. Insight and intuition they may have possessed; but that which is the basis of their assurance is the word of the Lord. And the word of the Lord is that the traitorous people of Israel shall suffer at the hands of a conquering nation; whether the prophets name the nation or not, there could be little doubt who was meant.

Now, the response of the prophets to the threat of Assyria is not the same in all details in each one of the prophets, and these variations in their thinking will give us some trouble. But there is one fundamental truth which each one of them proposes, and it is such a startling truth that we cannot afford to risk slighting it. I say it is a startling truth, although it has circulated for so long in the world which reads the Bible that it has lost much of its original pungency. Or shall we say that we look upon it as we look upon so much of the biblical revelation, as something which had its place in its own time, but has lost its urgency because the world has moved so far? This fundamental truth is simply stated by Isaiah: Assyria is the rod of the Lord's anger, the staff of His indignation. This is the basic prophetic utterance upon international relations which has been conventionalized into insignificance. It has been conventionalized because the modern world, even the modern Christian and Catholic world, is slow to confess that the principle has any validity for our day. It should not be difficult for us to put ourselves in the place of the ancient Hebrews and to enter fully into their mind, for the words they uttered in response to the prophets are familiar, and we have heard the like of them in our day: It is not the Lord, it is not He. It is someone else who brings this evil upon us, but not the Lord whom we worship and serve. It is not the bitter fruit of our evil deeds that we taste, not the breath of His hot anger that we sense. It must be a breakdown of diplomacy, a failure of strategy, a collapse of the military machine; but it is not the Lord. If wicked and godless men afflict the righteous, it cannot be the paralyzing stroke of His right hand, which Isaiah saw raised against His people. The Hebrews would gladly admit the prophetic principle if it were applied to another people, and they could appreciate the poems of Nahum which hymned the fall of Nineveh. But the Lord could not let this happen to them. National guilt, as we said above, is a terrifying idea; and its terror is magnified because it is accompanied by national blindness.

The prophets do not mean to justify the conquests of Assyria. But what happens to Assyria is little concern of theirs, and no concern of the people of Israel. Of Assyria they could say: "If I wish him to remain until I come, what is it to thee?" Their conviction of the moral will of the Lord in history leaves them no doubt that Assyria also will collide with the divine justice; but this collision is outside the scope of their thought – although they do not ignore it – because the Hebrews cannot do anything about it. And this is the tremendous and startling force of their ideas about Assyria, that no one can do anything about it except the Lord Himself, who will act when it pleases Him. It is He who has unleashed this power, and it is He who will restrain it. Before Assyria the Hebrews are helpless.

This has, of course, extremely practical implications. The foolish wars of the little western kingdoms were finally halted when this menacing colossus planted its huge booted feet right in the midst of their cities. Against Assyria it was unite or perish; but when the dilatory kingdoms finally aroused themselves to action, it was unite and perish. To the prophets, hope of salvation through foreign alliances was beneath contempt. It was a denial of the saving will and the power of the Lord to believe that salvation could come from foreign nations. The military resources of the nations were a ridiculously inadequate means of defense. The wealth which they hoped would finance their campaigns would only fatten the plunder of the spoilers. The Lord, and not Ashur, rode at the head of those advancing columns, and He was irresistible.

We have to pause for a moment, to attempt to translate this into modern speech, before we can seize its significance. We have to imagine any one, in any modern state, who would be so bold as to say that God was on the side of an attacking foe. We admire Lincoln for the wisdom with which he hoped, not that God was on the side of the Union, but that the Union was on God's side – wisdom from a professed unbeliever which has often been beyond the reach of believers. We have to imagine our modern hero saying this when the attacking foe is as flagrant an aggressor as was Assyria, whose imperial motives were ethically no loftier than those of Blackbeard and Henry Morgan. To imagine this for ourselves is to see at once that it is impossible. It does not happen and it is difficult to see that it will happen. Men cannot so detach themselves from their native environment and view things from the elevated point of vantage which is more proper to God than to men. Yet the Hebrew prophets did so; and modern scholars insult them by calling it "political insight." Men often learn wisdom from defeat; but the gift to see the defeat as justified before it happens is so rare that we need not regard it as normal in human thinking.

We have to add to this the implications: that defense is hopeless, that diplomatic and military measures are folly, that the aggressor poses a problem which cannot be met by such frail human means. As we shall have to point out, the Hebrews themselves were not blind to these implications; and the prophets, at least in some instances, suffered the consequences we should expect for saying such things. In our own more tightly knit modern political societies, even the most broadly liberal and tolerant government could not and would not tolerate such subversive speech in a time of national peril. Its conscience, if such a government had a conscience, would not permit it. The state, as such, could not allow this possibility without surrendering its own sovereignty, the very thing which enables it morally to gird itself for war. For if such a speaker told the truth, the state is false to its citizens in demanding that they hazard their goods and their lives in a cause which is not only wrong, but is lost. But the state simply cannot admit that it is wrong to that degree; and this is what the prophets insisted that the Hebrew state should admit. In doing the things that the very essence of the state requires, the Hebrew state opposed the will of the Lord.

This should not be understood to mean that the prophets were simply antimilitaristic, or that they saw the advantages of an imperial government over the futility of the squabbles of petty kingdoms too self-conscious of their sovereignty. One might, perhaps, erect a pacifist philosophy out of the writings of the prophets, but they did not look at the question on this high moral level. They meant that a community which is morally and religiously corrupt cannot by any means escape the consequences of its corruption. For such a guilty society, the use of human means only augments its guilt. It has lived on the assumption that the will of God does not govern human life, and it enters its mortal struggle endeavoring to frustrate the will of God by its own strength. For it is the will of the Lord that the wicked should perish, and perish by their own devices. Neither did the prophets mean that the Hebrews should adopt the homely principle of American politics and unite with those whom they could not overcome. Ahaz of Judah thought to escape the peril by invoking the help of Assyria; to Isaiah, this was a supreme betrayal of the Hebrew faith. It was a compromise with evil, a surrender to the world as it was embodied in the power and majesty of Assyria, a confession that the world was governed not by the will of the Lord, but by the will of the great king. Assyria was the rod of divine wrath, but it should not be raised to a divine dignity. Assyria herself did not recognize the hand of God in her deeds, and those who truckled to her were likewise unbelievers.

Does there not seem, then, to be an intrinsic contradiction in the attitude of the prophets? What, after all, were the Hebrews to do in the face of this monster, if they could neither die nobly fighting it nor live ignobly by compromising with it? We may as well admit that, on the merely political level, the words of the prophets have not that fine satisfying consistency which we see in an elaborate political philosophy. There is no splendid peace plan of which they could say: Do this, and live. Had political philosophy ever produced any such plan, this would give us reason for thinking that the words of the prophets have no significance. They dealt with the reality of evil, and there is no machinery which will infallibly eliminate evil. They invite, as we have pointed out, to repentance; but we ought not to understand this in a crass sense, as if, in the hypothesis of a national change of heart, the Assyrian warriors would drop their weapons, suddenly blunted, and fall at their posts. What the prophets meant was that Israel, by a national change of heart, could live through this catastrophe as the people of the Lord and emerge from it, not unscathed, but religiously and morally integral. They could not promise, in the Lord's name, an immediate glorious future.

The meaning of the prophets will be seen more clearly if we recall some of the popular beliefs of which we read in the Old Testament, and some of the promises which were made by false prophets. At some time in early Hebrew history arose a belief in "the day of the Lord." This was the day on which the Lord would manifest Himself to the world in all His might and glory, and would smash the enemies of His people, and would set up His people as lords of a universal empire. This popular hope had no connection whatever with the moral will of the Lord; He would do this solely because Israel was His people and He owed it to Himself, so to speak, to vindicate His supremacy as God by vindicating the supremacy of His people. It was on the basis of this and similar beliefs that we find prophets assuring the people that there was no real danger: the men of whom Jeremiah says, "They say all is well, all is well, when nothing is well." In the confidence of this belief, many of the Hebrews must have felt assured that no harm would touch them, that the hand of the Assyrian would be stayed before it touched the inheritance of the Lord. How much attention did they pay to Amos?

> "Ah, you that long for the day of the Lord!
> Why should you want the day of the Lord?
> It is darkness, and not light."

When this false security was destroyed, is it any wonder that the foolish Hebrews lost all faith in the Lord? No, the prophets promised nothing so easy as this.

But here they differ in detail. In Amos, for instance, there is scarcely a cheering note; his brief little book is dominated by the inevitability of the coming fall of Israel. Hosea offers more hope, for he is, as we have seen, the prophet of divine love; but this hope is not for the immediate future. The best he can promise his people, if they return to the Lord, is a period of trial like that through which they passed from Egypt to Canaan. Micah also is more impressed with the inevitability of the coming disaster. But in Isaiah we find a more complex attitude, and this must be treated at greater length.

There is no question in the book of Isaiah about the corruption of the people of Judah; his words are as harsh and unsparing as those of Amos. There is no question about the inevitability of the Assyrian victory. He has no use for military and diplomatic measures which are planned to avert the disaster, for they will not succeed. But what does he recommend? Faith. Faith in what? one might ask. And the only answer Isaiah gives is: faith in the Lord. Against the coming danger he counsels, explicitly, political inaction. The men of Judah should neither resist Assyria nor make a compact with Assyria; they should put themselves in the hand of the Lord. If this is not impractical, then the word has no meaning. Of course the king of Judah and his advisers could not accept such political nonsense, and they did not. And because they refused it, Isaiah said that they had effectively denied the Lord, denied that He is God. It is a tremendous act of faith which he insists that they make, more tremendous than most men can make even in their personal life; but there are times when one either makes the supreme act of faith or abandons faith altogether. What Isaiah demanded was that Judah suffer national martyrdom; Judah not only would not do this, it did not even understand what he meant. The practical men won the day; thirty years later, an Assyrian army marched through Judah and took forty-six fortified cities before it threatened the holy city itself. Isaiah was still there to witness the failure of the practical policy.

At this point, the second collision of Isaiah with the Assyrians, we meet one of the strangest turns in the whole of prophecy. In his early career, when Tiglath-Pileser had conquered Israel and Ahaz of Judah had submitted to him, Isaiah spoke of the disaster which would follow; a generation later, when Sennacherib ravaged the whole country and laid siege to Jerusalem, Isaiah showed serene confidence that the city would not fall into the hands of the Assyrian. Not a few modern writers have seen in this change of attitude a weakening of his high moral purpose, an acceptance of the popular belief that Jerusalem and its temple were inviolate, that there was a limit beyond which the Lord would not permit the Assyrian to go. It is too easy to charge with inconsistency a man whose words are preserved in a disordered collection of fragments, and to say that his attitude wavered in a conjunction of events which we are unable to disentangle; for there is no more knotty problem in Hebrew history than the course of Sennacherib's campaign against Judah. We cannot untie this knot here; but we believe it is important, if one is to be fair to the prophet, to remember that we cannot reconstruct the exact historical background of his words. It is important also to remember that Sennacherib did not actually take Jerusalem, although he extorted a heavy indemnity. Effectively, Judah was conquered, and remained conquered for almost a hundred years. But the holy city was spared, and that without any national regeneration; and it was a prophet who encouraged it to hope that it would escape. That, briefly, is the problem.

Now we can agree that there was a change in the attitude of Isaiah. But we ought to notice that there is no evidence that he treated the deliverance of Jerusalem as a reward of virtue. In fact, the word "deliverance" is misleading here. The experiences of Judah, as described in the annals of Sennacherib, were the kind of deliverance mentioned by Amos: It is as if the shepherd rescues from the mouth of the lion two shank bones or a piece of an ear. It was not a very glorious manifestation of the saving hand of the Lord, indeed, which left the country bleeding and in ruins, stripped of its mobile goods to meet the indemnity demanded by the Assyrians, and securely tied down in a state of vassalage. Here a remnant had survived, as Isaiah had said thirty years earlier; but this sentence was more of a threat than a promise. God had stayed the Assyrian's hand because He had chosen to do so, to the extent that the city and the temple yet stood; but the threat also still stood, and if the twenty-second chapter of Isaiah comes from this period, the prophet's intransigence was still unaltered. We might grant that the prophetic vision of Isaiah was limited compared to that of Jeremiah, for he does not seem to have visualized the possibility of a complete destruction of the Hebrew state; but if what we have already considered are revolutionary elements in Hebrew thought, we should not be surprised that the complete revolution, which we find in Jeremiah, did not occur all at once.

When Jeremiah enters upon the scene of Hebrew prophecy, seventy to seventy-five years after the encounter of Isaiah and Sennacherib, the great empire of Assyria was coming to the end of its days. In the middle of his career the oppressive conqueror crashed to ruins; he had overreached himself, extended his resources past the breaking point. Hatred lent strength to the peoples who fought Assyria, and the Babylonians and the Medes leveled Nineveh to the ground so thoroughly that it was never inhabited again. Xenophon and his Ten Thousand passed by its ruins two hundred years later, ruins which must have been massive; there is something pathetic in the ignorance of this educated Greek about the site, which he calls vaguely "an ancient city of the Medes." Into the political vacuum created by the sudden disappearance of Assyria there entered the Neo-Babylonian kingdom under Nebuchadnezzar, one of the great figures of the Old Testament, a man about whom clustered legends. As far as Judah was concerned, the international scene had not changed, for Babylon intended to take effective possession of the empire of the Assyrians.

Neither had the character of Judah changed. We have already mentioned the attempt which was made to regenerate the kingdom through a code of law. Jeremiah is our witness that whatever change was effected was superficial. Of all the prophets, none shows more certainty that the final hour is at hand, that Judah must go down as Israel had gone down before the Assyrians a hundred years earlier. None shows a deeper conviction of the utter corruption of the Hebrew nation, a corruption which is primarily religious. Because the people of the Lord have abandoned the Lord, their moral fiber is rotten, and the Lord has rejected them. Nothing was more sacred than the temple, the ark of the covenant, the law of the Lord; of each of these institutions Jeremiah says that they will vanish and be forgotten. This was the burden of his words almost from the time he began to speak. He saw the coming of a foe from the north before it could be determined who that foe would be. It had to happen, because the condition of the people of the Lord was such that the Lord could no longer tolerate it. In some detail, Jeremiah singles out each class of the people: the monarchy and the court, the priests, the prophets, rich and poor, great and small – although, unlike Isaiah, he does not have a special message for the women – and shows how each of them, in its own way, is everything it ought not to be. His words are less a plea for repentance than a declaration of hopelessness; we have all heard of the Ethiopian who cannot change his skin and the leopard which cannot change its spots, Jeremiah's figures of the ingrained guilt of the people of Judah. There is no possible escape from the menace from the north, which Jeremiah does not name until the identity of the foe is clear beyond all doubt.

We have noticed that some scholars find a lack of clarity and consistency in the words of the prophets during these international upheavals; but no one can say that the words of Jeremiah are obscure or ambiguous. He has only one recommendation: yield. The horror which Isaiah had of compromise with the aggressor does not appear in Jeremiah, although he is not really thinking of a compromise. But he is conscious of the futility of resisting the Lord. When the Babylonians laid siege to Jerusalem, his counsel to the king was surrender, and to the individual soldiers to give up the struggle and desert, to choose "the way of life" rather than "the way of death." If they were to defeat the Babylonians so thoroughly that no one was left except a few wounded in tents, these few would rise up and burn the city.

In these words of Jeremiah the thinking of the prophets about international relations reached their logical climax, as did the response of civil authority. The officers of the state demanded his life. The siege of Jerusalem was the supreme agony of the Hebrew state; the city was strongly fortified and occupied an excellent defensive position. Could it but hold out long enough to discourage the besiegers, there would yet be political life in the Hebrew state, even though it would be a brand snatched from the burning. But here was the prophet, weakening the hands of the men of war by his oracular pronouncements that the city should surely fall. Jeremiah barely escaped with his life. We can see that the civil and military authorities could not have done anything else, just as Jeremiah could have done nothing else. Here is the essential clash between the word of God and the word of man, the will of God and the will of man, the religious and the secular. Is there any way out of this clash? None that we can see.

When Varro by his reckless blundering had led the flower of the Roman army to annihilation at Cannae, the senate thanked him "because he had not despaired of the republic." This was the crime against the state second only to treason; indeed, it leads by a kind of moral necessity to treason. This was the crime of Jeremiah. The state had lost any claim to loyalty, because it was no longer what it was supposed to be. It had become, like the temple itself, a den of brigands. It failed even in its secular purpose; the prophets, we have seen, would not admit that it could ever have succeeded, because of a deeper failure, the failure to surrender to the will of the Lord. Jeremiah had to despair of the state because he hoped in God; if there were no moral will in history, if the Lord were indifferent to the character of His people, then He was no different from the gods of Canaan. How can the state admit such a principle, unless it is willing to yield its absolute claim upon the allegiance of its citizens? And we are not concerned here with questions of detail, of an unjust or foolish law or an error in policy; we are concerned with the fundamental claim of the state to allegiance, the claim which Jeremiah rejected.

Jeremiah despaired of the state because it was no longer the people of the Lord. Ezekiel, his younger contemporary, and a man gifted with a most extraordinary visual imagination, described the chariot of the Lord as departing from the temple after the Lord's own emissaries had kindled the fire which would consume Jerusalem. The Lord has removed from His people, and there is nothing left to protect them; in fact, He Himself has set the torch to the city. He departs from them because they are "a rebellious house," not governed by His will; He departs because they have done all that they could to expel Him. So the state is no more than a piece of driftwood upon the stream of history, to be carried at random by forces which it cannot control. Jeremiah despaired of the state because, by secularizing itself, it had lost its sacred character.

And what was left? The words of Jeremiah seem to be less revolutionary than anarchic. The institutions of Hebrew religion had their roots in patriarchal times, a thousand years earlier; they had grown from the great experiences of the past – the deliverance from Egypt, the covenant of Sinai, the settlement in Canaan. In these institutions the people had the Lord as their God. Now they go, and nothing replaces them. Hosea had said: "They shall sit many days without king, without prince, without sacrifice," without any of the sacramental means – if we may use the word loosely – by which they communicated with the Lord. No doubt this does give the religion of Jeremiah an anti-institutional cast; but we have to remember that he spoke of a concrete system of institutions which had been perverted by its users into a superstition. Not reform, but destruction: this was all he expected, and all he promised. The old must be swept away entirely before there could be talk of anything new.

Like Isaiah, Jeremiah had nothing to offer except faith in the Lord. This faith, as we shall see, gives rise to a hope for the future; but it is not a hope for the present or for the immediate future. Hope in the Lord demands that one be ready to await the time of His good pleasure, whenever it may be. But there is no hope for the nation as such. Many writers have said that Jeremiah marks the beginning of personal religion, the religion of the individual man as opposed to institutional religion. Jeremiah had no intention of founding a new personal religion. What he saw was the end of the institutional religion which he knew. Now a man had to find God by himself the best way he could; but he would not find God at all unless he sought the God of the Hebrews, the God of their fathers, the God who had spoken through His prophets, the God who now destroyed the people which He had made. This, certainly, is a new emphasis upon the personal element in religion, for the individual is cast adrift, cut off from the security which institutional religion gives him. It was unfortunate that it had to be, but the institutional religion was giving its adherents a false security. The crisis of the state was also a crisis for each individual member of the state. At such a time a man maintained his faith in the Lord by a total yielding of all secular hopes and desires, or he rejected the Lord. Those who had seen Him only in the institutions and the external features of the Hebrew religion and the Hebrew state were not very likely to see Him when these things ceased to exist.

After the Babylonians came the Persians; the Neo-Babylonian Empire did not long outlive its one vigorous personality, Nebuchadnezzar, and it surrendered, not very valiantly, to an even greater empire builder, Cyrus, king of the Medes and Persians, whom history calls the Great. Under his benevolent despotism the Jews were permitted to return and resettle in Palestine. A Jewish community lived once more, but it was not the kingdom of old. Hebrew national life had come to an end, and Palestine was never again under Jewish rule, except for one brief deceptive period under the Maccabees, to exist as a sovereign nation. The Lord had made this people, and the Lord had taken it away; no man would rebuild it. As we shall see, there were prophets who saw in this restoration the foreshadowing of a great future, and a step toward that future; but the future itself still lay beyond vision.

Was this the end of the people of the Lord? Was it for this that the Lord had led Abram out of Mesopotamia, and their fathers out of Egypt? Was it for this that He had smitten the Canaanites, and chosen David as their king? Was all their glorious history, the history of the deeds of the Lord, to reach its climax in this inglorious failure? These are questions which troubled the men of Israel, which wrenched the soul of a great patriot like Jeremiah; and they are questions which trouble the modern readers of the Bible also. What is the meaning and purpose of this sad story? To what does it lead? Why should the Lord have chosen a people only to permit them to frustrate His designs?

We ask these questions because, like the men of Israel, we are ignorant of the will and purpose of the Lord. Like them, we are inclined to accept the people of Israel, their polity and their religion, as a necessary datum in history. We think that, once

God has chosen them, He has committed Himself to a certain course of action. If this course is altered by the foolishness and the malice of men, we believe that He can bring good out of evil, but we also think that this change is a frustration of His will. But what is His will? His will is that men should know Him, for He speaks to them. His moral will is that they form their life according to the standards which He sets, for He gives us these standards. It is not His will that He should depend upon any mere human being for the accomplishment of His purposes. We cannot suppose that the necessary depends upon the contingent for its reality. Unhappy Israel, the vessel of election, came to believe that the Lord needed it, that He could not do without it. Their history shows this, at least – if we need it demonstrated – that the Lord is supreme. It shows that His moral will admits no qualification. We do not know that things had to happen the way they did; we can only do our best to make some sense out of the way they did happen. To the prophets, the Lord was never more gloriously triumphant, never proved more brilliantly the one true God, than when He struck down, through impious hands, the people which He called His own. This will never make sense to anyone who has a lower idea of what is primary in human life than the prophets had. The Lord will never demean His divinity by compromising with evil. If His people are evil, He will not have them; "if thy eye scandalize thee, pluck it out." Perhaps only such a demonstration could show the pure and unmixed goodness of God, the consuming fire with whom none can dwell. For men are readily inclined to attribute to their gods their own easygoing morality. Those who stood at the shattered gates of Jerusalem waiting to be counted by the clerks of Nebuchadnezzar could affirm with feeling that God resents it if He is esteemed a being of easy morals. The holiness of God appears not in His triumph over human might, but over human wickedness; and the history of the Hebrew state is such a triumph – not the kind we expect and desire, but the kind of which we had better be aware.

St. Ignatius Loyola, writing of the discernment of spirits, said that in a person disposed to good the action of the good spirit was quiet and tranquil, and the evil spirit caused disturbance; in a person disposed to evil the evil spirit is at home, and it is the good spirit that must enter violently. When one has read the history of the Hebrews, one reflects that the impact of God upon human life is indeed a violent impact. The vision of Elijah is inverted; God is in the whirlwind and the earthquake, not in the gentle breeze. For the world of men sets up a positive resistance, a wall of separation, a wall compacted of human philosophy and human sentiment. God breaches this wall, but things fly apart when He does it. After all, what is worth preserving in human institutions, if they are a barrier to the meeting of man with God? Christians who forget that Jesus said that He came to bring not peace but a sword are sometimes mildly scandalized at the tone of much Old Testament history and prophecy; they are innocent souls who have little idea of the manner in which men receive God. There is probably no point of contact between the divine and the human which it is more difficult to see than that which we have considered here. It was hard for the Hebrews to believe that God would turn the world over into the hands of a wicked and barbarous nation. Surely, they thought, Israel, with all its faults, is the people of the Lord; there is much good in it – indeed, when it is contrasted with the rest of the world, it seems to contain all good. But it is not good enough. Amos, speaking in the name of the Lord, said that the Lord would punish Israel because He had known them.

These are some of the elements of a biblical theology of history. Between the belief in an inflexible moral will which governs the course of human events and a philosophy of history which explains all by immanent principles there is little room for compromise. It is not a comfortable theology. "Call not holy," said Isaiah, "what this people calls holy." This theology permits one to find no security, to have no faith except in the Lord alone. It affirms that faith in man and his works is the worship of false gods.

THE HOPE OF THE FUTURE

THE failure of the Hebrew state as the people of the Lord, and the despair of human institutions as means to establish a society governed by the will of the Lord leave a spiritual vacuum. Despair and destruction are not a satisfying conclusion. Something more is postulated not only by the hope that springs eternal in the human breast, but by any concept of the Deity which rises above the level of nature. Now it is to be noticed that the collapse of the Hebrew state brings this postulate into sharper focus. Men can for a long time accept the world as a substitute for God; they cannot do so when their world is dissolved about their heads. Then they must either openly accept God on His own terms, or openly and finally deny Him. The word "crisis" is perhaps overworked in modern times; but it is a fact that God comes in a crisis, and only in a crisis, for His coming is a crisis by definition.

We spoke earlier of the cyclic theory of history which was formulated expressly by the Greeks, and which, without philosophic elaboration, lay at the basis of Mesopotamian religion. In such a theory, human events are a recurring pattern which never advances. From a philosophical point of view, such a theory is both more scientific and more historical than the imbecile myth of progress. Toynbee's massive array of the rise and fall of civilizations is the most forcible argument for the cyclic theory that has ever been presented. But the cyclic theory and the evolutionary theory of progress have this decisive difference from the biblical view, that both of them suppose a world in which God is neither present nor active, in which the course of human events is entirely determined by human and physical factors. In the cyclic theory, Israel had come to the full turn, and that is all there is to it. What befell them was the work of the necessity of history, and there was no personal moral will involved. In the theory of evolutionary progress, Israel was like the dinosaur; it failed to develop a response to meet its environment. Either theory supposes that Israel, once dead, will stay dead; in neither theory is there room for its survival, or rather its resurrection. For it lived on, not as a nation, but as a people and a faith. The God of Israel, far from perishing with His people, grew greater by their fall. They lived, and their faith lived, because their God is a God of hope. Despair of men, which we have considered through three chapters, is not despair of God unless one thinks God is no better than men; if one thinks He is better, then true hope in God is not possible unless one despairs of men.

In the Hebrew faith, events tended not to a circle, but to a term: a term which God wills and intends, and to which He directs everything. It was a shock to them that their own destruction should be a step to this term, but the basic faith of Israel was strong enough to withstand this shock. All their traditions showed them that there had to be something more; and the belief in a future took form most distinctly in the very period when faith in the present was being shattered on the rocks of events. We shall have to see what hope the future held for the Hebrews, what form it took, by what process they believed that it would be realized; for this hope is the ultimate key to Hebrew belief and Hebrew history, which is unintelligible without it.

Before we try to put into words the form and substance of this hope, let us collect some of the scattered pieces of which it is built up. The conventional theological treatment of this matter starts with what is called "the beginning of the Gospel": the words addressed to the serpent in Genesis 3:15. We have already alluded to this passage, and we have seen that at the very least it indicates, in the mind of the Hebrew storyteller, a deadly opposition between man and evil, personalized in the serpentine tempter. It is less a promise of victory than an assurance that man will not succumb; it is, perhaps, not much, but it is a good deal more than nothing, and with this minimum assurance we can go on to other passages where the hope of the future takes a more definite shape. When Abram was called out of Mesopotamia by the Lord, to what was he called? To what end was he promised a progeny numerous as the stars of the sky and the sands of the seashore? For this, at least, that God should put Himself in touch with man through Abram and his clan. The obscure phrase, variously translated in different Bibles, which is more precisely rendered, "In you all the nations of the earth shall bless themselves," most probably means that Abram and his clan shall be a formula rather than a medium of blessing: all nations shall bless themselves with the words, "May God do to us as He did to Abram." Again, it is not much, but it is even more than we find in the primitive story of man. Abram is a model of the divine good pleasure, a sample of the blessing which God gives to man, an ideal which shall appear desirable even to the nations who know not the Lord.

We find little trace of development of the hope in the centuries which lay between the patriarchs and the foundation of the Hebrew monarchy. This is not surprising; these were the centuries, as we have seen, in which the Hebrew nation and Hebrew institutions were formed, and attention fell more upon the present than upon a remote future. Furthermore, these centuries were, in a manner, a realization of the future as the Lord had promised it to the patriarchs; they were the morning, the youth of the Hebrew people, and youth lives in the present. Not until the dynasty of David was securely set upon the throne of Israel does the promise break out again, this time with a new brilliance and clarity, in a form which is retained throughout the course of Hebrew history. This is the conviction that the Lord had identified Himself with the dynasty of David. We have to recall that the ancient king was the incarnation of his people, the personalization of his nation, to understand the significance of the covenant of the Lord with David and his line. The identification of the Lord with the dynasty of David meant that the kingship and the kingdom which it incorporated were imperishable, as the Lord Himself was imperishable. It meant that David lived on as an ideal, even in his degenerate race, and that the ideal would realize itself one day in another David. As God had intervened in human affairs to bring Abram out of Mesopotamia, the Hebrews out of Egypt, and to set David upon the throne of united Israel, so He would again intervene to finish the work He had begun: He would make the dynasty of David the greatest of all dynasties. For a king who was the anointed of the Lord, adopted by the Lord as His son, could not be less than the greatest. So with the monarchy the hope of the future put on the robes of a king, and subsisted in the minds of men in this external form.

We have already adverted to the Sumerian and Semitic belief that the god was king of the city. The Hebrews also believed that the Lord was king of Israel. When the monarchy was first proposed, Samuel answered in the name of the Lord: "They have not rejected you, but they have rejected me as their king." Human kingship was not possible in Israel until it was conceived in a manner which did not infringe upon the kingship of the Lord. Actually, the speculative problem was never too clearly solved. Mesopotamian kingship did not infringe upon divine kingship because the king was an earthly counterpart of the celestial king. The Hebrews, as we have seen, could have no such idea; their king was a charismatic leader. The kingship of the Lord was above and beyond all human kingship. We can see how the kingship of the Lord is saluted in Psalms 92–99 (93–100); there, without stretching the imagination too far, we may see three aspects of His kingship. The Lord is king as creator, a warrior-king who is victorious over the forces of chaos. He is the cosmic lord of nature, who directs the forces of nature to His purpose. He is the supreme judge, who punishes the wicked and vindicates the righteous. In a word, the Lord is king of the world, and therefore king of Israel. Hence His kingdom is as eternal as Himself, and not communicable to any human ruler; it is not subject to defect, not liable to downfall as is human kingship, even the kingship of Israel. If one human ruler fails to administer the kingship in the manner the Lord wishes, He will commit it to another. It was the Hebrew belief that He would finally commit it to an ideal ruler, another David.

There seems to be no reason in the nature of things why this ideal ruler should appear most prominently in the words of Isaiah, but he does. Perhaps it is because Isaiah spoke at a time when the kingdom of Israel was near its end, and the dynasty of David was shortly to experience the greatest peril which it had faced since its foundation. Or – and there are those who think this is the compelling reason – it was because the dynasty had fallen so far from the ideal even of a good secular ruler; we have already considered the deterioration of the Hebrew monarchy. In any case, it was Isaiah who, after the idea of the eternal dynasty was proposed, gave it its most brilliant formulation. He presents the ideal king in four titles: "Wonderful counselor, divine hero, father forever, prince of peace." Counsel, as contrasted with the blundering folly of the Hebrew kings; courage and victory, as contrasted with their cowardice, their ignoble diplomacy, their lack of leadership; a father, as contrasted with their avarice and tyranny; and a prince of peace, which demands a little explanation.

The word which we translate by "peace" in the English Bible can really be rendered by no single English word; it designates a state of complete well-being of body and mind, of internal and external order: within the person, within the community, between communities. It is a rich word, conveying the notion of satisfaction of all needs and desires; and it is this that the ideal ruler shall bring once and for all, stable peace. The same ruler appears again as endowed with six gifts of "the spirit of the Lord": as a charismatic ruler, he is inspired by the divine impulse to govern in a perfect manner, with wisdom and understanding, with counsel and might, with knowledge and fear of the Lord. Other prophets and poets also allude to this ideal ruler; Jeremiah, for instance, gives him the title, "The Lord is our righteousness." In some of the Psalms the language and the ideas of Isaiah and of the dynastic promise are repeated with poetic embellishments: the ideal king is adopted as the son of the Lord, whose rule extends to the ends of the earth, who dispenses peace and justice and governs in a manner worthy of a divinely elected monarch.

A king is nothing without a kingdom; and since the Lord rules all the earth, His kingdom also must embrace all the earth, and

His chosen king must rule over all men. This was indeed a bold ambition for the prophets and poets of little Israel to frame, even in the days of David and Solomon; but they did not think that it would be realized by the force of Hebrew arms. In the preceding chapter, we referred to the ancient Semitic idea of a world state, which was realized by Assyria. Some scholars think that the Hebrew idea of the world kingdom of the Lord was modeled on the Assyrian empire. But since the idea is older than Assyria and is found in the Old Testament, at least rudimentarily, before the eighth century, we must judge it unlikely that Assyria is the model from which the prophets drew. But the Hebrew idea, we think, took form when it did as a reaction to the Assyrian conquest. The Hebrews regarded the Assyrian world state as an arrogation of the divine kingship, an attempt to submit the kingdom of the Lord to human rule. Prophecy put these words in the mouth of the great king: "The heavens I will mount; above the stars of God I will set my throne; I shall take my seat on the mount of assembly, in the recesses of the north; I shall rise above the clouds, I shall rival the Most High." Yet the idea of the world state retained its peculiar fascination, a fascination which we have sensed in our own day. Hebrew belief transfigured the idea into a world kingdom under the sovereignty of the Lord, and passed it on to the Western world as a counterweight to the idea of the secular world state which Alexander brought from the East.

The Lord Himself would establish His world kingdom, because He could do nothing less if He were to manifest His divinity to all men. All owe Him their fealty, and it could not be supposed that He would not exact His due. The phrase "kingdom of God" or "kingdom of the Lord" is not common in the Old Testament; but the idea, the image in one form or another, dominates the Hebrew visualization of the hope of the future. Strangely enough, as the present is dimmed, the hope of the future glows with more brilliant colors. We say strangely, for some interpreters have thought that the Hebrew hope of the future was kindled from the ashes of the past. They have forgotten that the psychology of nations, like that of individuals, does not so easily build new hopes out of the ruins of frustration. Within limits, as long as the individual or the nation retains its basic strength substantially intact, hope remains; but realism sooner or later forces one to weariness and despair. These interpreters would be hard put to it to find convincing parallels to the growth of the Hebrew hope in the Lord at the same time that He destroys their national life. This hope grew out of a faith in a God who more and more distinctly revealed Himself as unique, not so much in number as in character. But the opinion that many biblical descriptions of the kingdom of the future are no more than inflated national ambitions has some superficial attractiveness, and it leads us to consider the imaginative vesture which the kingdom wears.

If one reads, for instance, the second part of the book of Isaiah — that is, the last twenty-seven chapters — one is impressed by the extravagance of many of the descriptions of the kingdom. For those who are not professional biblical scholars, it is necessary to recall that the historical, literary, and religious background of these chapters is not that of the Isaiah of the first part, but of the latter half of the sixth century, the period during which Babylon fell to the Persians and Cyrus permitted the Jews to resettle in their own territory. The position of these chapters in "the book of Isaiah" creates problems concerning their literary origins into which we need not enter here, for one reads them intelligently if one is aware of this background, whoever their author may have been. Now the kingdom and the Jerusalem here depicted are drawn with magnificent traits; but it is a magnificence which is, at first glance, entirely external. It is a kingdom of surpassing wealth, of supreme power, imposing its will on the nations of the world and drawing tribute from them. It is a victorious kingdom, for the Lord has prostrated its enemies under its feet. It is a kingdom in which all material satisfactions are granted; in a word, it has some of the appearance of that kingdom of which we said earlier that it was implicitly a denial of the will of the Lord. This estimate of these chapters and other similar passages has some extraneous support. If one consults the writings of the Jews of the New Testament period, one finds the idea of the kingdom there intolerably degraded into a grossly materialistic state of well-being; the desire of luxury and of ease and a vindictive envy of the nations more powerful than Israel are vented without restraint. The Gospels and other sources of Jewish history are evidence that there flourished among the Jews of the period a vicious nationalism which masked itself under the ancient beliefs about the future kingdom of God. Jesus and the Apostles, when they preached the kingdom of God, found it necessary to speak with caution and qualification, in order that the message of the Gospel might not be confused with this national and worldly conception.

We have made the difficulty real, but not so real, we hope, that we shall be unable to place these passages in their proper intellectual and religious context. There are a number of traits of Hebrew thinking which we must recall if we are to read these passages with sympathy and understanding. Of these we may mention first that the Hebrews were a material-minded people, and their books are material-minded also. We do not intend this word in the unpleasant sense which it suggests to a modern reader. We have already mentioned that the Hebrews viewed reality in the concrete and the particular; they lacked a logic and a philosophy which would have enabled them to reason in abstract generalities. More than this, they had no well-defined idea of spiritual reality; we have already noticed that, while they were well aware that there is a vast difference between the created reality and the uncreated reality, they could express this difference only in picture, in image. If one wishes to attract people, one approaches them through their own desires; unless one does this, it will never be possible to elevate their desires. To the Hebrews, purely spiritual blessings were unreal. This generalization is, of course, quite sweeping and somewhat misleading. Such words as righteousness, justice, truth, kindness, fidelity, holiness in the Hebrew vocabulary show that we must not oversimplify. But even these words were not thought of in the abstract, but in the concrete: they represent the person or the act which is righteous, just, true, and all the rest. The concrete reality in which we apprehend these things is a material reality: man and his world, in which the effects of the divine attributes are seen, heard, touched. It is a different point of view, another pattern of thinking from that in which modern civilized man moves; we cannot reconstruct it in our minds, and we need not, but we must be aware of the difference and acquainted with its significance.

Hence the blessings of the future are presented in the mode in which the Hebrews could most easily apprehend them. These external blessings are not merely metaphors of spiritual blessings, although they have often been so interpreted. They rather describe "the good life," as it is most readily understood by the man of simple ideas and simple desires. The good life is, of course, more than this; it rests upon a basis of higher reality. We have already seen that the goods which the Hebrew kingdom sought to procure for its subjects were merely material and temporal, and that the prophets were fully aware that these were not the goods which the Lord promised; to identify the good life with these things is to accept the gods of Canaan, for material good is all that these gods promised. We cannot easily suppose that the hope of the kingdom of the future is the same hope as that which was repudiated in the kingdom of the present. The Hebrew community was intended to be a society governed by the will of the Lord; what makes the future kingdom a realized ideal is that the will of the Lord attains its end. These splendid blessings are the fruit of the harmony between man and the Lord. More important than the external glory of the future kingdom, if uttered in less elegant language, is the moral regeneration which is demanded and presupposed before this good life can be conferred upon men.

We must enlarge upon this feature of the kingdom, because to omit it is to see the kingdom in a false perspective. We may take two images which occur in the prophetic writings as typical of the many which contain, if less explicitly, this idea of moral regeneration. The first of these is the new covenant of Jeremiah. We have already indicated the place of the idea of "covenant" in the origins of the Hebrew nation. We have noticed also that Jeremiah is the prophet who speaks most frequently and most frankly of the passing of the external institutions of the Hebrew community. The covenant, however, does not pass away, but is transformed into a higher union of the Lord with His people. The old covenant was written upon tablets of stone; it was external in its formulation, just as any agreement is identified with the instrument which records it. The new covenant is written upon the tablets of the heart. Just as the old covenant transformed the external conditions of Hebrew life and made them different from the external conditions of other peoples, so the interior covenant transforms the individual person within himself. The old covenant was accepted by the people acting as a body through their representatives; the new covenant is accepted by each one for himself. Written upon the heart, it becomes the principle which dominates his thoughts and his desires; for the "heart," in Hebrew idiom, is the seat of thought and desire. God reveals Himself to each one in the tablet of the heart, as He made Himself known to Moses when He gave him the tablets of stone; and so each one shall "know the Lord," and will not learn of Him from His human representatives, priests and prophets. "Know the Lord" is a Hebrew phrase which is not easily translated; it signifies to recognize Him in His true nature, to perceive what He is. It means to experience the divine reality, as a man is said to "know" his wife. And, in this context, it means to acknowledge His supremacy, and therefore to submit to Him, to do His will. This knowledge of the Lord each one will enjoy. Jeremiah was painfully aware of the failure of the accredited representatives of the Lord to communicate the "knowledge" of Him to the people; and he envisaged the time when the Lord would communicate Himself to each one, as He did to Jeremiah himself.

A similar figure is employed by Ezekiel. The heart of the people has become a heart of stone, hard and unfeeling. The Lord will change this; He will restore to them a heart of flesh, which will be delicately sensitive to Him. They are dead, though they appear to live; when their heart is renewed, life will return, the good life which comes from submission to the will of the Lord. The heart, we have noticed, is the character; a man is what his heart is, for out of the heart come his thoughts, his plans, his ambitions, and it is to the heart that the Lord speaks. The change of heart is a transformation of the whole personality; this change the Lord Himself will work, not by a new institutional formula, but by touching the heart as only He can do. Then the evils which afflict human society will be entirely removed. There will be no obstacle to the divine will, no serpent in the garden. Once moral evil is removed, there will be no other evil to fear.

A second trait of Hebrew thinking which we must recall is derived from their political experience. We have adverted to the existence of conservative circles among the Hebrews which tended to identify the way of the Lord with a fixed manner of life; this ideal manner of life was the pastoral life of their fathers. Civilization, city life, agriculture, and commerce they regarded as inventions of Canaan from which the Hebrews should abstain. That the kingdom should be the vehicle through which the future blessings are proposed shows us how much this conservative belief had lost ground. The kingdom of the future is unintelligible as an ideal unless life under a monarchy had come to represent the highest form of life in society, offering far greater possibilities to realize human powers than the simple tribal community of herdsmen. At its best, the monarchy offered a much higher degree of security, both individual and social. It maintained a defense against enemies from abroad, and it was equipped to check enemies within. It imposed law and order upon society, and set up a machinery by which each citizen could hope to receive justice and the vindication of his rights. The smoothness of human relations within an ordered society facilitated the exchange of goods and services, and made possible a much fuller enjoyment of the resources of nature. Life under the kingdom was civilization opposed to barbarism; it was peace, security, prosperity opposed to strife, uncertainty, penury. It was, or ought to be, all those things which the simple but lawless desert life could never contain. The nomad's hand, like Ishmael's, was against every man, and every man's hand was against him. We have already noticed that it is probably not mere coincidence that the lines of the ideal king are drawn most sharply at a period in which the historical kings receded most from the ideal. The failure of the Hebrew monarchy to do its work made its possibilities stand out with greater clarity. But the prophets did not and could not dream of an ideal which would be a return to the restlessness of the nomad; so far had they come from the patriarchs. The good life could be found only in an ordered society; order came from authority, and authority was nothing if it was not the will of the Lord governing the life of men.

The kingdom of the future also borrows some traits from other sources. Prophecy did not have to spin the picture out of thin air. Hebrew tradition told of a state of integrity and harmony: Paradise, in which God had placed man in his creation. The conditions of Paradise will be reproduced in the kingdom of the future; in particular, we notice that God once more dwells familiarly with man, and that man is at peace with the animal world, of which God had made him lord. For the kingdom is more than a moral regeneration of man and society. As we have seen, sin is a cosmic disorder which ruptures the harmony between man and nature. The restoration of man is cosmic as well as moral. Nature also is renewed, and the earth becomes once again a "garden of delight." When man and God are at peace, man and nature are at peace. The Lord will create a new heaven and a new earth. The earth will joyfully yield its fruits in marvelous abundance, and man will enjoy them without toil and without surfeit. The picture is material-minded, yes; but we ought not to miss the fundamental truth which the prophets try to affirm through the picture, that the integrity of man and the world is maintained by the harmony between man and the will of God.

A third, and perhaps the most difficult trait of Hebrew thinking is the relation of the future kingdom to the non-Hebrew world. Readers of the Bible will remember the "burdens of the nations," those tortuously obscure passages about unknown peoples, which, however, are very clear expressions of hostility, dire predictions of the supreme evil to come. These readers have often been scandalized at the xenophobia of the Old Testament, forgetting that modern civilized man, especially in time of war, is capable of breathing a fire against his enemies which surpasses in virulence anything in the Old Testament. If the Bible reader is historically minded, he will recall that xenophobia was universal in the ancient Semitic world, and will reflect sadly that the Hebrews were no better than their neighbors in this respect. We need not deny that the Old Testament generally takes a more narrow view of the alien world than we like to think that we ourselves take; the point to notice is that the Old Testament contains the elements of a wider view, which occasionally finds a voice. The problem is not lightened by the tender language in which the Lord speaks to Israel in the second part of Isaiah. These passages are instances of what we may call, paradoxically, the "humanity" of God, a trait which many readers of the Old Testament fail to observe. The God of the Hebrews is not exclusively stern and austere; He appears in attitudes of delicate affection. But these passages speak of His affection for Israel in contrast to His attitude toward foreign nations.

For the Hebrews, the foreign nations were the enemies of the people of the Lord, and therefore of the Lord Himself; we have to state this, because it cannot be denied. But it must be qualified at once by what we have seen of the foreign nations as the instruments of the moral will of the Lord. Enemies of the Lord they may be, but not merely because they are enemies of Israel; they are His enemies because they are not subject to His will. Israel too is an enemy for this reason. Consequently, the law which is operative in the history of Israel is operative also in the history of the nations; belief in the moral will of the Lord means that they too will experience His justice. They must fall, because they lack the principle of survival. Ultimately the Lord will be victorious over them. Furthermore — this also we have noticed — the identity between the nations and the gods of the nations was close; the Lord vindicated His unique divinity by overthrowing the nations and their gods. His overthrow of His own nation was, as we have seen, His supreme victory; but the gods of the nations were not clearly demonstrated to be utterly impotent until they had lost their power to confer material blessings, to give their peoples victory in battle.

Is not this idea vitiated to some extent by the notion that the Lord's ultimate victory over these nations is also a victory for Israel, that in the ideal kingdom of the future they appear as subject and tributary to Israel? Is not Israel hoping that the Lord will give them the empire which He takes away from Assyria?

As we have conceded, the Hebrew view is narrow in some respects, and this may be one of the instances in which it is narrow. Nevertheless, the Hebrews would say that it were better to be a subject in the kingdom of God than to be a king in Sheol. They found it difficult to conceive that the nations would have the same place in the kingdom of God as themselves, the people of the Lord. Let it be; they found it difficult, and it would be captious for us to find fault with them. The full equalizing impact of the Gospel has not yet struck the Christian world; until it has, the Christian world need not disdain the ancient Hebrews because the scope of their vision was not fully human. No doubt, the full meaning of "the people of the Lord" does not appear in the Old Testament as it appears in the New Testament; but it is not so obvious that we should think them blind for failing to see it. It was something that the nations should be defeated and subjected to the Lord. If one wishes a contrast between the Old Testament and some truly narrow views, one need only look at some of the later Jewish literature, where the nations are promised nothing but torture and annihilation.

The most striking statement of the attitude of the Lord toward the nations is found in a little book where it is usually overlooked by Bible readers, the book of Jonah. It is overlooked because the attention of Bible readers is diverted to an altogether accessory literary feature of the book, the episode of Jonah and the great fish, which the English Bibles have dubiously made into a whale. Whether one accepts the story of Jonah and the whale as historical has become a test of fundamentalist orthodoxy. Modern students of the Bible, observing the historical and geographical background of the book, know that Jonah is a parable, as fictitious a composition as the Prodigal Son or the Good Samaritan; and they seek the truth which [illegible] there conveyed in the form of a story. This truth is not too subtly presented. Jonah is commissioned to speak the prophetic message to the Assyrians, the most hated and feared nation of the world, in Nineveh itself, the city of the great king. The message is the message which so many prophets spoke to Israel: Repent or perish. Jonah, thoroughly a Hebrew, would rather die than bring the word of the Lord to the Assyrians;

but he cannot escape the charge, for even the fish deliver him from the depths of the sea. Wonder of wonders, the Assyrians repent and the threat is removed. Jonah, discomfited at the Lord's failure to annihilate the Assyrians, sulks under his gourd; but the Lord withers the gourd, and Jonah learns thereby the unsearchable depths of the Lord's compassion: "You are sorry for the gourd, the creature of a night. Shall I not have pity on Nineveh, a great city, which has a hundred and twenty thousand little ones who do not know their right hand from their left?" It was no ordinary Hebrew who could look at the capital city of the piratical Assyrians, stuffed with treasure looted from their subjects, served by the slaves they had captured, and see in its proud people ignorant little ones, demanding the compassion of the Lord. He was a Hebrew who had looked into the heart of the God of Hebrew belief and Hebrew tradition, and told what he saw. As the Lord had compassion on Israel, so He must have compassion on all whom He had made. If we think the Hebrews were narrow, let us remember that there were those among them who could rise to a view of humanity almost as broad as the view of the Lord Himself, from whom they learned it.

How is this kingdom of the future to be established? We must emphasize that the prophets nowhere speak of human means. Hebrew military strength was doomed to a final defeat; not even the most fantastic imagination dreamed that it could ever be the instrument by which the will of the Lord was to be imposed upon the world. There is little trace of what we would call evangelization. It is true that Isaiah said that instruction would go out of Sion, and the word of the Lord from Jerusalem, an utterance which could be paralleled elsewhere. But to the Hebrews, faith in the Lord was never a matter of assimilating a body of truth, but of surrender to a person. Even in such phrases as instruction and the word of the Lord, they had no notion of redeeming the nations from ignorance. Their prophets were not teachers. When Alexander conquered the ancient Semitic world, he saw himself as a missionary carrying Greek civilization, with its literature, art, philosophy, and vices, into the darkness of the ignorant heathen world, and he succeeded even more than he had dreamed. The Hebrews had nothing of this sort to offer, and not until they came in touch with the Greek world and Greek learning did they begin to think themselves possessed of a message for the mind. The kingdom was not a constitution, not a legal system, not a civilization, not a philosophy, not a political form; it was the realized will of the Lord imposed upon mankind, and a regeneration of the cosmos and of human nature. This could be accomplished only by the Lord Himself, and He is the agent of the final revolution, as Hebrew prophecy depicts it. We have said that a genuine hope in the future presupposes a despair of human resources; and the kingdom is an achievement of the Lord which is beyond the power of man. It is another personal intervention of the Lord in history, and it is the greatest.

We must ask ourselves, at this point, about the nature of the ideal king who is to govern this ideal kingdom; the question introduces us to the relations of this hope of the future with the New Testament. In its most simple terms, the question is: Is this ideal king a divine person incarnate, a God-Man? Also in its most simple terms, the answer is no. We have to recall that nothing is more revolutionary, more counter to human experience, than the fact of the Incarnation. We can add, parenthetically, that nothing calls for greater faith. If a man can believe this truth, he should be able to believe anything that his faith imposes upon him; and the history of the dogma shows how hard it has been for men to accept it, even when it is proposed to them with the utmost clarity. Are we to suppose that this most sublime and most unexpected of all truths is found in a few casual allusions which most obviously mean nothing of the sort? Are we to suppose that the Hebrews, who were taught to abominate a plurality of deity, could, without any intellectual adjustment, assimilate the idea of a divine father and a divine son? To ask the question in this way is, of course, to answer it; but the question is not loaded. We have to suppose, besides, that this great truth seeped into the Hebrew religious consciousness without a ripple, without the repercussions which it has had since the historical fact of the Incarnation; and this we find impossible to believe. The Hebrews had no doubt that God would intervene to establish His kingdom;

they had only a faint idea of the manner in which He would do it.

If this be true, is there not an essential opposition between the kingdom of the future and the Gospels? This is a serious question; and it is weighted by this fact, that the Jews of the Gospel age were not, as a group, spiritually prepared for the Gospel. Nevertheless, we have the undisputed fact that Jesus Himself took the kingdom as the governing idea, the framework in which He placed His own words. This He could not have done if the idea were in essential opposition to what He was and did. And we have already seen, I think, why He could speak in terms of the kingdom: because it was the final and universal realization of the will of the Lord, because it was a regeneration of man and his world, because it was the work of the Lord and not of man. What He added, among other things – for who shall encapsulate His words in a single phrase? – was that the kingdom must exist in the individual person before it can exist in human society at large. But we cannot speak at length about Him without departing from our subject, which remains the Old Testament.

R. H. Strachan has called the word "eschatology" uncouth; perhaps we should apologize, then, for asking whether the kingdom is eschatological, that is: is it conceived as realized upon this earth, within the confines of time, or does it carry us beyond the limits of space and time? Strange as it appears to us, it seems that the Hebrews did not ask themselves this question. We do indeed find it raised in the later Jewish writings to which we have referred more than once, just as it was raised in the early ages of the Church; there was a considerable number of Christians, which included more than a few great names, who thought that God would finally establish a reign of His saints upon this earth. Happily, the opinion has died. One does not wish to be too apodictic in a matter of such delicate interpretation; but it appears that the distinction is meaningless in the minds of the writers of the Old Testament. The kingdom is simply in the future, and we have to let it go at that. If the question can be answered, we would venture the opinion that the vision of the prophets did not reach beyond space and time; the framework of their hope of the future was the known framework of the Hebrew monarchy.

It was this kingdom, expanded and idealized, through which the will of the Lord would impose itself upon the world. They had much to learn; but it is astonishing how much they had learned.

The question of the relation of the Hebrew hope to its realization requires yet another reference to Hebrew thought patterns. What we have in mind will be clearer, perhaps, if we mention an old and honorable treatment of this aspect of the Old Testament. The Old Testament was regarded not only as a prediction of the New Testament in whole, but also in detail. It predicted not only the future, but also the steps, the phases in which this future was to be realized. Consequently, by collecting a sufficient number of texts, it was possible to find a great many details in the life of Jesus foretold, enough to identify Him when He appeared. We know now that such exegesis is fantastic. It is impossible to imagine that God secretly revealed the future course of events in detail to the men of old, and that they distilled in cipher such details for the public as would sharpen its curiosity. If the sacred books were composed as a jigsaw puzzle to be assembled by the ingenuity of Christians who know the finished picture, then this manner of interpretation might stand; but we have to suppose that God spoke sense to the Hebrews also, and there is no sense in a fragment of a jigsaw puzzle. How the Old Testament points to the New and leads to it, prepares and disposes for it, we shall have to make some effort to say before we can call our work complete; but we do not mean to say that the Old Testament predicts the New in the sense that it foretells details with studied obscurity.

Hence the thought pattern to which we refer is the pattern which sees the future as a whole, the course of events telescoped into two dimensions, without depth. The analogy is well worn, but I use it because it is still good, of "foreshortening of perspective." It is of some importance to understand this; for the prophets speak of the kingdom as distant, as imminent, as already beginning to be realized. The author of the second part of Isaiah, for instance, speaks of the resettlement of Palestine in 537 B.C. as the first step in the establishment of the kingdom of the future. We do injustice to a man of a great mind as well as a great soul, a man who had the word of the Lord, if we think that he saw in this event the beginning of the end. But the puzzling question is: what did he see? That he saw the kingdom of the future, and saw it within the framework of Hebrew institutions, we have noticed. In addition, he experienced the first sign of a hopeful future for the Hebrews which had appeared in history in fifty years; a people apparently dead had arisen, the Lord had breathed life into the dry bones. The bond between the people of the Lord and the land of promise had not been severed. In this event, the saving will of the Lord asserted itself, the same saving will which would finally bring the kingdom of the future to pass. He, with other prophets, has the gift of seeing the future implicit in the present, just as the Hebrew storytellers see the present as the recapitulation of the past. This, which seems to us indifference to the hard facts of chronology, is a characteristic of Hebrew thought which we have to accept; it is rough on history, but it exhibits a fine sense of the unity and continuity of events which arises from the Hebrew awareness of the presence and the activity of God in events. It was a Hebrew who said that with the Lord a thousand years are as a day, and a day as a thousand years; and the prophets knew, although they could not find the words for it, that the Lord is outside the scheme of time. They could see the attributes which would establish His kingdom present in each single manifestation of His power.

We have collected our scattered elements, and in doing so we have, we think, gone a long way toward putting them together. We seem to have answered the question which we proposed in the preceding chapter: to what does the sorry history of the Hebrew monarchy tend? The Catholic puts his hope of the future in one word, which he has borrowed from the Hebrews: "salvation." What was the Hebrew idea of salvation, of deliverance? It was deliverance from evil of every kind and description, and in the first place from the corrosive and fundamental evil of his own malice: a regeneration of man. It was deliverance from the evil which he suffered because of the malice of others, whether they were the men of his own fellowship or external enemies. It was deliverance, finally, from the evil which arose out of a hostile nature, insubordinate to man because man is insubordinate to God. Evil in all its forms would be subject to "judgment"; the figure is drawn from the legal processes which detect evil and remove it. But judgment, in the Bible, often suggests something which is less obvious in our own use of the word. When the Psalmist prays, "Judge me," he asks that he be given his rights, victory over his enemies. Judgment for the Hebrews is less a dispensation of justice than a victory for the right and the good. The judgment which they expect is a world judgment, a judgment of nations; for the nations, as we have seen, were for them the embodiment of the forces of evil, the only reality which the gods of the nations possessed. Judgment was a final and conclusive demonstration that the Lord alone is God, and there is none like Him.

Salvation is deliverance from evil; it is also the acquisition of good. At the risk once more of oversimplification, this good, as it is represented in the kingdom of the future, seems best summed up in the Hebrew word which has no English equivalent, the word which we translate "peace": order and well-being, the order which would permit the simple peasant to sit under his vine and under his fig tree, with none to terrify him. It was order imposed from above, for it was created and sustained by the governing will of the Lord, which was no longer opposed. It brought security and peace of mind.

It is true that, if we ask what the Hebrews meant by "the good life," we are puzzled and disappointed. Plato could think of a spiritual level of existence at which man would find his happiness in the noblest use of his highest power, his mind, in the contemplation of Ideas, of truth as it is in its ontological purity unmixed with sensible qualities; and the Idea which dominated the whole of reality was the Idea of the Good in its purest and highest form. Theology and mystical experience have borrowed much from Plato. But Plato was one of the great minds of the race, and an intellectual snob without shame. He had no thought that his good life was within the reach of mankind in the mass, who would never rise above the level of their sensible desires. For him, the good life would come by education; it was not a moral regeneration. Frankly, the good life as Plato described it with such genius would have left the Hebrews unmoved, as it leaves most men unmoved; for it carries them into a world which is, to them, unreal and unintelligible. For the Hebrews, the good life was simpler and more popular; it was freedom, under the sovereignty of God, to do those things which a man could do and wanted to do, without fear or hindrance. The important thing was that it was a life of union with the Lord who dwelt among His people, a surrender to a person and not to an Idea: a person who responded to love with love.

Here, then, is the ideal of Moses and the monarchy brought to realization: a society governed by the will of the Lord. As we take our final look at it, we are impressed by the Hebrew conviction that it is the work of the Lord alone, not of man. It is preceded by judgment, the collapse of nations and of human institutions, none of which have the stability to resist their own internal processes of decay. None of them nor all of them put together will produce the good life; for the good life is out of the reach of human wisdom and human strength, it is the good supremely desirable and supremely unattainable. To strive for it is to strive to be like God, and this is the fatal folly of man, as it was in the beginning. It is to build a tower which will reach to the heavens. It is to put one's trust in flesh, which withers as grass; only the word of the Lord endures forever. The Lord will establish His kingdom not because man has failed to do it, but because man cannot do it.

But this kingdom is not the Hebrew Utopia. There are certain striking omissions in it, and some of them we shall have to consider; but they are due to the basic character of the kingdom. And this basic character, if we can find words to summarize it, is this: it is not a kingdom in which human welfare is paramount. God does not, as the Hebrews saw it, bring to pass this judgment and this kingdom in order that men may live the good life. They do, but the prophets were looking at something other than the best thing for man. They looked at the kingdom as a fulfillment in time and space of the divine reality, of the holiness of God Himself. It was something which God – if we may so speak, paraphrasing their ideas – had to do because His own inner nature required it. Being what He is, He must finally provide that good overcomes evil; there must be an end to the cyclic struggle between the two. This is His "glory," as the Hebrews used the word, that He shows Himself to be "holy." Nothing less than this cosmic upheaval will prove it. When the will of the Lord is supreme, then all things, man and nature alike, will have reached their term. Whatever this may mean for man, he can hope for nothing better; and he must face this future, at once terrifying and consoling, with a sweeping act of faith in the power and will of God for good.

THE WISDOM OF THE HEBREWS

WE HAVE given our attention, almost exclusively, to the Hebrew state, and we have tried to see the significance of its origins, its course in history, its fall. We have looked at the Hebrew state as a religious entity, because, unlike the modern state, that is what it was, and in its religious character lies its peculiar interest. We have observed its collapse, and we cannot but be more keenly aware of a spiritual vacuum which we have sensed from the very beginning of our consideration of the religion of the Hebrews: the absence of what we call personal religion. What do Hebrew history and Hebrew institutions – monarchy, priesthood, prophecy, sacrifice – tell us of the meeting of the soul and God, of the attitude of the individual Hebrew, "the common man," toward the Lord whom these officers represented? Very little, it seems. We have adverted earlier to the strong social sense of the ancient world; it would be true, if exaggerated, to say that the ancients did not think of religion except as a social function, and were convinced that man could not find God except in the society of his fellows. How, then, was the Hebrew to find Him when the external form of his religion, which was identical with the state itself, crashed to ruins, and that at the hand of the Lord Himself? This historical crisis was a crisis in the personal religion of the individual Hebrew, and it brought to light elements which were less prominent in simpler and happier days. We shall endeavor, in the chapters that follow, to distinguish some of these personal elements.

The absence of personal religion in our preceding chapters has meant that we have attended but little to the morality of the ancient Hebrew; again, we speak of the individual man. We have, indeed, dwelt upon the law which governed Hebrew society, upon the moral will of the Lord, and we have not failed to notice the distinctive and superior character of Hebrew morality; but it has been social morality in this sense, that it is identified with the way of life of a people as such. But we have not paid much attention to the existence of the individual conscience; we have spoken more of a national, a collective conscience, corresponding to the national and collective character which the law and the moral will of the Lord imposed upon His people. In the same way, we have seen how the vindictive justice of the Lord operates against the nation as a whole.

This perspective is imposed upon us by the books of the Old Testament themselves, and it is not a false perspective. The religious history of the Hebrew people from its origins to its final catastrophe is the history of a collective personality; the prophets commonly imagine Israel as an individual, and address Israel as an individual. If we want to study the personal religion of early Israel, we must study it in the spiritual adventure of the nation as such; for the spiritual adventure of Israel is typical as well as historical. It is the story of a spiritual tragedy, but redeemed by the element of hope which we have seen; the hope, however, does not take away the tragedy, which consists in the total failure and destruction of a vital human entity. What we shall have to say about the personal religion of the Old Testament is formulated against this background of the story of the Hebrew nation.

We shall have to begin from a point which, at first glance, seems to have no apparent connection with this story, for its roots lie deep in the ancient world; we speak of "wisdom." We put the word in quotation marks, for it renders a Hebrew word which is not easily translated by a single English word. The Hebrews used the word which we translate "wise" to designate skill in the arts and crafts: a wise carpenter, a wise mason, just as in modern Arabic the physician is "the wise one." In such contexts, the word means that the man knows his trade, that he possesses the sureness and the dexterity in its pursuit which come from good training and sufficient experience. When the word "wisdom" is applied to life itself, its meaning is much the same.

The wisdom which shows itself in the proper management of one's life and affairs is far older in the ancient East than any of the books of the Old Testament, and the sage appears almost at the beginning of literature in both Egypt and Mesopotamia. We can trace his career more easily in Egypt than in Mesopotamia, and it is to our purpose to look at him here; for the wisdom of the Hebrews owes no small debt to the wisdom of Egypt. In both Egypt and Mesopotamia, reading and writing were never skills possessed by the general population; the complex system of writing employed made this impossible. Hence we meet very early the class of professional scribes, and, likewise very early, the schools in which the candidates for this class were trained. These scribes were not members of the rich and noble classes; the nobility looked at the scribes much as the knights of Richard the Lion Hearted looked at the clerks. But the scribes were closely associated with the nobility and the royal court, for in no place was their skill more necessary than in those offices where public affairs and large private businesses were administered, and where the administration depended upon the accurate keeping of records. The scribes were the eyes, the ears, the memory, the hands of the men who steered the destinies of Egypt. They were themselves a social class, and they exhibit the snobbery peculiar to those who are just beneath the great. Quite often, the scribes were the real administrators of business and government, and in any case their possession of all the vital information made their advice very weighty. In ancient art we see the scribe with his stylus and tablet at the side of the noble as he surveys his estates, or of the king as he counts the spoils of victory; he is a slight obsequious figure, with an importance far out of proportion to his modest manner. And the scribe knew it. It was possible for a scribe to advance very far, even to reach the office of vizier in Egypt, in which he was a vicar of the king himself. But in order to achieve the full possibilities of his profession, the scribe had to be "wise";

and this wisdom was taught him in the scribal schools along with his reading and writing. It was taught in the same way that ethics were taught in the elementary schools in past generations, before progressive education made ethics superfluous; the young scribe learned his letters by copying out maxims from collections of wise sayings of scribes of the past.

We have a number of such collections from ancient Egypt, fewer from Mesopotamia, and their character is largely the same throughout. The elder scribes communicate to the younger what they have learned from their experience about the way a wise man should comport himself. Actually, the maxims add up to a fairly comprehensive code of conduct. The young scribe, a member of a lower class who was intimately associated with the upper classes, needed constant vigilance, a studied attitude which would never allow the wrong word to escape his lips. Furthermore, he was constantly in touch with lower officers, whose envy could ruin his career. So the code of conduct can be summed up in one precept: Give offense to no man. It is a frankly utilitarian code, for one avoids offense in order that one's career may suffer no hazard. But utilitarian morality can carry one quite a long way. We smile when we read that the scribe must eat and drink with moderation at the great man's table; if he feels the stirrings of appetite, he must put a knife to his throat. The utmost circumspection is required if he should have to speak with the great man's wife; Potiphar's wife, apparently, was not the only sexually frustrated female in Egyptian palaces. With the great man he must always agree, especially when the great man is angry, and he must not propose difficulties except when the great man is in a state of benevolent euphoria. He must always be affable to those beneath him, for he never knows when the turn of fortune will put them above him. One may see in these maxims no more than an ancient manual on how to win friends and influence people; but it seems that the code could produce a courtly gentleman.

The sages were capable of deeper reflections than this. Some of the collections of maxims were written in times of national crisis, and their authors attempt to find some basis for retaining their peace of mind in the face of calamity. They are not too successful;

the buoyant Egyptian spirit, sustained by Egypt's warm sun and equable climate, fell easily into despair when the stability of its external life was shaken. Few passages of any literature have the piercing pessimism of the Dialogue of the Man and his Soul, in which the man, desirous of committing suicide because of the evils of the world, is dissuaded by his soul: "Death is in my sight today like the recovery of a sick man, like the odor of myrrh, like sitting under an awning on a breezy day," and so on. We do not know which party won the debate. A document from Mesopotamia exhibits a similar pessimism, but within a different framework. A man is torn by doubt because he is afflicted with illness and other evils, despite the fact that he has never failed in his duty of worshiping the gods. In his anguish, he wonders whether man can ever know the will of the gods; perhaps what he thinks good is evil to them, and what he thinks evil is good to them. Is a man better off because of his piety? This doubter, apparently, was rescued from the slough of despond by the intervention of his god Marduk, who cured his illness and raised his head; were there other sages who had the same doubt, but experienced no such divine intervention? But, in the existing literary remains, these deeper reflections are the exception; most of the wisdom consists in maxims which communicate skill in the management of one's life and affairs. In spite of the emphasis placed upon personal ambition and personal success, that system of conduct is not entirely vicious which directs a man to live in harmony with his companions and associates.

The connections between the wisdom of Egypt and the wisdom of the Hebrews cannot be traced directly, except for a few literary parallels; but modern scholars feel certain that the connection is there. When the Hebrew monarchy was established, there were no precedents in the history of the Hebrews for the administrative form of its government. The long-existing bureaucracy of Egypt was a ready-made model, and more recent discoveries have shown how closely David and Solomon followed Egyptian procedure in the names and functions of their cabinet officers. There is little reason to doubt that professional scribes who arose to assist the officers of the monarchy also followed the Egyptian model, and that they even employed Egyptian copybooks. This does not mean that there was no native wisdom, for all peoples have a native wisdom, the collective experience of earlier generations synthesized in proverb and maxim and handed on from father to son. But it does explain why written collections of wise sayings should have appeared in Israel in the tenth century, the time of David and Solomon, to which Hebrew tradition assigned the first written collection of wise sayings.

The greatest of all wise men was Solomon, to whom the Lord Himself gave wisdom, and with it all other good things. Solomon spoke three thousand proverbs and wrote five thousand songs; he discoursed of trees and beasts and birds and fish and reptiles; he solved perplexed cases, and kings and queens came from afar to marvel at his wisdom. The ideal wise man he certainly must have been, for was not his life blessed with all success? And so all wisdom was attributed to him, and his name was placed at the head of almost every collection of wise sayings which we have in the Bible, although few if any of the things in these books can be attributed directly to Solomon.

These books of "wisdom," it will help us to recall, are Proverbs, Job, Ecclesiastes, the Wisdom of Solomon, and the book by Ben Sira which we call by the sonorous (and misbegotten) name of Ecclesiasticus. The last named was written in the second century before Christ, and the "Wisdom of Solomon" about a century later. Ecclesiastes probably belongs in the same period. Of the other two we can only say that they are older; in any case, we see that the fruit of wisdom matured rather late on the Hebrew literary vine. But, as we have seen, there is no form of Hebrew literature which can trace its ancestry back so far; and we need not think that these were the earliest works of the Hebrew sages.

Of these books, that which most resembles an Egyptian or Mesopotamian collection of wise sayings is Proverbs; it is also the oldest of the Hebrew wisdom books. The typical proverb is a sentence of two members, usually antithetic; besides, it was the mark of the wit of the sage to couch his saying in a wordplay, or in a form the meaning of which was not immediately apparent, the riddle. Such wise sayings are exchanged in the story of Samson and his Philistine groomsmen. Many proverbs are obviously the answer to the question, "What is like X?" or "Why is X like Y?" The book of Proverbs is simply a collection of these pearls of wisdom, strung together with no attempt to match them. The collection is preceded, in Chapters 1–9, by an essay on wisdom; in this more sustained effort we have a transitional form leading to the other wisdom books, which are longer compositions: collections of essays, or a single work built up of discourses about a single topic, like Job.

We have already indicated what wisdom meant to the Hebrew, but we have to qualify these remarks; for wisdom also received the peculiar stamp of the Hebrew belief, even if, in substance, it remained skill in the management of one's life and affairs. The Hebrew sages say more than once that the fear of the Lord is wisdom, or the "beginning" of wisdom: rather, perhaps, what we would call the "essence" of wisdom. No one is wise who does not fear the Lord, and who does not arrange his life and affairs in the spirit of that fear. Wisdom is properly the prerogative of the older generation; it is something which a father should possess, and should deliver to his son. A young man, in Hebrew wisdom, is a fool by definition; but, if he listens to his elders, he will get wisdom in due time. If he does not, he will remain a fool all his life, and there is no fool like an old fool.

But cannot this wisdom be found in a more orderly and codified form than the instruction of a father to his son? In the centuries after the fall of the Hebrew state, the sages identify wisdom with the written will of the Lord, the Law which He gave to Moses. More and more the Law was understood as a complete code of conduct; it was the wisdom which the Lord had given the Hebrews, and he who knew the Law knew all wisdom, for he knew the will of the Lord. This was not, however, the view of the earlier sages, for whom wisdom was still the collective experience of the past; it was admitted, of course, that it was the Lord who ultimately gave wisdom.

Readers of the Bible have often been offended by a certain rigidity in the concept of wisdom. The sages appear to divide all mankind into two great classes, the wise and the fools, and they do not imagine a passage from one class into the other, once a man has definitely chosen one or the other. The young man, we have noticed, is a fool by age and state; but he can learn wisdom by following instruction. Once a man has become a fool, there is no hope that he will ever become wise. In the same way, it is not to be thought that a man who has received wisdom as a gift from the Lord will ever reject it. And so we sometimes think that we detect an unctuous smugness in the sages, a sense of self-righteousness and a contempt for those who lack their wisdom. They are narrow and intolerant, and show little or nothing of compassion. So, at least, many have judged them. But there is a substantial body of truth beneath their oversimplification. They were convinced of the importance of the critical decision in human life, whenever it comes: the decision which turns the life of a man in one direction or another and which, once made, is irreversible. They believed that it was of the highest moment that the young man should know that he faces such a critical decision, and that he should be taught to see its inescapable consequences. For it is characteristic of the young to be heedless of the future, heedless of the fact that a hasty decision has permanent effects. No doubt such critical decisions can be patched up; no doubt a man can sometimes escape the consequences of his folly. The sages, however, were not concerned with instructing the young man how to patch up his life, but how to direct it so that it would remain whole and entire, in no need of patching. The tone of their doctrine is pedagogical, not speculative, and it has its proper place and function.

To self-righteousness the sages must plead guilty; it is the characteristic vice of those who are good, but not perfect. On the other hand, it is necessary to keep the difference between good and evil, between vice and virtue, clearly in mind. There is much maudlin sentimentality in some compassion, which does not imitate the compassion of Jesus, who saved people from sin without ever stooping to sympathy for sin. Morally, one man is never as good as another; if he is, then those who attempt to live by a moral code are wasting their time and their trouble. Why should the murderer be more worthy of compassion than the person whom he attacks? The sages were hard, and the world needed a more humane — or shall we say a more divine? — view of the ugly reality of sin; but they did not make the mistake of confusing sin with misfortune. Sin is folly, and the sinner is a fool; the compassion which denies this is a false compassion. One need not deny the reality of human malice in order to rescue a man from his malice; indeed, it would be no rescue which did not recognize the true nature of the evil from which the sinner must be delivered. This the sages knew, and they were wise in their knowledge. They lacked a realization of the possibilities for good in human nature, of the attraction which the good exercises even over the fallen human will. And, despite their conception of wisdom as a charisma, a gift of God, they did not see fully the truth that human goodness, if it exists at all, is the work of God rather than of man. But they did see that there is an essential and irreconcilable hostility between good and evil, not merely in the abstract, but in the concrete and the individual; this realization is something which many modern thinkers could learn from them.

They lacked also, it is to be feared, a perception of the weakness of human nature, even when it is endowed with wisdom. This statement needs some qualification; after all, Solomon, the wisest of the sages, played the fool in his latter years, and thus furnished the horrible example of what could befall the wise man. The sages knew this, but they knew also that it should not happen, that wisdom was a principle of stability in the moral life of a person. Even if a wise man acted the fool, he had within himself that by which he could recover his moral equilibrium; the fool had no such point of balance. Perhaps we should not say that they did not perceive the true depth of human weakness, but rather that they taught how a man could by wisdom overcome his weakness and fix his unstable desires. Again, they are pedagogical first and foremost.

We have taken notice earlier of the opinion attributed to Socrates and Plato that sin is ignorance, and virtue is knowledge: that a man wills evil only because he has never learned what is good. If his mind is trained, then he will always choose what is good. In modern times, the same opinion lives on in the belief that education will deliver man from his iniquity. The wisdom of the sages does seem, at first glance, to be involved in the same fallacy. For wisdom is an intellectual virtue, even if we take account of the fact that the Hebrews did not distinguish intellectual and moral virtues; the synonyms of wisdom are "discernment," "understanding," and the like, which seem to put the root of virtue where Socrates put it, in the mind. Likewise, sin is called folly. It is prudent to do good, imprudent to do wrong. In this also there is a substantial underlying truth, just as there is in the Socratic view of virtue, and the sages emphasized this truth. "The simplicity of the virtuous man is mocked," wrote Gregory the Great, sadly aware that it is more frequently virtue which is identified with folly. Jesus said that the children of this world are more shrewd in dealing with their own kind than the children of light, and St. Paul wrote that the wisdom of this world is the foolishness of God. And so the sages taught the young man that the height of folly is to do wrong. They seem to present sin less as an offense against the will of the Lord than against human intelligence. The sinner is a fool, to whom one cannot talk sense; he is like a child that knows neither good nor evil. He is shortsighted, improvident. For a quick small gain he hazards a permanent vital loss. He is thoughtless, heedless, witless. From his folly proceeds nothing but misfortune, disaster, final destruction, and he brings it all upon himself. If the young man will but learn that evil is folly, he may hope to escape all these things. It is not so much that virtue is knowledge; it is rather that sin is foolishness which is the doctrine of the sages.

For the sages really had no esteem of knowledge for its own sake; wisdom is practical knowledge, knowledge which issues in action. Even among the sages we find none of the intellectual curiosity of the Greeks. It is true that Solomon is said to have discoursed about trees and birds and beasts and fish, which would have brought his wisdom near the point which Aristotle attained in his treatise on animals. Ben Sira, who knew of Greek wisdom at least by hearsay, sees his ideal sage as knowing the wisdom of the ancients, penetrating the meaning of riddles and proverbs, traveling in strange lands, pouring out wise sayings, acquainted with the knowledge of the Lord, which is the Law. But, as we have had occasion to point out, the sages are pedagogical. It was the part of a wise man not to attempt what is above him, not to peer into mysteries. Wisdom was not the fruit of discovery and invention; the sages were anti-intellectual, in our sense of the word. Their wisdom was essentially conservative; the true and the pure wisdom was possessed by the men of old, and the sage was he who had best assimilated this wisdom handed down from generation to generation. It was, as we have called it, collective experience; the sage might add his own little bit of experience, but it was "in the same sense and in the same dogma." With the Egyptian sage, he thought the Greeks were children, always seeking something new.

We moderns would have found the intellectual atmosphere of the sages intolerably stuffy, and it is doubtful whether we can ever arrive at a true sympathy with them. We are not ourselves, of course, free of the struggle between conservatism and radicalism, between tradition and discovery, and we never shall be, for they represent two constant and opposing trends of the human spirit; if we knew how to moderate them, we should be wise indeed. St. Thomas Aquinas learned much more from Abelard than he did from Abelard's great and orthodox adversary, St. Bernard of Clairvaux; yet Bernard and Thomas are both Doctors of the Church. For the sages, wisdom was not a venture into the unknown, but a firm stand upon the known. From such an attitude science and philosophy can never arise. The wisdom of the sages had its place in a world where there were no fixed moral standards, and something of their wisdom is always in place as a counterweight to evolutionary morality. But something more than their type of wisdom is needed to maintain fixed moral principles in a constantly and rapidly changing world, to avoid the confusion between morality, which does not change, and manners, which do. Something more is needed also to meet the advance of the human mind; some, like St. Bernard, can meet it by flight from the perils of intellectual adventure, but it is not possible for all to do so.

We have not yet succeeded in defining the wisdom of the sages beyond the point at which we started: skill in the management of one's life and affairs. Perhaps we shall not succeed. The Hebrew sages accepted as their own the principle which we found basic in Egyptian wisdom: Give offense to no man. If we examine their wisdom in detail, we shall be impressed, as many have been, with its pedestrian level. We smile when we read the graphic warning of the sage against the strange woman, whose lips drip honey. We are amused at the earnest and frequent admonitions not to go bail, even for one's dearest friend. We look with some disdain upon the conventional exhortations to industry and thrift. We might even be tempted to say that the wisdom of the sages is, in summary, a knowledge by which we recognize those things which will get us into trouble. And we cannot fail to see that the motive which is given the young man is, frequently enough, a motive of self-interest. If he does what is right, he will succeed in his enterprises and will avoid the dangers which threaten the indolent, the laggard, the fool.

The sages have no doubt that the wise man will never experience misfortune, and that the fool will certainly experience it. Wisdom is a sure path to happiness, to success, to good fortune. In the world of the sages, it seems, virtue always has its reward. Solomon asked only for wisdom, and with it received riches, long life, and victory over his enemies. The wise man may be sure that the same thing will happen to him. Not a few students and readers of the Bible have been appalled at what they call the crass eudemonism of the sages. They think that the world of the sages is not only an unreal world, but that it is not even a good world; man, they say, should do what is right because it is right, and not because he expects to gain thereby. Some of these criticisms are not altogether pointless, and we shall have to examine in their proper place some Old Testament writings which go beyond the doctrine of the sages. But we do not wish to see their wisdom summed up as ultimate folly; and so we ought to try to see, if we can, what is contained in this element of their teaching, even if it repels us when we first look at it.

We spoke earlier, and in more than one context, of the Hebrew belief in an integration of the moral will of the Lord with nature and with human events. We tried to see how this belief is expressed in several different ways. We should be able to see that the sages are witnesses to this belief, even if it should have to be granted that they have formulated it less nicely than the prophets. Put in its simplest form, their belief means that, supposing the moral will of the Lord, it is impossible that a man should be better off by departing from the way which that will sets for him. The Hebrews believed firmly in the primacy of good; the whole universe itself was good, as the Lord had made it, and there was nothing wrong with it that could not be reduced to the rebellion of man against the supreme moral will of the Lord. When man is in harmony with the Lord, he is in harmony also with the things which the Lord has made, and his life should go well.

As a general law, this statement can scarcely be denied, unless one wishes to deny that there is any such thing as morality, that there is any difference between good and evil. But the sages, it seems, do more than state a general law; they apply it to particular cases. If it is so applied, then it should be at once obvious to them, we think, that this general law has to be related to other general laws. And one of these laws which we have already considered – not to mention others – is that the God of Israel is not a god of material and temporal benefits, like the gods of Canaan. And there is the fact of experience, which the sages seem to ignore, that virtue is not always rewarded, that the fool is not always led away to disaster. It is rather easy to say that they did not know or refused to consider these things; if so, they hardly deserve the name of wise, and we ought to find some reason in their words which escapes their facile critics.

There is reason in their words. There has been, especially in modern times, much high-sounding talk about disinterested morality; but there really is no such thing. One may visualize happiness in many ways, some true and some false; but the mind rebels at the idea that morality should issue in ultimate unhappiness. "Disinterested" morality consists in elevating one's idea of happiness, not in surrendering to despair. The principle of the sages is valid, and upon it one can erect a loftier structure. The philosophers have long distinguished the "honest" or moral good, the "useful" good and the "agreeable" good, and have so formed their ethics as to establish the primacy of the "honest" good, to which the useful and the agreeable must often be sacrificed. But the philosophers ought to know — and the unthinking man knows it, if the philosophers do not — that good is ultimately one, and that the honest good must, in the long run, be identified with the useful and the agreeable, even if, in the short run, they cannot always be achieved in a single action. The sages, in their own way, affirm not only the primacy of good, but also its unity.

Nor is their world so unreal as its seems. What assurance can they give of a peaceful and ordered life? None, one might answer, expressing the vast despair of our own day. And if all hope of such a life is gone, then all striving for it comes to an end; men do not, in the aggregate, attempt the impossible, although there are always individuals who do. We spoke above of the despair of the prophets of human institutions and human endeavor, and it might appear that the optimism of the sages cannot be reconciled with the prophetic idea; but the sages are dealing with affairs on a personal level. Concretely, there is no assurance even of a minimum of peace and order, within a limited area and a limited time, except in the substantial moral integrity of a group of people. This may be the best one can hope for, but, if it is the best, it is worth the effort. The individual has no hope of peace and order in his life except in wisdom; he certainly has no hope from folly. It will help us to remember that the wisdom of the sages comes from a relatively stable social and political scene, in which violent upheavals were the rare exception. It is not so cosmic a view as that of the prophets, but it has its modest place within its limitations. The sages were sure that wrongdoing, folly, corrupted the life of a man. There could be no profit in it; even wickedness could not prosper if it did not have the good on which to fatten itself. If all men were fools, then things would be desperate indeed. But they are not, although the sages were realists enough to recognize that the fool we have always with us. But the wise man, they were sure, would be neither richer nor happier, he would live no longer and no better, if he exchanged his wisdom for folly.

In justice to the sages, we ought to point out that their idea of success and prosperity is moderate. We said earlier that the Old Testament never rose to the revolutionary pitch of "Blessed are the poor"; all the same, the curses which the prophets launched against the amassing of wealth had not been unheeded. The sages neither expect nor promise great wealth as the reward of wisdom. Both prophecy and wisdom unite in the belief that the poor are the special favorites of the Lord. Where superficial smartness might say that poverty proves lack of wisdom and abandonment by the Lord, Israel's wise men believed that the Lord gave special care and interest to those whom He had allotted less than their share of the world's goods. He makes Himself their champion and judge, He vindicates their rights against the rich and the tyrant, He gives them the necessities of life; but He does not make them rich. Perhaps in this belief we are approaching the revolutionary statement of the Gospel; in any case, we ought not to say too quickly and too simply that the sages have a morality of self-interest.

No doubt the wisdom of the Hebrew sages, in the last analysis, is disappointing to the modern reader. We come to it after two thousand years in which philosophy, science, and the revealed religion of Christianity have operated to form the world of thought in which we live. We are conscious of the gulf which separates us from the world of the sages; the wisdom which they prized so highly seems to us mean. We feel that the sages, even without intending it, were making a stab in the direction of a philosophy, and that their effort was not felicitous. They exhibit the Hebrew belief in the will of the Lord as the supreme governing force of human life which we find in Hebrew law, prophecy, story; but we cannot see that they propose this belief with the same clarity and strength. Has wisdom any message for us, any meaning?

Perhaps what the sages say has been said better by others; perhaps the intrinsic value and significance of their wisdom have been assimilated by other literary forms. We do not find them wrestling with the great ideas; they were concerned with the small, the petty things of life: the daily affairs of the household and the market place, and the way in which a man might discover peace, order, satisfaction in these pursuits. It is of such small, petty things that human life is made up: the large issues, the great ideas, heroic endeavor are not a part of the normal life of the average man. What the sages do is to focus the Hebrew belief in the supreme moral will of the Lord upon these petty affairs of small people. To the Lord, these petty affairs are significant, and they ought to be significant to the people concerned. For it is in these petty affairs that they must realize their destiny, whatever it may be. It was wisdom to know that the management of one's life and affairs is important, and that what happens to a man is determined, in the last analysis, by what he is. Despite the past two thousand years, many of us do not seem sure just what wisdom is; and the sages could well permit themselves a smile at those who have thought that wisdom is philosophy, science, knowledge, learning. They had a name for those who think so.

THE MYSTERY OF INIQUITY

THE wisdom of the sages was an easygoing wisdom, in the intellectual sense; as we have seen, it exhibits no intellectual curiosity. It does not, consequently, reach the really profound problems of human life and conduct, and it will not satisfy a truly reflective mind. We have remarked that it is suitable to periods of stability; but it has not the inner strength to withstand crisis, for it has no answer to crisis, no prescription of what to think or what to do when the security which it takes for granted is dissipated. Such a crisis, in Hebrew history, was the fall of the kingdom of Judah, the end of the Hebrew monarchy and the people of the Lord. It is in this period that we find a voice which asks a question which the sages cannot answer, and this voice is probably the first to do so, although other voices later asked the same question.

The voice is that of Jeremiah, and the question is: "Why does the way of the wicked prosper?" We have to recall that Jeremiah is above all the prophet of agony: not the weeping prophet, as he has been called by those who have read little or none of his book, and as is indicated in the word "jeremiad," defined in the dictionary as a lament or tale of woe. We cannot tell whether his question was directed at a particular problem or at the general problem. Did he ask it of his own personal enemies, who did not experience the punishments with which he threatened them? Or did he ask it of the nations which were to conquer Israel? For even if they were the rod of the Lord's wrath, the fact remained that they were wicked and that they did prosper. Or did he ask it of men in general? It is the question of a man who thought himself overwhelmed by an irresistible torrent of evil; why does it happen? Why cannot the Lord do something to stem it? The answer which came to Jeremiah is curious, if it can be called an answer; we can state it here, for it will not take us far in our consideration. It was: if you cannot race with men, how will you race with horses? The answer of the Lord, when the prophet protests the unbounded success of evil, is that he can expect worse to come.

Several psalmists ask the same question, and they give the traditional answer of the wisdom of the sages: the prosperity of the wicked is not enduring. Disaster and death shall take away all their prosperity. The obvious subsumption, of course, is that the psalmist too shall die; and so we must consider that these poets and sages, when they speak of death, do not speak merely of the dissolution of the human organism, but rather of the manner of death. For the wicked, death is a terror, because it means the loss of all the things which they prize; not so the man who said to God, "You are the rock of my heart, my portion forever." Death comes to the wicked in its most horrible guise, as "the king of terrors"; he comes early, or he comes in the blow of an enemy, in the slow corrosion of a wasting disease. The wicked sees his wealth dissipated and his children destroyed before him. So the answer of the sages to the question could well be identified with the answer of the Greek sage who said, "Call no man happy until he is dead." Disaster lurks always for the wicked, no matter how secure he may seem; but wisdom should protect a man from such sudden disaster.

This simple doctrine was not enough for an anonymous writer who possessed the most profound mind and the most eloquent gift of language which we have in the Old Testament; for there can be no doubt that the book of Job is the supreme effort of the Hebrew literary genius, as it is one of the few great classics of world literature. One never quite succeeds in capturing the mind of its author, which always soars out of our reach, astonishing us to despair by the clarity of its vision and the magnificence of its expression. Every student of the Old Testament thinks, at one time or another, that he has found the formula of the book of Job, that he has created the perfect summary of its thought; and always, when the book is read again, we find that it says more than its critics can tell us. We shall not be so foolish as to attempt here to synthesize such a monument of art; as well attempt to summarize a symphony. But we shall have to do the best we can to tell what the book says.

The author begins with an old story, a fragment of folklore, about a rich and good man who was struck by disaster and lost his wealth, his children, and his health. Neither he nor any other man knew why this happened to him. But the storyteller knew; it was done to prove that a man could serve God without self-interest. And so the Lord permitted Job to be assaulted by the "Satan," whose name means "the Adversary," a kind of heavenly Grand Inquisitor. When the demonstration is finished and the Satan confuted, then the Lord restores to Job all his possessions in greater measure. Such was the story, and it must have been a story of the sages. As such it showed that a man could serve God without self-interest, and that God could prove the wise by adversity; if they withstood the trial, He would not abandon them. But the author of the book, with a marvelous dramatic sense, seizes the moment when Job is in the depths of his miseries to ask what a man ought to think about such things. To give his presentation reality, he introduces three of Job's friends, his "comforters," to debate the problem with him. In order to understand the book, we have to concede to the author his case: the case of a man of integrity who experiences total ruin. We must admit that it is possible for a good man to experience all the ills of life without final repair; for Job has nothing to expect but death. The story of folklore, of course, granted him a rehabilitation; but the author quietly ignores this happy ending, because he knows, and he expects his readers to know that things do not happen that way; one who has a collapse of fortune such as Job's cannot expect to have everything restored to him.

We have one more inquiring mind who proposed the problem to himself: the author of the little book called Ecclesiastes, "The Preacher," although why it should ever have received this title no one knows. Like the book of Job, it is anonymous; the author masquerades as Solomon, but he expects no one to take him seriously. Solomon was a man who lived long and much; he was an apt mouthpiece for the random reflections of this book. Everyone has heard the refrain of Ecclesiastes: "Vanity of vanities, and all is vanity." For this is the general impression of the book: that the endeavors of man are vain and profitless, that he can achieve no lasting good, that death is the end of all his efforts. The world is full of contradictions, and there seems to be nothing that makes one man better than another. The writer catalogues, with a grim satisfaction, the ills and troubles which beset mankind, and sees no escape from them, no way in which a man may find security. The little book has often given scandal to its readers, and it is not to this day a book that is much read and quoted. We have to understand its writer as spiritually akin to the writer of Job, and to see that he voices the emptiness of earthly life and worldly goods. These are not the things the human spirit craves, and the pursuit of them is folly. But what does the human spirit crave? The author of the book or one of its editors has interposed in the course of its reflections a number of wise sayings drawn from the traditional wisdom of the sages; these are in the spirit of the author, even if they should not be his own. For he is not a moral anarchist who denies the difference between good and evil; he is convinced that man must do what is right. But why must he do it? And what effect does it have upon his personal life, upon the world of men, if he does right? Ecclesiastes does not know.

Let us pause for a moment and try to formulate this problem in our own modes of thought and speech. It is a problem which has long agitated, in the abstract, the philosophers and the theologians; it is the problem of evil, which can be posed in several ways without changing its substance. It is the problem, in the concrete and individual case, which confuses the mind and tortures the heart of those who suffer evil. For evil is the irrational and unintelligible; it is the corruption of good and the corruption of being. It has no reason and no justification for its existence, for if a thing exists at all, it ought to be what it ought to be; and there is nothing which can explain why it is other than it ought to be. Evil is nothing, but it is a kind of malicious embodied nothing; it is pure destruction, and it tends to destroy all that is. Yet, by a paradox, there could be no evil unless there were something good. Reason cannot accept the fact of evil, but experience cannot deny it. How can it be?

One cannot attribute it to God without destroying any idea of divinity one might have; but how can one attribute it to a lower agent without, in some way, imperiling the supremacy of God, His power and will for good? One cannot attribute it to some blind and unintelligent force, for such a force would be neither good nor evil unless it were directed by some intelligence; and we cannot think that blind force is ultimately either equal to intelligence, or superior to it. One cannot attribute it to intelligent choice, for a choice means nothing unless it arises from an appetite for good; an appetite for evil would be an appetite for nothing. We cannot attribute it to error, for the mind must be corrupted by evil in some way before error is possible; the function of the mind is truth, and the mind cannot be diverted from its function by anything within itself. We overstate the problem somewhat because, in the abstract, thinkers have oversimplified it, and by multiplying words have obscured its reality and its urgency; if they have not solved it, at least they have hidden it. But it keeps popping up, because it is always present in the concrete and the particular; and the philosopher, however brilliant and incisive his mind, will ask as quickly as the uneducated man: "Why does this happen to me?" For it is the instinctive cry of distress of a man in the face of the unreasonable and unintelligible fact of evil, and all his speculations will not give him a final answer.

The writers of the Old Testament, of course, look at the problem in the concrete and the particular. Job is a man in whose life there is no correlation between moral goodness and general well-being. He has done all that he ought to do, yet he is nothing of what he ought to be. In his story is the wonder of Ecclesiastes why a man cannot achieve the good even when he tries to do it, why he seems unable to escape the pervading evil of the world. Neither of them asks the question of the Mesopotamian sage: perhaps what appears good to man is really evil, what appears evil is really good; who knows the mind of the gods? They did not ask this, because their Hebrew faith would not permit them to ask it. The Mesopotamian sage doubted, at least for a moment, whether there is any difference between good and evil; the Hebrew could not do this, for he believed in the supreme moral will of the Lord. For him, the problem was the apparent ineffectiveness of this moral will in human life; if the will of the Lord is for good, and if His power is supreme, why does not the good that He wills come into being, and why does He not annihilate evil? We cannot read the words of these ancient Hebrews unless we share their own awareness of the immediate reality of the problem of evil, and hear with them the anguished voice of humanity crushed by this monster which it cannot conquer; we shall not sympathize with them if we permit the devious logic of modern thinking to disguise the harsh fact which it cannot explain away.

This is the great issue which Job and his friends debate. And, to understand Job's friends, we have to recall the doctrine of the sages; for they are the ultimate corollary of the doctrine of the sages, carried beyond its scope to the point of absurdity. They assert that there is a correlation between the morality of a man and his well-being, that Job, as he stands, is impossible; that there is and there can be no such contradiction in terms as a good man whose condition is evil. Their doctrine admits no explanation of Job except that he is a sinner who experiences the just punishment for his crimes. This, hinted in their early discourses, finally becomes an explicit charge. We are reminded of the words of the Apostles related by St. John: "Lord, who sinned, this man or his parents, that he should be born blind?" The question contains a patent absurdity, but the too simple doctrine of the Apostles and of Job's friends did not balk at absurdity.

We do not, however, wish to write off Job's friends too easily. They have a coherent theory of evil, based both upon Hebrew belief and upon experience; they are convinced that evil is entirely the work of human malice. Were men all that they ought to be, the world would be all that it ought to be. But, like all theories of evil, their theory runs up against a blind wall; for this general rule fails in individual instances. Job was all that he ought to be, but his world was all wrong. Why? They have no answer for it. They do not even appeal to another principle of the sages, that Job may suffer for the sins of an ancestor; in such a man as Job the principle obviously has no application. They do not suppose that he is a victim of blind chance, of the law of averages; for this would suppose a world governed by no moral principles of any kind. One must enter the question more profoundly; and this the author does through the speeches of Job, his hero, although, as it has often been remarked, Job is a dramatic figure, not the mouthpiece of the author.

It is Job who generalizes the question. His own experience is typical of the experience of many. Why should any man be born, if it is only to meet such a miserable destiny? Job is faced by an awful and mysterious fact: God treats him as an enemy. He can conclude nothing else, for he too thinks, with the sages, that such experiences as his are the treatment due to an enemy; misfortune comes from "the wrath of God." But why is God his enemy? The question recurs throughout the discourses, and Job stabs desperately at the possibilities. Perhaps he is an enemy of God by nature, like the monster of chaos whom God vanquished in His creative act. Perhaps God takes pleasure in building up man for a fall; perhaps this is all He ever intends. And Job will not be satisfied with any dialectic which attempts to put the responsibility elsewhere. Reviewing in a few epic lines the whole sweep of human catastrophe, he asserts that God does it; if not He, who else? For the Hebrew belief in the divine supremacy will not allow anyone else to share in the divine government of the world. Then, almost inclining to the skepticism of the Mesopotamian sage, Job marvels that he cannot prove himself right before God. If he had a human adversary, he could appeal to a judge; but God, who has shown His enmity, is both his accuser and his judge. This is to say, equivalently if not formally, that justice is simply what God wills it to be.

This is bold language, not entirely in accord with the "patient Job" of popular imagination. It is language which some modern writers like to call "blasphemous"; they forget that the Hebrew Bible addresses God throughout in language which a modern Christian would never utter, for fear he might shrivel up where he stands. The approach of the Hebrews to God, as to each other, was direct and simple. Job, in the tortuous complaints of his discourses, is seeking an idea which is the key to the problem, if he can only find it: what is God? What kind of being is it that afflicts him for no cause that he can discover, and who permits – the Hebrews would say accomplishes – the myriad revolutions of human life which cast men up and down so helplessly? The thought occurs to him that God is power, as the ancient Semitic peoples thought of their gods, but power without control, blind and capricious, not amenable to reason or compassion. This thought Job cannot abide, for such a god is not a god at all. His mind rebels at the suggestion of a supreme irresponsible power. Justice cannot be simply what God wills it to be.

Certain of this, Job issues a solemn warning to his friends. They think they speak on God's behalf; let them take care, for He does not need to be defended by falsehood. Their assertion that Job is wicked does not justify God, for Job is not wicked, and God knows it. It is a falsehood to defend the ways of His providence by affirming that the world is all it ought to be; for, if God is just, He knows that it is not. Job still does not know why it is not, but he is sure of this: to assert that divine justice is perfectly realized in the historical world is to mock justice, to deny the difference between good and evil.

It is a great advance to refuse to accept the existing world as an argument against the justice of God; and the author of the book is poet and theologian enough to show us that this advance is not easily made. But Job still knows no reason why God treats him so. Now he toys with another idea. If there were something more to hope for, some ultimate vindication of his innocence, then his present condition would seem less intolerable. For in the eyes of all men, as in the eyes of his friends, he stands condemned. The poet knows, and speaks with feeling, of the universal instinct which finds total misfortune revolting. Human compassion is a jewel as rare as it is precious. Men are more inclined to accept the doctrine of Job's friends in one form or another, and to shun the victims of misfortune as the accursed of God, as the prisoners of their own failure. Therefore Job desires that his integrity might be demonstrated.

It is here that he voices in a strangely obscure manner a desire that there might be something more for him than the present life, that he might look forward to a reconciliation with Him whom he knows only as his enemy. Yet he stops short. This is a hope which his faith in God does not give him. But the very conception of the idea, joined to his assurance that God is infallibly just, affords him a bit of grim consolation. We are amazed that the author skirts the question so nearly without getting into it. May we not think that he was unwilling to speak of a future life as an easy answer to the difficulties of the present life? He would not have found that proposition reasonable which asserts that it makes no difference how topsy-turvy the present life is, as long as God sets it right side up in the world to come. He would have interposed that the same power which can introduce order and justice into the world to come should be able to introduce it into the present life. And this is, substantially, what Job says. The desire of a future life arises spontaneously from the depths of Job's soul; this much, at least, the urgency of evil demands, even if the desired future life does not satisfy the mind entirely.

But the poet does not follow up the suggestion which he has raised. Rather the later words of Job only reaffirm the problem in more pressing terms. Again Job takes a more general view of an unjust world, filled with human malice and human misery, and with no visible proportion between the two. "From the city the dying groan, and the wounded cry for help; but God does not hear their prayer." There have been many who have thought this, but have not dared to say it; the writer of the sacred book has said it for us, so we need not scruple to repeat his words. There is the fact, of which God is as well aware as we are: many in all kinds of trouble and sorrow call on Him for help – He does not hear their prayer. The wave of misery rolls on unabated, the malice of man rages on unchecked; God does not hear their prayer. There are many smug and prosperous Christians who find the words of Job blasphemous, because they have never fallen to the depths where they feel quite sure that God does not hear their prayer; may the good God never let them fall so far, for it is doubtful whether their faith in the Great White Father would survive such an experience. They will tell us that God always hears our prayers, and we believe that He does; we cannot agree with them that He always manifests His attention, that He either makes things right or, at least, makes us feel good. We cannot be sure that God will not answer us as He answered Jeremiah: "If you cannot race with men, how will you race with horses?" This candy-stick religion is the sort of thing which made Job curse his friends. Let us not dishonor the wisdom of God by supposing that He cannot tell good from evil, that there is nothing really wrong with the world.

After Job and his friends have had their say — and the mysterious Elihu, who enters the book from nowhere and returns thither — there is one more speaker who must be heard. The Lord Himself, of whom much has been said, should have a chance to speak for Himself. And He does speak, as the occasion demands, out of the whirlwind. The speeches of the Lord appear to be magnificent poetry, but not altogether relevant to the discussion; are they not an assertion of that which Job denied as the key to the problem, the divine power? This they do assert, but much more; they assert, in their peculiar Hebrew fashion, the divine wisdom. The wisdom of God appears most patently in nature; this Hebrew poet sees nature as a system of paradoxes, baffling to human intelligence, but coherent. Most things in nature man does not and cannot understand; yet he cannot deny their existence, nor can he deny that this bewildering and complex organism retains its vitality and achieves its purpose by paths which man cannot trace. The Lord hurls a challenge at Job and at all who ask the same questions: if you know a better way to do it, let us hear it. The modern man, of course, finds little wonder in most of the things which the poet mentions; he sees in these lines the childish awe of the ancient before natural phenomena. The modern man would list other wonders, but it would be a false pride that would forbid him to share the awe of the Hebrew poet before these wonders. Despite the ingenuity with which modern man has discovered the secrets of nature and harnessed its resources, he is still faced by a baffling complexity which he cannot entirely analyze. Like the poet of Job, his response to the wisdom of God in nature ought to be an act of humility.

This is the key, the answer which the poet gives, if we can call it an answer; for it leaves the speculative problem hanging in the air. We still do not know what to think about the mystery of evil; the poet shows us only what we can do about it, how we can live with it without renouncing either our faith or our reason. The wisdom which is great enough to govern the visible universe in all its complexity must be great enough also to govern the course of human events. This, one might say, is not an argument; it is not intended to be. The poet is not trying to make the mystery of evil intelligible; one must confess the limits of one's reason, and commit oneself to faith in a God who is great enough, wise enough, just enough, powerful enough to administer a world which exhibits such flagrant disorder. There is no other principle of stability in which the mind can find repose. We have no answer to the problem; the consoling truth which the speeches of the Lord communicate is that we do not need to have an answer, if we have faith in the wisdom of God, in His power and will for good.

We call it faith, but the author spoke of a theophany, an appearance of God to man. While theology distinguishes very carefully between faith and knowledge, between faith and vision, we, aware of this distinction, may permit ourselves to use the terms more loosely, after the manner of the Hebrew poet. The faith in which his hero finally rests is a vision, because it is a new insight into the nature and character of God. We hesitate to employ the much abused modern term "religious experience," because of its abuse; but we have to find some word, and an experience of God is the best we can find. It is an experience which God Himself grants, because no other can grant it; it is the skirts of His robe, the touch of His hand, "the whisper of a gentle breeze." It is "knowing" Him, as the Hebrews used the word. It is the knowledge of who and what He is that makes all human problems, even our own, small and insignificant. The author of this book, apparently, thought that a man could not so "know" God unless he had first known evil, unless the weight of the mystery of iniquity had crushed him nearly to nothing; unless this spiritual void be first created, there is no room for God in the soul. Some who have known God better than most have said the same thing. This overwhelming combat with evil is the spiritual crisis which determines whether a man shall know God or deny Him.

We are not wrong, we believe, if we find this spiritual crisis in the life of Jeremiah, although it is not set forth in formal debate as it is in the book of Job; it is highly probable that the life of Jeremiah was one of the sources from which the author of Job drew. We have referred earlier to the doubts and fears of Jeremiah, which made his career as a prophet, especially in its final years, a living agony. As a prophet, he spoke of the inevitable downfall of his people; it was clear to him that it had to happen, because the Lord could not tolerate inveterate and obdurate malice. It was clear to him also that this downfall would be externally the work of a godless world power. In addition, he was a man of affectionate and delicate sensibilities, who loved his people and his land, and who was cut off from them because of his hostile message, which he hated to deliver. If we could create in our own imagination the stress of this crisis, we should not wonder that his attitude vacillates in devious ways. The fall of Judah was the moral will of the Lord in action; but this raised as many questions as it answered. The moral will of the Lord demanded much more than the fall of Judah in order that it should be perfectly realized; and how was this bloody conquest to advance its realization? We have noticed that Jeremiah, with the rest of the prophetic company, had a vision of the future; but he saw no connection between the fall of Jerusalem and this great future.

Jeremiah, however, found something which enabled him to face the hopeless present with an undiminished confidence in the future. This was the knowledge of God of which the author of the book of Job wrote, a knowledge which Jeremiah gained through an interior struggle as terrible as that of Job. Some have spoken rather disdainfully of the struggle of Job as fictitious, and they find Jeremiah more admirable because he is historical—as if the author of Job could ever have written of such an experience from mere hearsay and imagination. But the experience of Jeremiah is related in the story of his life, as told by himself and others, and is not transformed into a poem. From this knowledge of God Jeremiah gained the profound insight into the problem which his life and his words show: evil cannot be explained away, nor can it be expelled by force or by any other human means. Man, like Jeremiah himself, like the kingdom of Judah, can overcome evil only by suffering it, by permitting it to overwhelm him. Let others try to avert it by war, by diplomacy, by all sorts of plans and devices; he knew that these would fail, and that the kingdom of Judah would fulfill its destiny only by falling before the sword of the conqueror. He could, therefore, look upon this terrible prospect with calmness, even with satisfaction.

But it is not, by any human standards, a reasonable attitude. It is instinctive to resist evil by all the means at one's command, to flee from it; it is neither instinctive nor prudent to think that one conquers it by embracing it. Jeremiah had no other advice for his people except that they should embrace it. They did not, of course, accept his advice, for they were men of wisdom and prudence to whom this advice was folly. They could not see, any more than he could see, how their salvation would be found in the destruction of all that they valued; lacking his intense faith in the power and will of God for good, they could not possibly have found his advice anything but subversive.

The same mystery appears more clearly in the figure whom we call the Servant of the Lord, mentioned four times in the second part of the book of Isaiah. We have already noticed that the background of these chapters is the years between the fall of Jerusalem to the Babylonians and its restoration by the Persians: from 587 to 538 B.C. We call this figure the Servant because the prophet gives us nothing which would indicate his identity. He is a man with a mission, and the mission is "salvation"; we have already looked into the meaning of this word in the Old Testament. His mission is not a mission to the people of Israel only, but to the nations beyond Israel as well. His image is modeled upon the Hebrew concept of a prophet; this, at least, is most easily deduced from his description. For the means by which the Servant will accomplish his mission are not the means of the king and the warrior; he will speak to men, but not with the authority of the ruler. Indeed, the prophet expressly excludes any means which involve display or violence; the Servant will do his work softly and quietly. As the image of the Servant grows more clear in the prophet's mind, it is darkened; hostility appears, opposition which the Servant must overcome and will overcome, because the Lord who has chosen him is with him. Finally, the darkness bursts into the vision of the fifty-third chapter of Isaiah.

There the Servant appears as a marvel, a mystery, an incredible phenomenon. For this chosen Servant of the Lord is seen to lack all human attractiveness, to be reduced to insignificance. Men turn from him in horror and dread – not, as some have foolishly thought, because he was ugly and deformed, but as Job was abandoned by his friends: because the hand of the Lord has touched him. It has touched him in ways which the prophet has not described clearly, because he did not see them clearly; but the hand of the Lord has laid upon the Servant an intolerable burden of suffering, so great that he finally succumbs under it. The language of the prophet more obviously implies that the Servant suffers violence at the hands of men, and this is not unlikely; the servants of the Lord in the Old Testament often had to face violence, or the threat of violence. However it happens, the Servant dies painfully and ignobly, and no one attends to it.

But the prophet sees that this is the doing of the Lord, and that the death of the Servant is invested with tremendous significance. For his death has brought healing, salvation to many, even though they are unaware of it. In his defeat is his victory. His death is an atoning death, an act of submission to the Lord which the Lord accepts on behalf of those who, in some mysterious way, share it. And the death of the Servant is not as desperate as the death which Job foresees for himself; in a way which the prophet does not explain, the Servant himself shall look upon the fruits of his atoning death. The Servant, like Jeremiah, can do nothing with the evil which threatens him except submit to it, yield to it; and it works itself out upon him. He is not himself guilty; the wrath of the Lord is not aimed at him, as it was aimed at the iniquitous people of Israel. Yet God treats him as if he were angry at him, as Job said of himself, and he is reckoned among the wicked. But, in submitting to evil, he accomplishes the mission which the Lord has given him; through his own death salvation comes. Here is no speculative theology of vicarious atonement; the prophet has seen this truth, that through the suffering of men other men can be spared from suffering. Evil still remains an irrational factor in human life; but man can meet it in such a way that what he does is the greatest thing he can do. There is no reason why this should be, and the mind of man does not easily accept it; but the Servant of the Lord, as conceived by the prophet, is the final answer of the Old Testament as to how men shall meet the evil which they cannot overcome except by surrendering to it, by becoming its victims.

Readers of the Old Testament have always found this vision, so alien in content to all human wisdom and human sentiment, one of the most difficult passages of the Bible to assimilate into their habitual thinking. We may conjecture that it is for this reason that so many efforts have been made to identify the Servant more precisely than the prophet did, as if the prophet knew who he was, but playfully omitted the name so that Bible readers could play guessing games. In consequence, there are few Old Testament characters with any remote similitude to the Servant who have not been proposed as the original of the prophet's portrait. Such proposals are indeed nothing but guessing games, and we need not discuss them seriously here.

Of more importance is the interpretation which presents the Servant as a personalization of the people of Israel. We say a personalization, an idealization; for it is absurd to suppose that the prophet meant the historical group which went to Babylon. Those who see the Servant in this way mean the nation as a continuously living entity, in its past, present, and future: not only as it existed, but as it was intended by the Lord who founded it. They say that this prophet saw that the final destiny of

Israel, as a people, was to be a victim; it was to suffer at the hands of the nations, and thus to deliver these nations themselves. This, they say, was the way in which Israel was to be a light and salvation to the nations, and this great prophet was the one who saw it most clearly. Proposed in this manner, the interpretation is not unworthy of the prophet, and altogether in the line of thought which we think we find in the prophets and the history of the Old Testament.

But the words of the prophet indicate that the Servant was more than an ideal personalization of the people. To make this clear, we have to recall that the Old Testament stories often exhibit what we may call "the ideal person": ideal in this sense, that the person represents a group and incorporates into his own personality the history and the traits of the group. Thus the patriarchs are not only the ancestors of the Hebrews, but in their character, their personality, their manner of life, their adventures, they exhibit traits and experiences similar to those of the Hebrews as a people. David is not only the founder of a dynasty, he continues to exist, in a sense, in each succeeding member of the dynasty; each king is a "David," even if he never attains to the stature of the ideal king who headed the line. The idea is not peculiarly Hebrew, although we cannot duplicate exactly the biblical cast of the idea elsewhere. We have already observed that the ancient king was an incorporation of the people itself.

With this "ideal personality" as a basis, we see how the prophet could visualize a man who was Israel, although he is a distinct individual person. He is Israel because in his own life and person he possesses in the highest degree the religious gifts and the religious mission of Israel, and because in his own career he fulfills the destiny of Israel. He is all that the Lord intended that Israel should be; in him Israel reaches its peak, its fullness. But he is a distinct person, and he means as much to historical Israel as he means to the nations. We know of no historical person in the prophet's experience of whom this could be said; and it hardly seems reasonable to suppose than any man of whom such great things are predicated should be otherwise obscure and unknown.

There is only one individual in the prophet's experience who would approach this ideal figure, and this individual is not historical; this is the ideal king of whom we spoke earlier, who is also an agent of deliverance. Yet the opposition between the two is so direct and formal that, at first glance, it seems impossible to combine them into a single figure. Can we be sure that the prophet meant to combine them? There is really no necessity for thinking that he did so. They are two lines of prophetic vision that lead to one term. The prophet must have found it as difficult as anyone else to see how there was room for the two; we may suppose that he proposed the line which he saw, because his prophetic inspiration would not let him keep silence. How the riddle was to be solved he could leave to time and to the good pleasure of the Lord. This much he knew: the Servant of the Lord, as he saw him, could not be combined with the exaggerated and worldly hope of the future which, as we have seen, was the essential defect of the popular Hebrew idea of the future.

It is an interesting but hardly a surprising fact that this corrective had little or no effect upon subsequent Jewish thought. The Servant scarcely reappears in later Jewish literature. There was no room for him. He departs so violently from conventional ideas that the Jews could fit him into no scheme of the future which they concocted. The ideal king and the ideal kingdom they could not understand either; but these at least afforded them some ground for a vision of the future which satisfied human desires; to human desires the Servant offered nothing.

The way in which the Jews ignored the Servant makes the appearance of the Servant in the New Testament all the more striking. I count seven explicit allusions and two implicit allusions to the passage in the New Testament. There are not many Old Testament passages which recur this often in the New Testament. As it happens, few of these passages are attributed to Jesus Himself; but no one can question the fact that the identification of Jesus with the Servant belongs to the most primitive stage of Christianity, and only the most captious critic would deny that the identification was made by Jesus Himself. For there was no other from whom the Apostles could have learned it.

And so Christianity has always seen in Jesus the "fulfillment" of these words of the prophet; He is the ideal Israel, who sums up in Himself the religious gifts, the mission, the destiny of the people of the Lord. And this destiny was to die. His words and His life reflect the same spirit which we believe we see in Job, in Jeremiah, in the Servant of the Lord: that there is no answer to the problem of evil, and no way to meet evil in the concrete, except suffering and death. We have seen men in all the ages try to shake off the burden by the most varied and ingenious devices, and they have all failed. Jesus alone came and said: Take up your cross. If you wish to live, die. If you wish to find joy, suffer. He did not explain it; He simply lived that way. If there were a better answer to the problem, if there were a better way to meet it, it is hard to think that the Incarnate God would not have chosen it. He did not make evil easy to understand or easy to bear; He showed only that it is possible to live with it, and to live well, to live heroically, without doing anything about evil except to suffer it. This is the mystery of the Servant, the mystery of the life and death of Jesus, that it is in yielding to evil, in becoming its victim, in being consumed by it, that man has his only hope of overcoming it; and, by the solidarity which links Jesus with all men and all men with each other, this victory over evil can be communicated to others who are ignorant of what happens on their behalf.

At the beginning of the previous chapter, we took up the consideration of the personal religion of the Old Testament. At this point, we feel that we have ended it — at least, we have followed it to its highest point, the point where man meets God: where human nature meets the divine nature in the Incarnation, and where the individual person meets God in the spiritual crisis of his combat with evil. This is what the Old Testament has to say about the power of the human person, the secret weapon which no one can take from him: his power to suffer and to die, retaining his strong faith in the power and will of God for good, which realizes itself in his own personal destruction. We ought to notice that this personal religion of the Old Testament follows the same path which we have pursued earlier; it is a negation of human powers and human values, it is the depth of the despair of man from which faith in God rises. For we deal now not with institutions and laws and such, but with the essential goods of the human person: his body, his spirit, his life, himself. These also accomplish nothing good; in their death is their life.

XIV

LIFE AND DEATH

WE HAVE had occasion to remark upon some of the strange silences of the Old Testament: strange, that is, to modern ears. To some questions which seem to us most urgent the ancient Hebrews gave no attention, either from a lack of curiosity or from an unwillingness to plunge into depths which they feared were over their heads. The almost total silence of the Old Testament concerning life after death astonishes most modern readers. No modern philosophy takes this question so casually; even the prevailing agnosticism examines it at length before it takes its stand and regretfully announces that the evidence does not permit it to affirm anything about life after death. To the believing Christian who accepts the teaching of Catholicism concerning life after death, the belief in survival and reward seems so vital to his faith that he cannot imagine a religion in which this belief would have little or no part; to him, denial or doubt of life after death is practically the same as denial or doubt of God, the height of irreligion. If he becomes aware that the Old Testament shows a great void of this belief, he will refuse to think about it, for he cannot think of such a void in what he conceives the word of God to be.

On the other hand, if he stops to reflect about the content of his own belief, he will perceive that there is very little in it for the understanding, and nothing for the imagination. As a Catholic, he believes in survival after death in a state determined by the merits of the individual; as a well-instructed Catholic, he knows that the popular fancies of heaven and hell are not only misleading, but false. If he recalls how little God tells us about life after death, how little the human mind is able to conjecture about it, he will, perhaps, be less shocked at the silence of the Old Testament about it.

At the same time, the Hebrew indifference to the life after death stands in sharp contrast to the beliefs of a people who were their near neighbors, and with whom they had numerous contacts over the centuries of their history: Egypt. The substantial structure of the Egyptian tombs has combined with the dry climate of Egypt to preserve the mortuary remains of ancient Egypt in abundance. One will scarcely find a museum so poor that it does not possess at least one Egyptian mummy. What the thousands who stare incuriously at these withered relics of a past age do not realize is that, in Egyptian belief, survival in the afterlife depended upon the preservation of the body. We have to attend to this fact, as we shall refer to this feature of Egyptian belief when we approach the question of Old Testament belief. For it is not easy to define what, exactly, survived death in Egyptian belief; in this, as in other matters, the Egyptians exhibited their quaint and characteristic capacity of thinking along parallel lines. Egyptian art often represents the human being as accompanied by an exact double of himself, called the *ka* (recently identified as *ku,* but we retain the less accurate and more familiar usage). It is inexact to call it a "soul," and not sufficient to call it an invisible double. Neither is it the "self," the "ego," or the "personality"; Henri Frankfort called it "the vital force." Its permanent departure from the body was death. But it needs the body as a seat; if the body is destroyed, the *ka,* with no place of its own, becomes a ghost, a demonic spirit. If the body is preserved, the *ka* continues to live its own proper life.

The place of this life is the realm of the gods; if we were to be exact, we should have to trace the different forms of this belief, but it is not necessary for our present purpose. For all these forms of life have one essential common feature: the life after death in the realm of the gods does not differ from earthly life. The activities and the pleasures of the dead are the activities and the pleasures which they enjoyed while they lived. Egyptian tomb paintings, which represent the dead at work and play, are an invaluable source of information for the historian of Egyptian culture. Here is the nobleman fowling in the marshes, dining with his friends, entertained by musicians and dancers; here is the peasant driving his oxen at the plow, or harvesting and threshing his grain; here are the craftsmen — masons, smiths, potters, spinners, weavers — producing the goods proper to their skills. These paintings are not merely decorative; they are the reality of the world of the dead, just as are the paintings of food and drink, tools and weapons. For the world of the dead was, so to speak, a shadowy two-dimensional world in which the picture was the reality, and the *ka* of the deceased could enter the picture. In this world, of course, the troubles of the present life were removed. In the early stages of Egyptian belief, even the social structure of the present life was transferred to the next; immortality was proper to the king alone, and was granted to his subjects only because a king must have subjects. Not until much later did belief in the afterlife reach the point where it demanded that every man be a king in the next world.

Even from this brief sketch, it should be clear that the Egyptian belief in the afterlife was not belief in another life at all; in fact, it is a denial of another life. To the Egyptian, the life of this world was good, and he asked no more of the gods than that they continue to grant it even after bodily death. Their belief was a denial of the reality of death, a denial that any change in the condition of human life was possible or desirable. It was as stout an act of faith in the goodness of this world as man has ever made. And it is a testimonial to the good life which the ancient Egyptian kingdom gave its subjects, great and small. In all Egyptian literature that has come down to us, there are only two or three skeptical voices; they may have spoken for many, but they come from times of stress and crisis, and they do not represent the ordinary belief of the Egyptian in normal times.

There was no real differentiation on moral grounds among the dead. The Egyptians spoke of a judgment, and a rather awesome process it was; the deceased entered the hall of judgment and took his stand before Osiris and forty-two assessors, while his heart was weighed in the balance against the feather of justice. In the background lurked the monsters who would devour his heart, should it be heavier than the feather. In spite of the searching examination of the deceased, what was important was to know the right answers. We have these manuals of instruction which were buried with the dead that they might know how to respond to the judges. If the ritually correct answers were given, the deceased was admitted to "the field of rushes." If we stop to consider it, there was no more reason why entrance into the next life should be conditioned upon moral differentiation than entrance into this life, for there is no difference between the two. If a man were worthy of life, he was worthy of the next life. And so the reality of guilt, of malice, of the human will for evil, was effectively denied. From this it should be evident that the Egyptian belief in the afterlife had no appeal for the Hebrews. We may credit them with enough intelligence to see that such a belief was opposed to the religion of the Lord, just as the religion of the gods of Canaan was opposed to it. Egyptian belief also affirmed the primacy of the goods of this world, and denied the decisive import of the moral will.

If we turn to the other great civilization which the Hebrews knew, that of Mesopotamia, we find there a blank concerning the next life which reminds us of the Hebrews. For, while Mesopotamia spoke of a world of the dead, it was not a "life after death." This is the way it is described in the poem of the descent of Ishtar into the underworld as translated by E. A. Speiser: "The land of no return, the dark house, the house which none leave who have entered it, the road from which there is no way back, the house wherein the dwellers are bereft of light, where dust is their fare and clay their food, where they see no light, residing in darkness, where they are clothed like birds, with wings for garments, and where over door and bolt is spread dust." This is gloomy enough; no more dismally hopeless picture of the destiny of man after death was ever imagined. Achilles, evoked from the underworld, said to Odysseus: "I would rather be the meanest slave on earth than reign king over the dead"; and when the Mesopotamian hero Gilgamesh found his dead friend Enkidu, the words of Enkidu were no more comforting: "If I tell thee the order of the nether world which I have seen, sit thou down and weep."

The Mesopotamian could not share the Egyptian folly of imagining that death was any other than what it seemed to be, the end and the term of this life. In such a view, of course, there is no need for moral discrimination, for all men die alike, and none is better or worse off than his fellow. Hence the Mesopotamian also affirmed the desirability of this life, but he affirmed it with a sad awareness of mortality. When Gilgamesh sought the plant of immortality, a goddess admonished him to be content with what life offers (as translated by E. A. Speiser): "Gilgamesh, whither rovest thou? The life thou pursuest thou shalt not find. When the gods created mankind, death for mankind they set aside, life in their own hands retaining. Thou, Gilgamesh, let full be thy belly, make thou merry by day and by night. Of each day make thou a feast of rejoicing, day and night dance thou and play! Let thy garments be sparkling fresh, thy head be washed; bathe thou in water. Pay heed to the little one that holds on to thy hand, let thy spouse delight in thy bosom. For this is the task of mankind!" In such words the Mesopotamian religion, as we sketched it earlier, comes to a fitting conclusion concerning life and death.

Now it is a striking fact, which it does no good to minimize, that much of the Old Testament exhibits an attitude toward death which shows no appreciable difference from the Mesopotamian attitude. Even in the story of the first human couple, the penalty which the Lord addresses to them is: "You shall die." There is no looking beyond this ultimate term. As what was promised them in the beginning was a continuation of life upon this earth, what falls upon them for their disobedience is the end of life upon this earth. The horizons of the storyteller and his hearers, as far as we can see, did not extend beyond those of Mesopotamia. There may be those who are shocked at this, but their shock cannot put ideas into the mind of the ancient Hebrew. And this innocence of the story of primitive man persists through the Old Testament until we reach its latest compositions: "Better a live dog than a dead lion," said Ecclesiastes, writing in a sophisticated age many centuries after the story of Eden was told; he had not learned anything that made life after death a more desirable prospect than life upon earth. In the chapters which precede, the factor of survival has never entered into our consideration of Hebrew beliefs – not because we have omitted it, but because it is not there.

It may help to understand its absence if we recall a few ideas about the constitution of human nature, as the Hebrews understood it; and we must bear in mind what we have already seen more than once, that the Hebrews had no philosophy and no science. They looked at man as they looked at the heavens, and saw no more than their senses could reveal. Readers of the Bible will remember how frequently the word "soul" occurs in the Old Testament; but they usually do not know that this word is a false translation of a Hebrew word which really cannot be translated, because it signifies an idea which we do not have. When we hear the word "soul," we think of the spiritual component of human nature, the principle of life, which survives the dissolution of the human compound of soul and body. The Hebrews had no idea of such a spiritual component principle. What the English Bible calls "soul" is usually best rendered as "self," although this also is subject to qualification. The antithesis between the Hebrew idea and the Greek idea has been pointed out by Wheeler Robinson: to the Greeks, the human person was an incarnated spirit; to the Hebrews, it was an animated body. Before one can believe in survival, one must think of something which can survive. To the Hebrews, life was the life of the body; when this ceases, life ceases totally.

They were aware, of course, that life was not identical with the body purely and simply; if it were, then the body would never die. So they spoke of the "self," which is more or less the modern "ego," the conscious self which thinks and acts and feels and suffers; when death comes, the "I" simply ceases to be, and there is nothing left but what the Hebrews called a "dead one." They also thought of the blood as the seat of life, for one can see a man's life leaving him with his blood. They also thought of the "spirit," which is the breath; God breathed into man at his creation, "and man began to live." When the "spirit" leaves a man, he is dead. When the body is inert, there is no "I," for there is nothing the "I" can do; the lack of any idea of spiritual activity made it impossible for them to conceive of any life detached from the body. The blood comes out and falls into the ground; it does not survive, obviously. The "spirit," the breath, is not a human person; it returns, in the words of Ecclesiastes, "to God who gave it," but it does not live. The only form of survival which the Hebrew mind could conceive was a restoration of the only life which it knew, the resurrection of the body; and there is no trace of this idea in the Old Testament outside of a few passages, and those obscure.

There is in the Old Testament an underworld, an abode of the dead. Our venerable Douay Old Testament has misled its readers since its first publication by giving this underworld the name of "hell," which suggests something altogether different. The King James Version more properly turned the Hebrew word into English by calling it "Sheol"; the word is meaningless to most readers, but in this instance that is an advantage. Compare, for example, the words of the Mesopotamian poet quoted above with these words of Job: "I go, never to return, to a land of darkness and blackness, a land of shadow, like gloom, of blackness without order, and when it shines, it is like gloom." One would think the Hebrew poet was imitating a Mesopotamian model, but he was not; the idea was commonly diffused throughout the ancient Near East. Or compare the words which the Anglican Church, quite mistaking their meaning, adopted as a part of the burial service: "There the wicked cease from troubling; there the weary are at rest. The prisoners also are at ease; they hear not the voice of the overseer. The small and the great are there, and the slave is free from his master." Job does not intend these words to be consoling; he is complaining that death is the great leveler which strikes all men alike and leaves all equally dead. To the man whose life is miserable the next world may appear desirable by comparison, as it did to the Egyptian poet who wrote the dialogue of the man with his soul; but the whole burden of Job's complaint is that he can hope for nothing except utter oblivion, and in it surcease from his present misery. It is still death, the total denial of life as he knows it. Or consider the brilliant description of Sheol in the fourteenth chapter of Isaiah: the tyrant dies and descends to Sheol, there to be greeted exultantly by other kings who have gone before him. All alike have fallen before the final conqueror, death; all are reduced to the same state, their pomp and the noise of their harps brought down to Sheol. But this is poetry, not theology. Sheol is an imagined nothing, the denial of terrestrial life. Its external features – the dust, the darkness, the doors and bolts – are obviously the external features of the tomb; Sheol is one vast sepulcher, in which all mankind lies down together. There is no moral discrimination in Sheol, for there is no moral discrimination in death. Sheol is not a form of belief in survival, an imagined afterlife; it denies the continuation of life as we know it, and of the future it affirms nothing.

In addition to the literary allusions to the state of the dead, we now have some evidence of Hebrew burial practices. These practices, in some details, are not in harmony with what we read in the Old Testament; in particular, the practice of leaving food and drink and implements in the grave reminds one of Egyptian uses, and suggests a similar belief. But it is extremely difficult to conclude from burial practices to doctrinal propositions, since there are few human activities which retain more archaic and meaningless rites than funeral customs. Without literary evidence such as we have in Egypt it is dangerous to argue to the beliefs of the Hebrews from their graves. In all probability, the Hebrews adopted the burial practices of the Canaanites with little attention to their significance. The Canaanites may have been affected by the burial practices of the Egyptians, though they did not share the Egyptian belief in the afterlife. Their grave offerings can be interpreted as signifying that the deceased in Sheol were thought to need food and drink and certain other necessities, or as a propitiatory offering which would prevent the deceased from coming back to haunt his thoughtless survivors. The Hebrew adoption of these practices was, consciously or unconsciously, an adoption also of the superstitions which lay beneath these practices. We have seen other instances in which the Hebrews adopted Canaanite superstitions; but the Old Testament shows us the peculiar faith of the Hebrews in the Lord which sooner or later expelled these superstitions.

We do not wish to exaggerate the Hebrew attitude toward death, still less to imply that it is an attitude of despair. Even more remarkable than the silence of the Old Testament concerning life after death is the casual way in which the Hebrews accepted death as the normal and inevitable end. There is none of the dark brooding over death which we find in Greek and Roman and modern hedonists. After all, Job is almost the only Hebrew who expresses any complaint or questioning about it; if he spoke for others besides himself, they cannot have been many. The "psalm of Hezekiah" has a similar tone. The Lord granted man his portion of years — threescore and ten were the ideal — and man had to make the most of them. When his time came, early or late, he ought to face death like a man; the Hebrews told the story of Gideon and the Midianite bandits with a certain relish, for these men faced death boldly, desirous that the blow be administered by a man rather than by a boy. The Hebrew religion, as we have seen, was not a religion of this world. "Eat, drink and be merry, for tomorrow we die" is quoted by Isaiah as a repudiation of the moral will of the Lord. The temptation to despair thus expressed must have been felt by more than a few; Ecclesiastes voices it in words which very nearly echo the words of the goddess to Gilgamesh (as translated by J. M. P. Smith):

> "Go, eat your food with gladness,
> And drink your wine with a happy mind,
> For God has already accepted your deeds.
> At all times let your garments be white,
> And let not oil be lacking upon your head.
> Enjoy life with the wife whom you love
> All the days of your empty life,
> Which he has given you under the sun;
> All your empty life."

We may find some explanation of the Hebrew attitude toward

death in their social consciousness; we have referred to this feature of their thought before, and it is often a key to what lies behind their words. Certainly the Hebrews regarded it as the utmost disaster for a man to die childless, or to die with the expectation that his family would be wiped out after him. A man lived on, in a manner, in his name, which was borne by his sons, "X the son of Y"; he lived on also in his good name, the memory he left of himself. It was not much of a survival, and Job could ask: "What does he care about his sons after him?" But in the normal life of the Hebrews it was an expectation that a man could cherish; "I shall not entirely die," said the Roman poet, thinking of his literary immortality. And that mysterious sense of solidarity which we find in the Hebrews enabled them, it seems, to think of themselves as living on, as long as the group with which their life had been linked continued to live. It is a sense to which we are not utter strangers, even if the modern concept of the dignity and the importance of the individual person does not permit us to share it fully. But anyone who has ever observed or felt the capacity of parents to identify themselves with their children, or of teachers to live vicariously in the careers of their students, will not have to be told that the idea of the immortality of the group is more than a figment of the scholar's imagination. This, of course, is not personal immortality; neither is it absorption into the Absolute. Nor is it entirely irreligious; the Israelite was a member of the people of the Lord, and he had faith in the immortality of the people of the Lord. As long as it endured, and his name and seed were reckoned among it, he was not entirely dead.

This reconstruction of the sentiments of the ancient Hebrew is largely speculative, and there is no use trying to make more of it. If it leaves us dissatisfied, we shall have to resign ourselves, because the evidence does not take us much farther. But it is not the whole story; there are some other indications which, faint as they are, suggest depths greater than we realize. Readers of the Psalms must have noticed the numerous lines in which the Psalmist expects life from the Lord, and he easily understands these lines, with their own Christian background, as expressing a hope of life eternal. Closer study of the text reveals that in almost every instance the Psalmist expects not life eternal but continuance of this present life, deliverance from the danger of death. But there are some lines which scarcely admit this explanation; they leave some questions unanswered, and indicate that the hope of the Psalmist did on occasion pass beyond the limits of his earthly horizons.

Let us consider first the words of Psalm 48 (49): the assurance of the Psalmist that the Lord will redeem him from the power of the nether world by receiving him. The phrase is similar to others which express the hope of escape from imminent death; but the context here is not that of petition for deliverance from danger. The psalm is a meditation on the vanity of hope in wealth. No man, however rich, can meet the price of the ransom of his life. No rich man need be feared, for death will take from him all his wealth; rich and poor, wise and fool die alike. In this context, the words of the Psalmist can hardly mean anything but a contrast between vain hope in riches and his own hope in the Lord; and since hope in riches is vain precisely because riches cannot ransom from death, then hope in the Lord must be wise because the Lord does ransom from death. The words of the Psalmist are not easy, and many commentators would suppose that we have a poem combined from poems; but as the psalm stands, it utters a confused assurance that the Lord can deliver even from the world of the dead. We cannot take it much farther, but it is a hope, even if it is formless.

A similar voice of hope is heard in Psalm 72 (73). This psalm also is a meditation upon the paradox of the prosperity of the wicked, and the Psalmist confesses that his own faith was nearly shattered thereby. But his faith was saved when he considered the ultimate failure of the wicked. In contrast to them, he has a sure hope:

> "Yet with you I shall always be;
> you have hold of my right hand.
> With your counsel you guide me;
> and in the end you will receive me in glory.
> Though my flesh and my heart waste away,
> God is the rock of my heart and my portion forever."

Here also there is no question of petition for rescue from the danger of imminent death. The meditation looks at the question in general terms; and the hope of the Psalmist means nothing unless it means a deliverance from death which is more than an escape from present danger. Again, we should not look for a more precise formulation. These two passages can easily be blown up into a well-developed doctrine of survival; we do not wish to make more of them than we ought, and we shall not if we remember such psalms as 29 (30) and 87 (88), where the Psalmist expresses clearly the absence of any hope of life after death. The Psalms, like the Old Testament as a whole, can and do reflect different stages of belief.

Now we have in Psalm 72 (73) a clear expression of a Hebrew belief which appears many times elsewhere in the Psalms and elsewhere in the Old Testament: the belief in union with God. The phrase is necessarily and disagreeably vague, but it is not without meaning. We mean union with God such as that described in the quotation of Psalm 72 (73), or such as that of which we read in Psalm 41 (42):

> "As the hind thirsts for the running waters,
> so my soul longs for you, O God.
> Athirst is my soul for God, the living God.
> When shall I go and behold the face of God?"

We grant that these words express a desire to take part in the liturgical worship of the temple, as is evident from the context; but it would be an unfeeling exegesis which would see in this impassioned language no more than a desire for the liturgy. For the Psalmist is manifestly filled with a sense of the living presence of God, and the liturgy is for him the satisfaction of his desire to praise God, to be near Him, to feel Him more intimately. Or let us look at Psalm 62 (63):

> "O God, you are my God whom I seek;
> for you my flesh pines and my soul thirsts
> like the earth, parched, lifeless and without water.
> Thus have I gazed towards you in the sanctuary
> to see your power and your glory.

For your kindness is a greater good than life;
my lips shall glorify you."

We have in the line, "Your kindness is a greater good than life," a statement of the idea which is implicit in this sense of union with God. To the Hebrew, life was more than animal vitality, more than human activity and energy; life was association with the Lord, who not only dwelt among His people, but joined Himself to each one of His people who sought Him. In possessing Him was a satisfaction greater than anything which merely human endeavor could obtain. And we think that this sense of union reached a point where the union was conceived to be something which could not be sundered except by rebellion against the Lord. Those who possessed the Lord and whom He accepted could not finally be parted from Him like those who had never known Him. For the Lord is everlasting, and so also are His love and His kindness.

We still have the question which we asked earlier: how could there be a belief in survival until there arises an idea of something which can survive? We have no answer; but we think we see the Hebrew faith in the love and kindness of the Lord, which trusts Him to remain always the kind of God He has shown Himself to be. If we join this to the idea we mentioned earlier, the idea of the immortality of the people of the Lord, we may think of the people of the Lord, in Hebrew terms, not as an aggregate of persons existing at any given moment of time, but as the unity of all those who ever appertain to it. It is faith, not doctrine; it defies formulation in terms of our own philosophy, but it affirms the power of God to accomplish what is humanly impossible.

We have already indicated that the book of Job points to such a faith, even if it does not reach the point where faith in survival is precisely expressed. We may think that the author himself was possessed of this faith; but, rather than state it formally, he preferred to heap up all the considerations which argue against its possibility, and to marshal against these the overpowering arguments from human life which make men cry out for such a faith.

For, without one word to indicate it directly, the book of Job is the most powerful argument which we have in the Old Testament for survival after death; but the author, for reasons which he knew, presented it subtly. Those who, like the friends of Job, are satisfied with the good things of this world, and find the Lord in them, cannot easily be brought to see the vacuity of the present life unless it is thrust down their throat; nothing but an experience like that of Job will ever convince them of the inescapable reality of the next life. For men do not look to another life until they have seen the futility of the present life.

We have noticed also that the poem of the Servant of the Lord, of which we spoke earlier, without any doubt envisages a triumph of the Servant over death; and the poet means more than an impersonal triumph, more than a survival of the Servant in his achievements. This, at least, is the obvious sense of the words. The Servant, of course, is not an ordinary individual; in fact, we have remarked that many interpreters believe that he is not an individual at all. If the Servant is the people of Israel, then it is quite intelligible that the prophet can speak of his death and resurrection; and his words would, in this hypothesis, have no reference to the question under discussion. But we have seen good reasons why the Servant cannot be so considered, and why, consequently, he must be thought to triumph over death; and the thought harmonizes with the ideas drawn from the Psalms which we have considered.

One more passage will illustrate both the existence of the hope and the tension between the later hope and the older absence of hope. We turn to the twenty-sixth chapter of Isaiah, recalling that most modern scholars think that this chapter is not the work of the prophet whose name appears at the head of the book, but of an anonymous later writer whose work was included with that of Isaiah. There we read: "Dead men do not live, the 'Shades' do not rise." The poet thinks of the collapse of his nation, and sadly accepts its finality; for there is no one who redeems from Sheol. We think of the vision of Ezekiel in the thirty-seventh chapter of his book. The Lord shows the prophet a field full of dead bones and asks him, "Son of man, shall these bones live?"

The prophet refuses to answer: "Lord, you know," but he obviously does not think that dead bones can live again. But the spirit of the Lord blows upon the dead bones, and they are joined together, and they rise, a mighty host. So the poet of Isaiah 26, when he considers the goodness and power of the Lord, abandons his despair: "Your dead will live, their bodies will rise, those who dwell in the dust will awake and sing joyfully; for your dew is a dew of light, and the earth will give birth to the 'Shades.'" We must ask, of course, whether this prophet, like Ezekiel, is not speaking of a resurrection of the fallen nation, depicted by means of this imagery, rather than of a resurrection of the dead considered as individuals; and we must grant that this is possibly the sense of his words. But the very choice of such an image, foreign as it is to the ancient and simple Hebrew ideas about death, is significant; taken together with other passages, it again suggests, if it does no more, the hope of survival after death. For the Lord does not abandon His people; and even those who have died still belong to His people.

With this background presupposed, when we finally meet a fully developed idea of survival it strikes us with a sudden surprise. For we cannot trace the development. Yet in the twelfth chapter of Daniel we read, with no introduction whatever, that the bodies of the just will rise to glory, and the bodies of the wicked will rise to shame. We have to recall what we said earlier, that Hebrew psychology could not conceive any form of survival except the resurrection of the body, because animal life was the only life which they knew. Scholars now think that this part of the book of Daniel, at least, was written in the second century before our era, and thus we find ourselves several centuries later than the prophets and the Psalms. The ingenuity of learned men has attempted to fill this gap in history, and to find the sources of this belief outside of the Old Testament and the religion of the Hebrews; we need not argue the point here, for their arguments are inconclusive. But neither are we able to show how it grew from early Hebrew belief; there it is. The literature produced by Jews during these same later centuries, which is not included in the Old Testament, exhibits the same belief in the resurrection of the body. In the New Testament, of course, the resurrection of the body appears as a generally accepted belief (except for that Jewish priestly party called the Sadducees) which is adopted by Jesus and His followers with no question.

But this was not the only form which the belief in survival assumed. The latest book of the Old Testament is almost certainly the book called the Wisdom of Solomon; it was written not in Palestine, but in Alexandria in Egypt, in the first or second century before our era. Alexandria was, at this time, the greatest Jewish center outside of Palestine; it was also a great center of Greek learning, and here Jewish religion and Greek learning met and mingled. Thus we can explain how the writer of the Wisdom of Solomon adopted an idea which is not biblical and not Hebrew: the idea of the immortality of the soul. For, as we have seen, in the Old Testament the "soul" is not a living being distinct from the person, and talk of its survival would have no meaning for the Palestinian Jew. But the writer of Wisdom had learned some Greek philosophy: not much, but enough to grasp the Greek idea that the soul is really the living being which communicates life to the body. The body is mortal, and the proper functions of the soul do not come from its union with the body, but from its own spiritual vitality. And so he sees the souls of both just and unjust surviving, one group unto bliss, the other unto misery. He could not have elaborated this idea without the aid of the Greeks.

Modern Catholic theology has incorporated both ideas, that of the resurrection of the body and that of the immortality of the soul, although in their origins the two ideas are not easily combined, and there is still some tension between the two. But the Catholic, whether theologian or not, is usually unaware of the tension, and there is no reason why he should be aware of it; the important thing is belief in personal survival, and this we believe. But it might be wise for us to recall that there are more things in heaven and earth than are dreamed of in our philosophy, and that we cannot imagine nor even properly conceive the manner of life after death. In this sense, our faith still gropes in a blindness not altogether dissimilar to that of the Psalmist who knew only that God was his portion and the rock of his heart, and that the love and kindness of God are better than life.

When St. Paul in his missionary travels first reached Athens, the intellectual capital of the Greek world of his day, he decided to speak in the *agora*, the market place where the philosophical schools met and disputed, where every man with an idea was free to lecture to anyone who would listen, where the Athenians spent all their time, as Luke ironically remarks, "in saying or hearing some new thing." Paul's discourse, as he thought suitable for this educated audience of philosophers and rhetoricians, was couched in more elegant language than he was accustomed to use, and included a few ponderous allusions to Greek literature. But when he mentioned the resurrection of the dead, some laughed, and others said, with freezing courtesy, "Let us hear more of this some other time." The response of the educated man has not changed much since St. Paul was laughed out of the *agora*. Absorption into the Absolute the educated man thinks he can understand, or Plato's intellectual souls contemplating the Good; but the crude Hebrew belief in the resurrection of the body is too, too unrefined for a mind trained in science and philosophy. Crude it is, and difficult it is; but it is definitely involved in a number of biblical beliefs, and these deserve some of our attention.

Let us consider the belief in sanction: a cosmic justice which rewards every man according to his works. The biblical belief, even in the early days when we can scarcely find any trace of belief in survival, is that what a man does with his life is important and definitive. Of primary importance is the moral will of the Lord; He sets up exact standards, not of secular achievement or merely human culture, but of moral and religious goodness. To attain these is the first duty of man. If he does it, he has done all, and if he does it not, he does nothing, whatever may be his power, his wealth, his learning, or anything else he gains. One may point out, of course, that in much nonbiblical Jewish literature the belief in sanction is little more than a desire for revenge upon the rich and powerful nations which ruled the Jews, and this we can grant; the belief in sanction can be perverted, as any belief can. It is an instinct of unredeemed human nature to think first of sanctions for others. But we are not talking about the degenerate productions of late literature; we are talking about the books of the Old Testament, and we have seen that this belief in the importance of the moral determination of the person is addressed in the first place to Israel, the people of the Lord. Any modern doctrine of the dignity and independence of the person is irrelevant if, unlike the Hebrew belief, it attaches no permanent significance to the actions of a man, if it thinks that God Himself is unconcerned. This is the supreme dignity of the human person, that God Himself treats it as important, and judges it upon its merits.

Here also is the final answer, as far as the mind can take it, to the mystery of iniquity. It is not altogether final; it does not explain why things are wrong in this life to say that they will all be made right in the next, as we have remarked earlier. But it does affirm the supremacy of good over evil, of right over wrong, of God over His creatures; and we risk losing our grasp of this affirmation if we ignore the importance of sanction. This supremacy must be maintained if the world is to remain intelligible. Faith in the power and will of God for good moves with inevitable necessity to some form of sanction which demands a life beyond the present.

But does it demand the resurrection of the body? Here we meet a paradox of the Old Testament. We have been at pains to show that it denies the lasting value of the goods of this world; at the same time, we have noticed more than once that its mental atmosphere is concrete, material-minded. Christianity, the spiritual heir of the Old Testament, is above all things a "spiritual" religion, "otherworldly." Now, this spiritual religion, bringing out what is implicit in the beliefs of this material-minded book, makes an affirmation which even the most crass modern materialist does not dare to make: an affirmation of the essential goodness and permanence of the animal life of man. We have noticed that the Hebrews had no idea of the "soul," and so they were never in danger of identifying man with spirit, and of denying the value of human life as it now exists. Flight from the world does not mean flight from matter and the material; and such a flight never occurred to the Hebrews. They accepted the world and human life as the Lord had made them, and they did not think that it was a divine mistake to create a being compounded of "spirit" and "flesh." For man was made in the image and likeness of God, and this statement did not refer to his soul alone. If human life was worth creating, it is worth restoring; if human actions were of permanent value and significance, then so is the human person. And the human person is "flesh."

We have devoted more attention than we ought, perhaps, to an idea which is scarcely characteristic of the Old Testament. We do so because the problem is there, and because the idea explains much that is implicit, because it is basic to the New Testament, and because it is a true development of the Hebrew belief about life and death. We, apparently, attach more importance to the idea than they did, because we have a formulation of what we believe; but our knowledge of our own faith will be deepened, it seems, if we realize that our belief in survival is a different expression of the same faith in the same God, of the same belief in the dignity of the human person and the decisive value of human life which we find throughout the Old Testament. If this earlier belief is placed against this broad religious background, perhaps it will not appear so crude and indelicate as many modern thinkers would have it.

THE PRAYER OF THE HEBREWS

WE HAVE put off, up to this point, the consideration of a feature of the Bible which might appear primary: the Bible is the great book of prayer for the Christian world. We Catholics learn, almost in our infancy, the Our Father and the Hail Mary, and these are the words to which we turn instinctively the rest of our lives whenever the need for prayer arises. So well do we know them that we have ceased to think of them as biblical in their language and contents. The Our Father we have learned from Jesus Himself, who thus answered the request of His disciples to teach them to pray. What we do not know, unless we are familiar with the Old Testament, is that the Our Father is drawn entirely from the religious thought and language of the Old Testament, that practically every phrase within it can be found in the Old Testament. When Jesus was asked to teach His companions to pray, He drew upon the book which contained all their faith and their hope, and assembled from it a prayer which is unsurpassed in its perfection and its simplicity, expressing, as no other prayer ever did, what a man ought to say when he approaches God.

We might not be inclined to think of the Old Testament as a book of prayer, but this title would describe it as well as any other. From the time when Abram first addresses the God who called him out of Ur of the Chaldees to the invocations of the books of the Maccabees, the Old Testament is filled with the words which men spoke to the Lord on almost every conceivable occasion. And one book, the book of the Psalms, is a prayer book;

it is and it has been the prayer book of Christians from the very beginnings of the Church. Jesus and His followers used the Psalms to express their own sentiments toward God, as the Jews had used them for centuries. The book which had been the prayer book of the synagogue became the prayer book of the infant Church. The Psalms, as they are arranged in the Divine Office, are the official prayer of the Church, to be recited by all those who have the duty of doing the work of the "Ecclesia Orans," the Church at prayer. The Mass is woven from biblical phrases, not only in its selection of readings from the Epistles and Gospels and other books, but also in the composition of the Canon of the Mass and other fixed portions, as well as in the "Orations," which change from day to day. So much has this biblical language formed our prayer that, if we wish to address God, we fall unconsciously into the formal and somewhat stilted style which we associate with prayer; it is a language far removed from the language of daily life, for we have come to feel that we should not speak to God in the same terms in which we speak to men. This language is different because it is biblical, made up of phrases drawn from the common English versions of the Bible, now more than three hundred years old. Without knowing why, we have come to think that God ought to be addressed in Elizabethan language. We shall have to point out that the development of a "language of prayer" is a departure and, we think, a deterioration from the biblical idea of prayer.

We said that the Bible as a prayer book might claim our attention first of all, because this is the way in which most of us know the Bible, even if we are unaware that the conception and the language of our prayer is so thoroughly biblical. But we have thought it wise to postpone it to now, because the prayer of the Old Testament arises from the religious beliefs and sentiments of the Hebrews; once we have some grasp of these, the prayer of the Hebrews immediately becomes more intelligible. Prayer is never a systematic exposition of belief, for it is too personal, too intensely emotional, too deeply rooted in the concrete realities of life for that. But prayer, when it is unstudied, is a more sincerely genuine expression of the truths we believe and the good things we hope for, of what we think God is, of our personal response to the divine, than is any manual of doctrine. We say "when it is unstudied," for many of the prayers in the Old Testament are as studied and formal as are the prayers in our own prayer books. But we believe that we shall find that the greater number of Old Testament prayers, even if they are not always entirely artless, are nearer to the spontaneous utterance of the Hebrew than are any of the prayers in a modern manual. We hope that the reflections contained in our preceding chapters will assist us in seeing the spiritual springs from which these prayers flow.

Modern students of the Psalms have classified them into various types of prayer, and this classification can easily be extended to the other prayers which we find elsewhere in the Old Testament. Hermann Gunkel's classification is now widely accepted:

1. Hymns or songs of praise;
2. Community lamentations;
3. Royal psalms;
4. Personal lamentations;
5. Personal thanksgivings.

These are larger groups, to which the following smaller groups must be added:

6. Blessings and curses;
7. Pilgrim psalms;
8. National thanksgivings;
9. Legends;
10. Psalms dealing with the Law;
11. Prophetic psalms;
12. Wisdom psalms.

This classification is not intended to signify that each psalm falls into any one class; many of the psalms, if not most of them, are mixed, exhibiting elements of one or two or three or even more classes. The point of the classification is that each type has certain fixed patterns of expression. A few words about each of these classes will help us to see what this means.

The hymns are songs of praise, and in them the Lord is praised for all that the poet finds laudable: in essence, it is His divinity, or some of His peculiarly divine traits. In particular, the poet finds the Lord worthy of praise because of His mighty deeds, whether they are exhibitions of His power in nature, as in Psalm 103 (104), or in the history of His people, as in Psalm 102 (103). Frequently enough, the historical allusions are more concrete than they are in the psalm just mentioned; Psalm 134 (135), for example, enumerates a number of the events which Hebrew tradition related of the passage of the Hebrews from Egypt to Canaan.

Community lamentations appear in Psalms 43 (44), 73 (74), 79 (80). In these the whole nation is threatened by some great danger, usually political; but the danger may also come from the forces of nature: drought, pest, plagues. One observes, in such petitions, that the poet recalls some past exhibitions of the Lord's power and good will as a motive why He should act in the present danger; and that the psalm often concludes with a note of thanksgiving, as if the danger had already passed while the prayer was said.

The royal psalms are prayers for the king; we have noticed earlier that the king is the visible incorporation of the nation. Such are Psalms 19 (20) and 20 (21). In Psalm 71 (72), the king of Israel is merged with the ideal ruler of the kingdom to come, in the sense that he is described in terms which are hardly applicable to a historical ruler; but, as the king was the visible incorporation of the nation, so also he was a visible pledge and symbol of the hope of the ideal kingdom to come. The psalms which speak of the kingship of the Lord, such as the group 92–99 (93–100), do not belong to this group, but to the hymns.

Personal lamentations are petitions for deliverance from some personal danger; in form and in content they resemble the community lamentations. Such are Psalms 7, 25 (26), 55 (56).

Personal thanksgiving may be seen in Psalm 29 (30). Blessings appear in Psalm 66 (67), curses in Psalm 108 (109). "Pilgrim psalms" is the name given to the group of Psalms 119–133 (120–134), which are apt for chanting by those who approach the sanctuary for worship. National thanksgiving is the counterpart of national lamentation; such prayers are found in Psalms 45 (46) and 47 (48). Legends, or historical psalms, are recitations of pieces of Israelite tradition, such as Psalms 77 (78) and 105 (106). Psalms about the Law are few; one is the longest and the least poetic composition of the whole book, the praise of the Law in Psalm 118 (119). Prophetic psalms, although modern scholars think they can identify the type, are rather hard to define; they are psalms which resemble, in form and in content, the prophetic "word," and thus they usually express a threat of judgment, a rebuke of sin, a promise of the ideal future; Psalms 82 (83) and 49 (50) are alleged as examples of this type. The wisdom psalms we have had occasion to mention earlier; they are meditations on the questions raised by the sages, such as Psalms 1, 36 (37), 48 (49), 72 (73).

There is scarcely one of the Psalms in which the element of praise does not appear, and this deserves our attention. Our own refrain, "Alleluia," the Hebrew "praise the Lord," is indeed a summary of the spirit of Hebrew prayer. For the Hebrews were keenly aware of the excellence of the Lord, and they never wearied of extolling it, nor did they seem to fear that He would tire of hearing about it. There was in the Hebrew prayer of praise a feature which is less meaningful to a modern reader of the Psalms: a feature which we may call the spirit of competition. The Lord was extolled at the expense of the gods of the nations. The gods of the nations, of course, were nothing, but they were imagined as the adversaries of the Lord, which, in a sense, they were; for the allegiance which belonged to Him alone was given to them. But He is even greater than the most extravagant claims which the nations make for their gods. From what we have seen of the conflict in Israel itself between the Lord and the gods of Canaan, the perpetual praise of the Lord was a profession that He alone could do the things which were worthy of God, that He alone could fulfill His promises, that He alone had the power to bestow the good life upon His worshipers. The need for the praise of the Lord was even greater when we recall how the Hebrews were crushed under foreign oppressors, each of whom vaunted the power of its gods in its own conquests. No small faith, we can imagine, was required to maintain one's allegiance to the Lord in the face of such magnificent successes. But the Hebrews were able to wait, sure that the gods of the Assyrians, the Babylonians, the Persians, the Greeks, the Romans would finally be proved false. These hymns of praise, which we sometimes find a bit too formal for our own tastes, are the Hebrew profession of faith, and they did for the Hebrews what the Creed does for us.

We can say, it seems, that the Hebrew prayer of praise is not altogether suited to our modern habits. Prayer, after all, is modeled upon human address, and there cannot but be some similarity between the manner in which we address a human dignitary and the manner in which we address the Deity. In a modern democratic society, it is not the fashion to greet its officers with profuse and embroidered testimonials of their wisdom, their strength, their goodness, and so forth, although there are still some traces of early ritual in our midst. But in the ancient Oriental culture in which the Hebrews lived, the gods were addressed in what is now called "court style"; indeed, it is difficult to see any difference between some ancient documents addressed to the king and the hymns addressed to the gods. Such invocations seem to us insincere, and they do not rise easily to our lips. Shall it be said that the Hebrew hymns of praise are "court style," the same kind of fulsome compliment which the ancient paid to his king to render him benevolent for the request which was to follow?

It cannot be denied that there is a human element in prayer, for prayer is the speech of a human being; nor can it be denied that prayer follows conventional forms, for it is human to employ conventional forms of address. But even the conventions rest upon some accepted truths; and it is an accepted truth that the excellence, whatever it may be, which raises a man above his fellows should be acknowledged in words. This lies at the basis of the court style, and it lies at the basis of the formulae of praise which we read in the Psalms. The external features of this conventional address vary from one age to another and from one culture to another, but the principle remains unchanged. The Psalms, compared with the simplicity of "Our Father, who are in heaven," may seem cumbersome; but each prayer, in its own way, gives utterance to that reverent submission which is the only proper attitude of him who approaches God. It is impossible to suppose that there can ever be a democratic form of prayer.

So the Hebrew hymns of praise issue from the fundamental Hebrew beliefs. The Hebrews see the glory and the beauty and the goodness of God not in the abstract, but as these things have been manifested in their own experience: in the deliverance of their nation, in the wonders of nature, in the experience of the individual person. For the reality of God, as we have had to point out more than once, is an experiential reality to the Hebrews, not reached by profound thinking or by instruction, but apprehended in the realities of life and the visible world. Some of the men and women whom the Church venerates for their intimacy with God have suggested something very similar; for they sometimes speak as if all prayer, even in its elementary forms, is mystical in character, a response to the near approach of God to the soul. Those who do not share this awareness of the divine immediacy will always find the Hebrew hymns of praise somewhat strange upon their own lips. The world is less marvelous to them, for they think that science has taken away its wonder. The course of human life is less mysterious, because history and psychology have explained the course of events to them. In very truth, they find it hard to praise God because they have never experienced His excellence; they have never stood before the divine glory, as one might stand upon the rim of the Grand Canyon, and given way to an involuntary gasp of admiration. No, we shall not accuse the Hebrew hymns of praise of insincerity, flattery, court style, once we perceive how spontaneously they rise from Hebrew belief and Hebrew religious experience.

We have long been accustomed to name the four ends of prayer as adoration, thanksgiving, atonement, and petition; the element of praise and that of adoration, it is plain, are very much the same. The element of thanksgiving need not detain us long, except that we should remark upon its prominence in the Psalms. The scope of thanksgiving is as wide as the worshiper conceives the power of his god to be; the Hebrews, as we have seen, placed no limit upon the power of the Lord, seeing it in the small and the ordinary as well as in the great and the spectacular. Thanksgiving arises from that sense of the divine immediacy to which we have referred, and to which we shall refer again.

The element of atonement, however, calls for a little more attention. We have to recall what we said concerning the words of the prophets about sin; and these words remind us that in ancient Israel the sense of sin could not have penetrated the Hebrews in general very deeply, or we should not expect to find the prophets speaking as they did. We can see their casual disregard of sin in their ritual, of which the prophets speak with such vigor; the superstitious cult which the prophets describe is malicious precisely in this, that it is based upon a belief that whatever guilt has been incurred can be removed by a mechanical performance of the proper atoning ritual. But in many of the psalms a sense of guilt is seen which is founded upon the doctrine of the prophets. If one reads those seven psalms which the Church has for so long grouped as the "penitential psalms," one can scarcely doubt the profound feeling of guilt which is expressed in some of them. Yet there is something missing; we feel uncertain whether the Psalmist, in speaking of himself as guilty, does not mean that he is a member of a guilty people. We might guess that the poet had apprehended the idea of national guilt, but not the idea of personal guilt. It is possible that this is the meaning of some of the psalms which confess guilt; as we have seen, the Old Testament speaks much more frequently of a national, a collective guilt than it does of personal guilt. Men like David, Solomon, Ahab, Manasses, Absalom and ladies like Jezebel were responsible agents, and so they were regarded; but the words of the prophets were less frequently addressed to such individuals. The ordinary Hebrew might think of himself as less than perfect, but he would not admit that he should be classed with sensational evildoers: a failure of self-understanding which we can explain, if we cannot excuse it.

The penitential psalms show that the Psalmist was often moved to confess his guilt because of some adversity: illness, for example, or the enmity of others. There is something not altogether dissimilar in the literature of ancient Mesopotamia, where also there appears a form of prayer called the "penitential psalm." The worshiper asks his god for forgiveness; he is sure that he must be guilty, because the god is angry with him, and he knows that the god is angry with him because the god afflicts him. But he does not know what his guilt may be; and so he professes sorrow for all and anything he may have done that has displeased the god.

We have remarked earlier that there is no strongly defined moral character in the gods of Mesopotamia and Canaan. And it is this that distinguishes the penitential psalms of Israel from those of Mesopotamia. Superficially similar in form as they may be, they are totally dissimilar in the fundamental beliefs upon which they rest. The anger of the Lord is never capricious; there is no question about the moral standards which His will imposes, and no doubt about why He is angry. The Hebrews knew that His anger would not be removed except by a change in moral life; they could not, like the Mesopotamian, rest serenely confident that the anger of the god had passed because there was a change for the better in the circumstances of life. It may be granted that affliction is not the loftiest motive for which a man may confess his guilt; but the Psalms are human also in this respect. And it is surely human to be aroused to a sense of guilt by trouble; in fact, there is practically nothing else which does arouse it in most of us. It is human also to wish to be delivered from trouble; this is not to say that the penitent wishes no more than this, that he views his wrongdoing only as troublesome to himself. Here there is not even a superficial resemblance between the psalms of Mesopotamia and the psalms of Israel. Suffering was educative, as Aeschylus also said; and it taught the evildoer the true depth of his wickedness, the difference between good and evil which is hardly learned except by experience.

The story of the sin of David exhibits some peculiarities of the Hebrew idea of repentance. David, when charged by Nathan, admitted his guilt, and was assured by Nathan that the Lord forgave his sin; but he must suffer for his sin, the child of his adultery must die. Against this threat David fasted and put on the garb of mourning until he heard the child had died, and then he abandoned his austerities. This surprised even his household; they questioned him, and he answered simply, "The child is dead." Surprising as it is, David did not intend these austerities as penitential. Guilt and punishment were one: if his guilt had been removed, there was hope that prayer might avert the threatened punishment. Once the calamity had arrived, the austerities had no purpose. For David, repentance took away the sin, but not the punishment; he was reconciled with the Lord, but the penalty must be exacted. The prayer for forgiveness is one thing, the prayer for deliverance from the evil consequences of sin is another; for the deliverance is not necessarily granted because forgiveness is granted. For the Mesopotamian, there was no forgiveness unless it were attested by a change of the anger of the god to favor, which could be manifested only by a change in the state of his own affairs. For the Hebrew, as we have seen, sin was a cosmic disturbance, which upset the smooth course of events in nature and in human life; a man could be reconciled with the Lord by forgiveness, but repentance did not of itself remove the disorder which sin had introduced into his life. We have already noticed that the sin of David was the point at which his life turned from success to disaster; repentance and forgiveness could not alter the awful course of events which his sin had initiated.

But the greatest importance of the penitential psalms is simply that they imply the possibility of repentance and reconciliation. We shall have to sum up, before we have finished, what the Hebrews thought God was; and we cannot forget how frequently He is addressed in prayer as "merciful and forgiving." His justice is equaled by His mercy, His anger is surpassed by His kindness; for His anger endures but a moment, while His kindness is everlasting. The power and will of God for good, His supremacy over evil, does not appear more magnificently than in His capacity to forgive the wrongdoer and restore him to favor. This is the way, and this is the only way in which evil can be finally removed from the sons of men, and a society of peace and order established. Not by annihilating the wicked, not by forcibly eliminating evil from among mankind is righteousness to be realized; the Lord wills to rehabilitate the world by turning the sinner from his evil ways that he may live. And we must admit that this is more difficult than the use of force; but the Hebrews believed that even this was within the power of the Lord.

To most people, prayer means asking God for something, the prayer of petition; and petition has a large place in the Psalms. The character of a man can probably be determined from the things he prays for as well as from anything else, but in this respect the Psalms are not too revealing. The Hebrews ask for everything, but the petitions are usually couched in general terms. We see the petitions most clearly in that class of psalms which is called "lamentations," either community or personal, in which the community or the person is threatened by some evil; here the petition is urgent, and the tone is anything but formal. Do the Psalms ask for spiritual goods? In the sense in which the modern Catholic prays for spiritual goods, no. They ask for forgiveness of sins, of course, for divine guidance and help. They confess human weakness, and they ask that the divine strength may supply for human weakness. That spiritual good which is sought in every petition is the divine good will and favor. If this be continued, there is nothing else that need be sought.

There are several qualities of the petitions of the Psalms which deserve our attention, although they are somewhat disconnected. We certainly cannot help but notice the confidence which is the prevailing attitude of the petitioner, despite a few examples such as Psalm 87 (88), one of the saddest compositions in any language, suitable to the mouth of Job. The Hebrews invoke the Lord with the assurance that He must give a favorable answer. He must help them because He has helped them before, or because He is able to help them when no one else can, or because His reputation will suffer if He does not help them, or because they are His own people, or because His good nature is such that He would rather help them than not. When Jesus told His disciples to pray with importunity, likening God to the man who helps his neighbor not because he wants to, but because he is tired of hearing him, He recommended a kind of prayer with which the Psalms had made them familiar. In many of the Psalms a set formula is employed in which the need is described, the motives for divine assistance are proposed, and then thanks are rendered for the favor received — as if the Psalmist had experienced the divine assistance while he was still asking for it. The Lord is thanked because there is no doubt that He will listen and do. Such hope, of course, issues from a strong faith that the Lord can do what He is asked, and is willing to do it; but in the Psalms the hope is rather experimental than deductive. Allusions to the wonders of the Lord in the history of His people and in the works of nature become commonplace. Even in those psalms which are personal rather than national the Psalmist appeals to the past favors of the Lord as a reason why He should grant what He is asked in the present. The Lord is not only believed to be a God who answers prayer, He is known and experienced as a God who does so; for His immediate presence in nature and in history is perceived.

We spoke earlier of the development of a peculiar "language of prayer" in modern devotions, a language which we employ nowhere else. We observed that it is peculiar not because it is biblical, but because it comes from a sixteenth- and seventeenth-century translation of the Bible, made in the days when words like "vouchsafe" could be heard in the streets. Many still believe that the Bible should not speak the language of daily life, but should maintain a tone and an idiom which are solemn, stately, majestic, distinctive — and unreal. With this belief we cannot agree, for the Bible is written in the language of daily life. Even Hebrew poetry is not as far removed from the common Hebrew speech as our poetry is removed from our prose; and the Psalms are poetry. But, though they have a certain poetic diction, they have something which is entirely lost in "Bible English" translations, and something which is lacking also in modern formulae of prayer: a tone of familiarity with God. One has to go beneath the conventional translations, or acquire a translation into modern English, to realize how shocking this familiarity is. We would scarcely address God in these words: "Wake up, Lord! How long are you going to sleep?" Neither do we address the Incarnate Word as His disciples did when they were tossed in the storm: "Master, does it make no difference to you that we are going under?" We, if we were in danger, would not say with the Psalmist: "What good would my blood do you? Save my life, because I cannot worship you after I am dead." When we recall the classical definition of prayer as "familiar conversation with God," we see how "familiar" the conversation of the Hebrews could be.

But such familiarity is not peculiar to the Hebrews; it is paralleled by the outpourings of such mystics as St. Teresa of Avila, who did not hesitate to chide Almighty God for not doing His duty. Perhaps we ought to hesitate, but there it is. There is no doubt that one grows more familiar with God as one gets to know Him better; and it is not altogether proper to think that He stands upon ceremony. There is a paradox between the familiarity which appears in the Psalms and the sense of reverence and awe which appears in the same collection; but the paradox is in us, not in God, for we have to approach Him from more than one direction. The God whose majesty imposes reverent silence is the same God who is addressed with impatient importunity as if He were a member of the family. But, after all, is He not?

The same familiarity appears at its peak in the books of Jeremiah and of Job, those two champions of the privilege of a man to speak his mind to God. It is difficult to pick out any particular passage of Job which exhibits this freedom of speech more than any other. The modern reader of the Bible would no doubt be slow to speak to God in the terms which Job employs, and we probably should not attempt to remove his scruples. But the modern reader ought to know that it is possible for a man to lay bare his innermost heart to God, and to give words not only to his anguish, but also to his impatience and his doubt, in the assurance that his plea, like the plea of Job, will be answered by a new vision of the God who seems so distant. Likewise, we find the language of Jeremiah in such chapters as 12, 15, and 20 a little too heady for our own use. Yet we can see that there is a place where one can uncover one's weakness and fears with the hope that the weakness of man will be fortified by the strength of God; for he cannot put on the strength of God who has not first learned his own weakness. There is often, we fear, something artificial and insincere in the way in which we give expression to our own sentiments; but in the books of Jeremiah and Job and in the psalms which are spiritually akin to them, man speaks to God with a directness and an unspoiled freedom which are a revelation to us.

There are, however, some features of this familiarity which many modern readers find not altogether pleasing. Some have said that they are annoyed by the tone of complaint which they detect in the Psalms; they feel repelled by the Psalmist's enumeration of his troubles, for this is not the way in which they themselves would speak. They have schooled themselves not to complain about their troubles, to maintain an interior and exterior serenity which is not in harmony, they feel, with the passionate complaints of the Psalmist. Part of their difficulty, of course, comes from the fact that they are likely, in reading the Psalms, to come upon a whole series of such poems, which were not written to be read consecutively. But there is more to their difficulty than this. Oriental peoples, ancient and modern, are much less restrained in the expression of their emotions, whether by word or by gesture, than Western peoples. The joy of festive occasions and the grief of mourning are both externalized in an uninhibited manner which the Western observer finds simply in bad taste. To these people there is nothing admirable in stoic impassibility; indeed, they feel that one who conceals his feelings is not responding either to the joy or the sorrow of the occasion as he ought. In their eyes, his restraint is in bad taste. Between such cultural patterns there is a gulf which can be bridged only by sympathy and an understanding that external behavior is not of the essence.

But we must admit that this cultural difference makes it difficult for the Western reader of the Psalms to understand why the Psalmist speaks in what appears to him a complaining tone. Perhaps he cannot make the words of the Psalmist his own. But he will do well to remember that not a little of the stoic restraint which he admires and practices is no more than personal pride and vanity, an unwillingness to admit that he can be bent by the winds of adversity; and he might then recall that many times men will not prostrate themselves before God because they are too proud to confess that they are at the end of their resources.

The Psalmist himself said in his security that he would never be disturbed, but he quickly learned better. Unlike him, we do not so quickly admit that the stupidity or the malice of our fellow men, or of ourselves, has brought us up against a stone wall; but we cannot sincerely ask for the divine assistance unless we truly believe that we cannot do without it. The complaints of the Psalmist, perhaps, we cannot make our own; but neither can we invoke God unless we share with him the spiritual awareness of human weakness from which these complaints arise.

Somewhat akin to this trait of the Psalms is that which many readers have called the "self-righteousness" of the Psalms. To understand this, we have to recall first of all what we said above about the division which the sages made of all men into two classes, the good and the bad. To the Psalmist, it was inconceivable that he should put himself in the class of the wicked, for the wicked do not even address God, and they care nothing about His law. For this reason, then, we find the Psalmist sometimes invoking the divine assistance on the ground that he is worthy of such assistance; God ought to hear him, because he is a good man. Here, certainly, the modern reader feels that he must part company with the Psalmist. The modern reader has been taught to approach God with the words of the publican upon his lips: "O God, be merciful to me, a sinner." He appeals not to the justice of God as a motive for answering his prayer, but to the mercy of God. He asks for help not because he deserves help, but precisely because he does not deserve it. In his mouth, the words of the Psalmist would indeed sound self-righteous.

This feature of the Psalms arises, again, from their religious background. When a man approaches God, he must feel some link, some bond of community with God; it may be more or less intimate, but it must be something which brings him nearer the Deity he invokes. The modern Catholic, for instance, approaches God as a member of the Church which is the Body of Christ, and thus as a member of Christ. His prayer is never merely his own personal prayer, for he never feels himself an isolated spiritual unit. He prays, as he lives, in virtue of the divine life which he receives from Christ through the Church, and his prayer, like his entire Christian life, is shared by the head and the members of the Body to which he belongs. This fundamental Christian truth and attitude cannot be translated, as it stands, into the Old Testament. The ancient Hebrew did know himself a member of the people of the Lord; his prayer and his life he had in common with the other members of that people. We have already remarked, more than once, the strong social sense of the ancient Hebrews, and we have noticed that it often stands in antithesis to the strong sense of the importance of the individual in our own culture. The Israelites were "servants of the Lord"; that is, slaves, members of His household, subject to His command and dependent upon Him for the necessities of life. Or they were "sons" of the Lord, members of His household, subject and dependent, but linked to Him by a more intimate domestic bond.

But that which made the Hebrew a member of the people of the Lord was not the same thing as that which makes the Catholic a member of the Body of Christ. Early in the history of the Hebrews the contrast between the people of the Lord and the nations who knew not the Lord was easily drawn. But many of the psalms come from a period when the national consciousness had been dissolved by the catastrophe which destroyed the nation. The wise men, as we have seen, found in the people of the Lord itself the division between the righteous, the true Israel, and the wicked. Membership in Israel of the flesh was not enough. Membership in the true Israel was the rock upon which the spiritual security of the Hebrew reposed; take this away, and there was no longer any link between him and the Lord. Job, as a victim of calamity, was judged by his friends to be cut off from union with God; and Job himself has no assurance that he is joined to God. Job and his friends are represented as non-Israelites, but their spiritual thinking is Hebrew. For Job, his awareness of his personal integrity, and nothing else, is the ground of community with God. If God does not recognize this, then Job is a spiritual castaway. The Psalmist also approaches God not only as an Israelite – for there are many false Israelites – but as a true Israelite, one whose life accords with the law which the Lord has given Israel.

What we have said here might not seem to agree altogether with what we said earlier about the penitential aspect of the Psalms. Perhaps it does not; the Psalms are a collection of poems, not a theological treatise, and they have not been collected with any master plan of inner unity. But we look for a basic consistency. And Israel always believed that sin did not remove a man irrevocably from the Lord, although one might say that this was clearer to some Israelites than it was to others. There was a difference, even for the sages, between the kind of sin which corrupts the character of a man and the kind which does not corrupt. They did not specify the difference precisely, but they were aware of it, as we also are aware of it. Christianity has advanced beyond the religion of the Old Testament in its hope of redemption from sin, in its belief in the plank which saves from spiritual shipwreck, as the Council of Trent called sacramental confession. At the same time, we know that there is such a thing as a definitive choice of that which is evil, a choice which human means simply do not reverse, because we do not expect a man for any human motives to reverse the course and direction of his entire life. The Psalmist never admitted – nor should he admit – that he had made such a definitive choice of evil. Even if he had sinned, he was not a "fool," in the biblical sense of the word. And this was the ground of his security. To us, it seems like trust in oneself; but those who believed that wisdom was a gift of the Lord did not think so.

We cannot leave our discussion of the Psalms without referring to that one feature of them which is, perhaps, the greatest stumbling block to the modern reader: imprecations such as those we read in Psalms 68 (69) and 108 (109), and the appalling simplicity of Psalm 136 (137): "Happy the man who shall seize your little ones and dash them against the rock." However the Hebrews may have felt about their Babylonian conquerors, we are not edified at the prayer that another conqueror may dash out the brains of Babylonian infants. Many are the expressions of dissatisfaction with such utterances, and many the attempts to rationalize them. But most readers, unaware of these erudite rationalizations, and unable to reconcile their belief in the word of God and their idea of Christian charity, find it easier to ignore these lines of the Psalms, and they certainly never make them their own.

Yet one cannot say simply that these psalms are un-Christian. They are un-Christian, of course, in the sense that the whole Old Testament is un-Christian; but in these criticisms, spoken or unspoken, the word is applied to these psalms in an unfavorable sense. We have to believe, if the Bible means anything to us at all, that there is a basic spiritual unity between its various parts; and when these psalms are called un-Christian, the word means exactly what it means when we say that the Babylonian epic of creation or the poems of Catullus or the writings of Voltaire are un-Christian: in opposition to Christian faith and Christian morality. To apply this word in this sense to any part of the Old Testament is to abandon any belief in the Old Testament as the word of God. Yet how can we reconcile these psalms with the words of the Gospel: "I tell you: Love your enemies, do good to those who hate you, pray for those who persecute and slander you"?

At the risk of sounding smug, we have to say, in the first place, that we must try to think of this thing without sentimentality. Many writers who have been piously shocked at these words of the psalms are not shocked at such affairs as the sack of Jericho, for instance, which we have described as a barbarous act of misguided piety. We think that, if it be lawful to commit such a mass murder, it is lawful also to pray that one's enemies be brought to death. But we cannot invert the proposition; if we find that the prayer of the Psalmist is morally irreproachable, it would not follow that Joshua's wars of extermination were also irreproachable.

There are a number of factors which have to be considered. The modern Christian attitude has often been summed up as "loving the sinner but hating the sin." T. E. Bird has called this a fallacy; without going so far, we may think it not an entirely felicitous formula. Sin exists only in the concrete, in individual persons; and wherever it exists in persons, it renders them hateful. Unless one agrees to this, it would appear that one does not distinguish between good and evil, and thinks the wicked man is as lovable as the man who is free of sin. The Christian obligation of loving one's enemy – and, by implication, the sinner – does not require that we cease to recognize him as wicked and therefore hateful. No higher model of Christian love can be found than Jesus Christ, whose love was not an affirmation of the goodness of men, but a desire to confer upon them the goodness which they lacked. Now, the distinction between sin and the sinner would scarcely occur to the Hebrews because, as we have often noticed, they looked at reality as something concrete and particular. What is primarily real, and primarily hateful, is the sinful man.

If we admit, however, that the sinful man is hateful, may we go a step further and speak of him as the Psalmist speaks of him? The question becomes even more pressing when we suppose that the Psalmist is speaking of personal enemies rather than national enemies, as it seems we must suppose in some contexts. Our answer depends on whether we may turn the question this way: Is one bound to desire the fulfillment of divine justice, or its frustration? If we take the obvious answer, then we ask what was, in the mind of the ancient Hebrew, the fulfillment of divine justice; and we recall at once the teaching of the sages. Divine justice was not fulfilled unless the wicked were overwhelmed by complete disaster; if he escaped disaster, it created a problem which, as we have seen, is one of the most worrisome questions of the Old Testament. But, from whatever angle the problem is viewed, the Old Testament never supposes that it can be solved by permitting the wicked to enjoy the fruits of his wickedness and to escape the consequences of his malice; this would be a world without a supreme moral will, in which there would be no difference between good and evil. The consequences of evildoing were as inevitable as the divine justice itself.

One asks, of course, whether the Hebrews should not rather, in the words of Ezekiel, desire not the death of the sinner, but that he turn from his evil ways and live. With this we can agree; and since we read it in Ezekiel, we ought not to suppose gratuitously that the Hebrews did not so desire. But we have noticed often enough a connection between the Psalms and Hebrew wisdom; and when the Hebrews spoke of the question in general terms, they adopted the great dichotomy of the two classes. As we have pointed out, this dichotomy did not envisage the passage of men from one class to the other. And so, in the same general terms, they do not envisage an escape for the wicked from the wrath to come. They see no future for Babylon, the very embodiment of worldly power, except a fall; and they do not foresee its fall in ancient warfare without the barbarities which were a part of that warfare. We ought to bear in mind that the benediction invoked upon Babylon's conquerors is equally valid, in Hebrew belief, for the Babylonian conquerors who dashed out the brains of Hebrew infants; in each case, the conqueror was blessed because he was the unwitting minister of divine justice.

It may help us to understand these passages if we remember that Christian charity does not forbid such words as those which Jesus addressed to the Pharisees, or the words of St. Paul, who asked God to strike the high priest and to reward Demas the coppersmith, who had done him much evil, according to his works. It does not forbid such quaint liturgical features as the solemn rite of excommunication, which is scarcely less horrendous than the imprecatory psalms. And, although the remark may be invidious, one does not feel that the Christian community has ever, on a large scale, realized the splendid ideal of Christian charity. Christians, like unbelievers, rarely turn the other cheek; when evil threatens their lives, their country, their goods, they defend themselves, as they feel morally free to do; they are aware that they may, within the limits of Christian charity, desire that others suffer evil and inflict evil themselves upon others. We are not, perhaps, so spiritually advanced beyond the ancient Hebrews as we sometimes like to think.

We said earlier that we ought to try to think of this without sentimentality. There is a world of difference between Christian charity toward the sinner and a sentimental sympathy for him. Christian charity finds him loathsome, but it will spare nothing in order that he be redeemed from his loathsome condition; it is all the more ardent because it finds the sinner such an abominable creature. Sentimental sympathy, on the other hand, is a sickly feeling that the sinner is not such a bad fellow after all, more the victim of misfortune than an agent of iniquity. We do not wish to feel very hard toward him, because we really believe that he and the world of his kind cannot be changed. We accept him, and we have no burning desire to change him. We cannot really hate him, even for what is hateful in him, because if we do, we hate ourselves also; for we are what he is. We are sympathetic to sin in others because we are sympathetic toward sin in ourselves. We find the biblical imprecations distasteful not because of our Christian charity toward the sinner, but because the tale is told of ourselves. We have not grasped the paradox of Christian charity, that one cannot really love the sinner until one has learned to hate him.

We cannot, most probably, make the words of the Psalmist our own. They reflect too sharply that ancient world of thought patterns so different from ours. But we shall learn wisdom from these psalms if we learn that sickly sympathy with the wicked is no true compassion, even to the wicked. We have had occasion to point out many times that the Old Testament never compromises with evil, and we meet the same hardness here. This is an Old Testament pattern which has lost none of its vitality in the modern world.

What can we say in summary of the Bible as a book of prayer? Prayer is what we are, and it is what we believe God to be. If we say that the prayer of the Christian world has been molded by the Old Testament, we should hardly exaggerate. For, despite the particular obscurities which we have mentioned, the words and the sentiments of the Old Testament are those of our own spiritual climate. It is no accident that Jesus and His disciples and the primitive Church prayed in the language of the Psalms and the prophets. We have not really advanced beyond them. For us, too, the language of the Psalms and the prophets is our profession of faith, the substance of the things we hope. Whether we know it or not – and many of us do not – in the public and private prayer of the Church we are still sons of Israel, approaching God in robes borrowed from the great souls of the Old Testament. The Old Testament will not be neglected nor forgotten as long as Christians continue to invoke God in the spirit and the language which they have learned in the New Testament.

XVI

THE GOD OF THE HEBREWS

WITH proper reverence, we trust, and with not a little apprehension, we finally approach that subject with which most works on biblical theology and religion begin. For this is the question to which the Bible leads, and the question which is most significant in the study of the Bible: who and what is the God of whom the Bible speaks, and who speaks in the Bible? Whether the answer to the question be theistic or agnostic, no one will deny that the answer is decisive for one's philosophy of life. For we face the supreme reality, the reality which, if it exists, gives value and meaning to the human and the secular: the reality which is the root of intelligibility and desirability. If this supreme reality is unknown and unknowable, then it is meaningless for human thought and human life, and the human and the secular themselves become the supreme reality. If we can succeed in synthesizing the Old Testament affirmation of the same reality, our understanding of our Christian and Catholic belief will be agreeably widened and deepened.

For we began by saying that the Old Testament is a book about God. Can we put in one word, one idea, that which is most proper to the God of the Hebrews? We have tried to see this God in contrast to the idea of deity which prevailed in the ancient world of which the Hebrews were a part, and it is against this background that we should be able to find what is most distinctive in the God of the Hebrews. Many writers have attempted to do so; most commonly, they have seized upon the unity and unicity of the God of the Hebrews as that which sets Him off most sharply from the gods of the nations. Ethical monotheism, belief in one God who imposes a moral order, has often been proposed as the essence of the religion of the Old Testament. This, however, is couched in language a little too metaphysical for the tastes of many Bible readers. It is rarely that the Old Testament lays emphasis upon monotheism as a speculative truth, although we cannot say that it is omitted altogether. The emphasis more frequently, we think, lies rather upon this, that the Lord is really God, that He is all that God ought to be; it is an emphasis upon the nature of divinity rather than upon its numerical unity. The distinction may be slight, but it is valid.

Others have found that the Hebrews, like the other peoples of the ancient world, saw divinity as supreme and invincible power. That the Lord is supremely powerful is accepted without question; when the prophet of Isaiah 58 asks, "Is the hand of the Lord shortened?" he speaks with irony; the thought could never occur seriously to a Hebrew. But we have already noticed that the author of Job did not find this idea of God satisfactory; and it follows, we think, from what we have seen of the Old Testament that power is only an external surge of the divinity which lies beneath it. The Lord is felt in His power, but He is not known for what He is. He is not known until the motives for the exercise of His power are revealed.

Rudolf Otto, whose work in this field has been extremely influential, identified the divine with the holy, which he defines as the "numinous"; that is, "a fascinating and fearful mystery." It is a mystery, because it lies outside human experience; it is nonrational, or suprarational, "wholly other." It attracts, while at the same time it repels; and so the response of man to the deity is bipolar. He is impelled to flee, but he is simultaneously drawn to union. There is much that is sound in this analysis, and it has a broad biblical basis; we shall have occasion to refer to it again, even though we believe that Otto has not taken sufficient account of some features of the God of the Hebrews.

But that this God is "wholly other" is of primary importance, and we believe that we have tried to bring this out. He is wholly other, in the first place, from the gods of the nations, who have neither divinity nor being; His grandeur is solitary and unrivaled, He alone is really God. He is wholly other, again, from the visible world of which man is a part; no cosmic force, nor all of them together, can be identified with Him. No image can represent Him, for his reality is not perceptible to human eyes. Not even man, who is made in His image and likeness, can see God in himself. God stands above and beyond all things that are not God, and He is not circumscribed by anything in nature or outside it. He is supremely free and independent. He is wholly other in the unmixed goodness which is His own. Niebuhr, in bringing "creatureliness" very near to sinfulness, has not been entirely faithful to biblical thinking, for the Old Testament, as we have seen, asserts the essential goodness of the things which God has made; but creatures, when contrasted with the goodness of God, are "evil," in the biblical sense of the word. And so the fundamental vice of humanity is "idolatry," the worship of a creature instead of this "wholly other" being, the failure to recognize the gulf between the holiness of God and the unholiness of creatures. He is wholly other also in His purpose and intentions, which are not directed to those things which men desire; His purpose and intentions run counter to human desire, and thus the conflict between man and God is initiated. He is wholly other in the means which He chooses to accomplish His purpose, means which man would never choose, even if man could scrutinize the deep designs of God. And so a merely humanistic evaluation of the life and destiny of man makes that life and destiny unintelligible.

This mysterious, "wholly other" being is, in Otto's terms, non-rational, in the sense that He escapes the comprehension of the human mind. The Hebrews, as we have pointed out, were innocent of philosophical speculation; modern thinking has devised "ways to God" through the analogy of creatures which the Hebrews did not know. But the knowledge of God which is the fruit of such speculation would not be what the Hebrews called "knowledge of the Lord." For this is the paradox of the mysterious reality, that it makes itself known to men; and when known, it is revealed as a vividly real personality. Does not the "wholly other" mystery of the divine seem to vanish when the Old Testament speaks of God in human terms: His eyes, His ears, His tongue, His arm, His hand, His wrath, His good pleasure, and such things? Yet the Hebrews who used this language were well aware that they were speaking of God improperly; but they had to speak of Him in this way, or speak of Him as an abstraction, as an impersonal and remote being. To do so would not give expression to the vivid and immediate reality of which they were conscious, and between the alternatives, neither of which describes the divine reality itself, their instincts led them to risk making God too much like themselves rather than to risk obscuring His vital personality. Where modern philosophers look for a precise formula which will synthesize the terms of the paradox, the Hebrews happily affirmed both terms. But, we must repeat, the knowledge on which the affirmation was based was not "rational" knowledge; it was a knowledge drawn from experience, the experience of God Himself.

This mysterious being cannot be "known," in the Hebrew sense of the word, unless He makes Himself known; as we have seen, God speaks to man. For speech is the means of personal communication. We know something of a person from what we hear of him, from what we see of him, from what he does; but we do not have that knowledge which is a vital union of possession unless we get it from the interchange of speech. The speech of God, of course, is not the speech of man; to hear it is a unique and indescribable experience. But "speech" is the word and the analogy which the Hebrews employed, and we cannot evacuate its meaning without removing an essential part of Hebrew belief. The speech of God reveals the character of this mysterious personality — not completely, for that would be impossible; even in men, there are hidden depths of the personality which are never revealed by speech. But God is known enough to be distinguished from all that is not God. By His speech the meaning of His actions is understood, His purpose and intention are revealed, His will is manifest.

This is the personal activity which means most to man: the imperious will of God. God is mysterious and "wholly other," but He is not remote. He is immediately present, He is the very atmosphere in which human life is passed, His concern in human affairs is greater than the concern of men themselves. We shall not find anything like this in the religions of the nations. There is another paradox here, which modern thought calls the paradox of an immanent and a transcendent deity, a God who is both within the world and outside it. Again, the Hebrews happily affirm both terms of the paradox. It was the fool who said that God does not see, He does not care. To the Hebrews, the will of God was the supreme cosmic force to which all other forces are subject. They affirmed this despite the problems it creates; for there are some problems which would be less baffling if we thought of God as a remote and uninterested spectator. But no problem is solved by removing it from the dominion of the divine will.

This will affects every activity of man. The whole Old Testament rebels against the division of the religious and the secular; and its attitude is extremely pertinent to modern times, when humanism and secularism have reached a peak which they have scarcely attained since the building of the tower of Babel. There is an irreconcilable conflict between the Bible and much of modern thought. Modern thought will accept the Bible as a handbook of personal morality, as a mine of apt quotations about God and human life, as an anthology of anecdotes to illustrate a point; but it will not accept the Bible as a whole, with its stubborn insistence upon the universal supremacy of religion in human affairs. Neither did the ancient Hebrew kingdom accept this universal supremacy; and Isaiah showed them his motto, "Swift is the spoil, speedy the prey." Total submission to the divine will integrates human life, on the individual and the social level; if the submission is anything less than total, then human life is shattered by the forces of disintegration which are implicit in it. There is no purely human substitute, whether law and government, military power, social and humanitarian activity, which will keep human life and society from flying apart if they are not submitted to the will of God entirely. The modern sense of the power of man over his environment and of the dignity and freedom of the individual can scarcely be joined to the biblical idea of the divine will. We like to think that the Lord leaves us to ourselves to realize the great powers He has given us, as if the world were a giant Erector set. We refuse to accept the biblical belief that we could not be in worse hands than our own, because we do not share the biblical belief in the guilt of mankind; and we do not see that such an assertion of human independence is idolatry, the worship of self.

The will of God governing human life is serious; if men rebel, He brings His power to bear upon them. The Bible does not attribute the afflictions of mankind to natural operations or to the defect of natural operations, as we do; these afflictions are the wrath of God. For if there is a moral will, they could not believe that God would remain inactive if His moral will were flouted. The will of God is for good; but the Hebrews, whose concepts and vocabulary were limited, said that, in certain circumstances, the will of God was a will for evil. They meant, of course, that it was a will for those things which men think evil: distress, defeat, "Sword, famine, and pestilence." But these things are not really evil; what is really evil is that man should not be submitted to the will of God for good. This will for good is irreversible, even if it accomplishes itself through that which men think evil. For by such means is the evil of rebellion removed, the obstacles to the divine will for good taken away. It is the purest secularism to believe that there is no connection between the relations of man with God and his relations with his environment, even if the relationship poses such problems as those of the book of Job. The problems, again, cannot be solved by removing such things from the domain of the divine will and explaining them exclusively in terms of natural or human causes. Is there evil in the city, asked Amos, and the Lord has not done it? When a man runs against that cosmic will, he bloodies his head.

We said above that the will of God is for good; and the proposition is worth repeating, for readers of the Old Testament sometimes forget it. We speak of what we have called the moral will; for this is the will which is directed to the supreme good of man, which cannot be realized in any degree by deflection from the moral order imposed by God. The divine will for good is, in the first place, a will that man should be everything that he ought to be, and nothing that he ought not to be; this is a will for his moral integrity and for his basic human integrity. In a world in which the evil will of man has disturbed the harmony of God, nature, and man, it sometimes seems that the supreme good of man, his moral and human integrity, cannot be obtained except at the sacrifice of his personal desires. Here again God is "wholly other," and His ways are manifestly not our ways. But as man cannot resist the will of God to achieve His purpose, so man cannot alter the election of the means to attain that purpose. He must confess, with Job, that he does not know a better way to do it, and accept with a faith which is nearly blind the truth that the justice of God, which he fears, is the will of God for his own good.

What we have said of the God of the Hebrews thus far in this summary seems to lean in the direction of an austere majesty; we have to remember that this God, who is so immediately present and so deeply concerned in human affairs, is also a most accessible God. We have pointed out earlier the familiar tone in which much converse with God in the Old Testament is carried on; and we can remind ourselves again that this is the common, indeed the prevailing tone. The Hebrews felt that the divine condescension by which God spoke to them was an invitation to talk back to Him; if He did not wish it, He could have remained in light inaccessible. But He did not remain there; and so He showed Himself a God who is compassionate beyond human understanding. For his iniquity man experiences not only the divine justice, but also the divine pity. The Hebrews constantly implore this in their prayers, in the assurance that God acts in accord with His revealed character when He exhibits pity. They knew that among men there are those who are too proud to ask pity or to accept it; for pity demeans a person. But they knew also that it is better for man to be demeaned before God; for God cannot show His compassion to those who will not accept it. For us who read their words, it is good to remember that the Hebrews thought of those who did not experience the divine compassion as fleeing from it; it is not the lack of pity in God that removes men from His kindness. With an extremely bold stroke of the imagination, Hosea represented God as hobbled by His own compassion.

Does compassion rise to the level of love? This is a difficult question to answer precisely. But we think at once of two titles which the Hebrews gave the Lord: the father of Israel and the spouse of Israel. In ancient Semitic culture, these titles could be employed as figures of authority or ownership rather than of affection, but in the context where these titles occur there is no room for doubt; the titles signify love. And the love which they signify is the most intimate and tender which men know. God did reveal Himself to the men of old as a God who loved them.

We must recognize that there is some obscurity in the idea. The philosopher's adage has it that love either creates equality or supposes it. There could be no thought, for the Hebrews, that equality between God and man was supposed. Could they believe that equality was created by such love as that of father and son, husband and wife? We cannot see that they did, for they thought of children and wives as inferiors, not as equals. The figures make the divine condescension very real, but it remains condescension, the movement from the superior to the inferior. And so such words as *mercy, kindness, compassion* are employed to designate the divine condescension rather than the word *love.* But the word is there, and the figure is there, even if it remains one of the great unfinished ideas of the Old Testament. We have to remember that this is a trait of the God of the Hebrews, and the atmosphere of familiarity and confidence which we have observed in the prayer of the Hebrews rests upon this childlike belief in the essential good will and kindness of the Lord whom they invoked. His anger is momentary, His kindness is everlasting; it is a human description of God, but the Hebrew faith would not be the same without it.

So the bipolarity of man's response to God, as described by Otto, has a basis in the Old Testament; but we have to modify Otto's proposition. That which makes God fearful is not His power and majesty, not even His "wholly other" nature, for the Old

Testament sees man, in his primeval state, living familiarly with God; the repulsion which separates the two arises from a sense of guilt in man. This guilt, despite Professor Niebuhr's learned exposition, is not merely a sense of creatureliness; it is an awareness of rebellion against the cosmic will. Rebellion makes man unworthy of God; it is hostility to God which arouses, humanly speaking, a counterhostility. God is not distant from man until man withdraws from God, in the biblical view. But the attraction, the "fascination," remains; for neither of the two poles neutralizes the other. It remains because man never succeeds in replacing the supreme good which he renounces by another good which satisfies him. He constantly pursues through devious paths the divinity which always eludes him, because he is seeking it in the world or in himself. Into the spiritual vacuum which man creates God moves, and appears in the ruins of human hopes and ambitions as that which man was seeking all the time. And the "fascination" is activated because God reveals Himself to the besotted vision of man as the person who is what man desires to be, and who has made man in His own image and likeness. So the Old Testament tends to the point where the "fascination" overcomes the awe, where perfect love expels fear.

THE OLD AND NEW

AT THE very dawn of Christianity, the relations between the Old Testament and Christianity became an acute question. For Jesus came into the Jewish world as the fulfillment of the Old Testament. The Jews who refused to accept Him as the fulfillment of the Old Testament were forced by the logic of their position to treat their sacred books as terminal, and themselves, ultimately, as the fulfillment of these books. The cleft between Judaism and Christianity took form very early, and it has remained to the present day. We no longer witness the type of controversy between Jews and Christians which was common in the infancy of the Church; many modern Jews and Christians are only vaguely aware of the basis of their separation. But they are divided not only on what they think of Christ, but on what they think of the Old Testament.

In the second century of the Christian era, there appeared in the Church a man named Marcion. Marcion reacted to the Jewish claims of the Old Testament in a startling manner. Let the Jews, he said, have their sacred books, for these books are Jewish; they are not Christian. Marcion asserted that the God of the Old Testament was not the God of the New Testament, that His character and attributes were contradictory to the character and attributes of the Father whom Jesus revealed. God had not revealed Himself to the Jews, their sacred books had no relationship to the New Testament, and had nothing to contribute to the faith of Christians. The Church, of course, could not tolerate such views, and expelled Marcion and his followers, thus affirming the unity and continuity of the two Testaments.

But the relationship between Old and New Testaments did not thereby become a settled issue. We do not intend to take the reader through centuries of discussion and dispute, because such a review would weary even professional theologians. The discussions were not concerned with the unity and continuity of the two Testaments, for this was an accepted doctrine of the Church; they revolved rather about the meaning of this unity, and its application to Christian belief and Christian life.

We have seen that the Bible was the prayer book of the early Church, as it has remained the prayer book of the modern Church. Outside of this, the Old Testament was considered in the early Church as a book which spoke of Christ. We are in danger of stating here the opinions of the Fathers of the Church too simply, and we are sensible of the possibility of rebuke; but we are trying to sum up in a few paragraphs a vast intellectual movement, and it is scarcely possible not to oversimplify. This view of the Old Testament was a reaction, in the first place, to the Jewish denial that Jesus was the Christ; but, in addition, these men thought that the Old Testament, since it is so much more extensive than the New, should tell a great many things about Christ that the New Testament does not tell. The further question, then, was: How does Christ appear in the Old Testament? For it is obvious that the Old Testament is not superficially concerned with Him. Let us pause and try to recapture the thinking of the Fathers of the Church about this problem. They saw no reason why the Old Testament should have been written except that it should speak of Christ. If it did not speak of Him, it would not be a Christian book, and the Jews and Marcion would be right. They saw that the New Testament appeals to the Old, and they believed that, if they could formulate the principles behind the quotations of the Old Testament in the New, these principles could be extended to the entire Old Testament.

There are two ways, the Fathers said, in which Christ can be found in the Old Testament, and these two admit subdivisions: in prediction and in preparation. The predictions may be, or may be thought to be, explicit and formal; if they are, nothing is necessary except to identify them. But even the Fathers could find relatively few of these within the Old Testament. Therefore most predictions were, they thought, uttered in type or figure; and this requires a little explanation.

This use of the Old Testament, called "typology," has a good foundation in the New Testament. In recent times the basis of New Testament typology has been closely studied, and we can now see more clearly its background in the Jewish interpretation of the Old Testament with which most of the New Testament writers were familiar. There is a fundamental similarity between Old and New Testaments which rests upon a community of ideas, of beliefs, of language. It is the same God whose saving will is revealed in each of the Testaments. Hence one can point out similarities between exhibitions of His saving power, as between the exodus of the Hebrews from Egypt and the exodus of the neophyte from sin through baptism; both were passages through water. Jewish interpretation, which sought the meaning of every single word of the Bible, found such similarities in the words themselves, "catchwords," or in merely external features of the narratives. The method and its purpose are intrinsically sound, for they rest upon a belief of the unity of Old and New Testaments which permits us to illustrate one by the other, and thus to arrive at a deeper understanding of the whole. A searching examination of the use of the Old Testament in the New reveals that typology is much more restrained than it has often been thought to be; unfortunately, these restraints were not always imitated by some of the Fathers who cultivated typology.

We alluded in our first chapter to the modern revival of this kind of interpretation. One takes a text the sense of which, understood by itself, is not concerned with Christ at all – so, for instance, the ark of Noah or the tabernacle which the Hebrews constructed in the desert. But, since the Old Testament, as these Fathers understood it, always and everywhere speaks of Christ, there must be some deeper meaning in these items; and so both the ark and the tabernacle are understood to signify the Church which Jesus founded, either in general or in some particular aspect. For the

Old Testament speaks of Christ not only in His life and person, but also in His mission; and it contains in type and figure the whole of the Christian dispensation. Many of the Fathers of the Church thought that God revealed the entire Christian dispensation to such spiritual giants of the Hebrews as Moses and the prophets; but the prophets could not communicate this revelation, because their people would not have understood them. Therefore they veiled the revelation under types and figures which cannot be pierced except by a spiritual understanding; Christians, upon whom the plenitude of the Spirit has come, are endowed with this understanding, at least those Christians who have advanced to a truly "spiritual" life. To the Jews and to more carnal Christians, this spiritual sense remains hidden, and therefore they never perceive the true meaning of the Old Testament; for this spiritual meaning is the true meaning. The Old Testament, properly understood, was thought to contain the fullness of divine revelation, couched in its own figurative style.

The intrinsic weakness of such a system of interpretation is evident; and it was this weakness which led to its abandonment. For it depends almost entirely upon the arbitrary judgment of the interpreter himself, who is by definition a man of spiritual understanding. One cannot argue with a man of spiritual understanding; one listens humbly. The system supposes that the Old Testament was written formally for Christians, not for the Hebrews, that the prophets spoke to men centuries removed, not to the men who stood before them. It supposes also that they deliberately spoke in riddles. Such a consideration of the Old Testament is simply impossible; and it would never have arisen, if these early Fathers had known any other way to think of the Old Testament as a Christian book.

Is it not a Christian book, if it prepares for Christ? This also was proposed by a few of the Fathers of the Church. The two systems were not thought to exclude each other; actually they do, if they are carried to their logical conclusions. For the idea of preparation, properly understood, signifies a progressive revelation of God to man. Man, taken historically, was not apt for the fullness of divine revelation – a proposition which was accepted by the "allegorizing" school also; but if preparation means anything, it means that the fullness of revelation was not granted even to a few privileged souls. There is a growth in the knowledge of God; each new revelation of God makes man more apt to receive the following step, which will take him yet farther. This interpretation of the Old Testament, at once more accurate and more fruitful than the theory of types and figures, was not studied very earnestly during and after the age of the Fathers of the Church; and the "allegorical" school degenerated into fantasy. By and large, those who took the Old Testament seriously throughout most of the Christian era looked at it primarily as a mine of evidence, of texts by which they might prove the divinity of Jesus and the truth of His claims.

In the sixteenth century, Catholics as well as the theologians of the Protestant sects dug into the Old Testament as a mine of theological evidence. Each side, as we saw earlier, accepted the Bible on the same terms as the word of God, and each sought to find in it arguments for its own exposition of revealed truth. This meant, of course, that most of the Old Testament was not seriously studied, because most of it had no relevance to the current controversies; in fact, the idea of the Old Testament as a whole, and even of its parts as distinct literary units, was not very prominent in the theological schools of the seventeenth and eighteenth centuries. Finally, some were discouraged by the extravagant claims made by theologians, and decided that a book which could be pulled in so many directions at once could hardly be the word of God at all.

We hesitate to exhibit hindsight by criticizing the work of these great men of the past, who achieved marvels within their limitations; we should be fortunate if we do as well within our limitations. But each age, as the Sovereign Pontiff has reminded us, can and should contribute something of its own to the understanding of the Bible. The Old Testament has been viewed as a Christian book, one that speaks of Christ; it is that, even if we cannot understand the proposition in the sense in which it was understood by so many of the Fathers of the Church. It has been viewed as a preparation for Christ; it is that also, even if the idea of progressive revelation which we formulate will not be quite the same as that of the Fathers. It has been viewed as evidence of Christianity; it is that also, even if we admit, regretfully, that this involves more than a search for proof texts. But above and beyond these, there are some points of unity and continuity between the two Testaments which are not contained in these formulae of the past, or, at least, are not too openly stated in them.

Let us consider first the proposition that the Old Testament is a Christian book. This we must maintain, even though its authors were not Christians. We maintain it because of the unity of faith and of spirit which governs the two Testaments. One need not abandon the Old Testament in order to accept the New; indeed, one may not. We maintain this despite the unparalleled novelty of the Incarnation, the great revolutionary event which overturns all human ideas and human values – except the knowledge of God. Novel the Incarnation was and is; but it is not out of character with the God of the Hebrews, although it is entirely out of character with any other idea of divinity which has ever entered the human mind. We do not say that the Incarnation was announced with studied obscurity in the Old Testament, that the prophets left clues to identify Christ as if biblical study were a treasure hunt; we say that they knew and spoke of a God who is the same as the God who took human flesh, and that they spoke of a world which was apt for this desperate remedy.

Many modern Catholics are not sure that the Old Testament is a Christian book. We have all heard the preacher's commonplace that the Old Testament is the law of fear, the New Testament the law of love. This fallacy becomes current because it is such a successful parody of the truth. Readers of the Old Testament know that it is false, and we hope that readers of this book have become suspicious of it. They know that the Hebrews would say that a God who is only fearsome is no true God; that a God who neither exhibits nor excites affection is no true God. If they turn to their Bible, they will find that the Old Testament expresses the love of God for man and of man for God in unrestrained language. They know, too, that a God who does not arouse fear is no true God; they are aware that the Old Testament contains nothing so fearsome as the New Testament doctrines of hell and judgment. A distinguished modern theologian, Father Jules Lebreton, once quoted with approval a more ancient distinguished theologian, Origen, as saying: "We have searched the Scriptures, and we do not find that God is called father in the Old Testament."[9] It is hard to understand how two men so learned should have overlooked or misunderstood at least twenty-six instances in which paternity or paternal traits are applied to God in the Old Testament; it is very dangerous to say that something is not contained in this bulky book.

On the other hand, the Old Testament never knew the love of God which is revealed in the Incarnate Son of God. It knew the divine condescension, but it did not know that God could empty Himself and take the form of a slave, becoming obedient unto death: love supposes equality or creates it. Neither did it know the capacity of man to love God, if man be adopted as a son of God. When Jeremiah and Ezekiel spoke of the transformation of the heart, they did not know the power of God to transform. In these, as in other things, the New Testament is novel, revolutionary. But the continuity is not broken. Those who knew the God of the Hebrews could recognize Him in the Incarnation; but they would see that they had not known Him very well. His character does not change, but its depths are newly perceived.

Christians are sometimes startled at the moral level of the Old Testament. Where Catholics have not escaped the influence of Puritanism or Jansenism, it is whispered that there are some parts of the Old Testament which really had better not be read. Religious communities which read the Bible in their dining rooms piously omit some lurid episodes. They probably have not considered that they agree in this with the peddlers of pornographic literature, who plead in their own defense that their wares contain nothing which cannot be paralleled in the Old Testament. Catholics are not quite sure of a book in which those who appear to be the heroes and heroines tell lies, steal, murder, practice polygamy – all, they think, with divine approval. It is easier to forget about such stories, and to believe that the Hebrews lived in a very special world under a very special dispensation. This, of course, makes the Hebrews entirely unreal and entirely meaningless for the modern Christian.

Again, we hope that the reader of this book has learned that the Hebrews were altogether real people with an altogether real God. They have heard of the moral will of the Lord, and they have perhaps seen that the tremendous moral earnestness of the Old Testament is of one piece with the moral earnestness of Jesus and the New Testament. They may be able to understand that the unenlightened moral insight of the Hebrews has no more effect upon the substance of Hebrew belief than the unenlightened morality of the Crusades or the Spanish Inquisition has upon the substance of Catholic belief. They will agree that God could not enter the world unless He had first created an atmosphere of moral seriousness. A merely human morality may be, at a given moment, higher than a morality based upon faith in a God with a moral will. But a merely human morality can never have any more force than there is in the good will of the men who have formed it; and the insight of a merely human morality can never exceed the capacities of the human intelligence from which it proceeds. A morality based upon faith in God grows both in strength and in vision, and it has no limit except the limits of the knowledge of God. And what limits shall we place upon the power of God to reveal Himself to man?

The Old Testament is a Christian book because it is a book of hope. We have referred earlier to the often-voiced despair of the ancient world, a despair which could be silenced only by worldly prosperity, which represented the summit of man's hopes. The Old Testament is the monument of the Hebrew belief in the power and will of God for good, which nothing can defeat. We ought to notice that this is not the simple and untested faith of the child. The hope of the Hebrews was indeed passed through the fire, and that not merely once; but each time it emerges stronger than it was before, with a clearer vision of its object. And thus we may answer the question: Does the Old Testament point to Christ? We cannot accept the idea that the Old Testament is a collection of clues which point to Him; but it points to the ultimate fulfillment of the power and will of God for good. It hopes for something to which Jesus is the answer. The ancient ideal of a society living in submission to the will of God is what Jesus established, the society which is in the world without being of the world, and therefore not subject to the corrupting influence of the world. He is the ultimate term of the divine condescension. He is the man who realizes in His own person all that the Hebrews hoped that man, led by the Lord, might become, and through whom other men reach their destiny. He is the true Israel, and all who know the Lord are members of Him; in Him Israel attains its destiny and dies, to rise again to a new and undying life. Yes, the Old Testament points to Him; for it is a book that always looks forward, and carries us with it in its forward glance until it reaches Him, and then it reposes, as if to say: "Here it is."

We said that the Old Testament is also considered as a preparation for the New. We might ask: Why should there be a preparation? Cannot God act without preparing the conditions for His activity? Is He bound by the conditions of space and time, so that the divine operation must be extended in space and time? And we must confess that we run up against a mystery. Certainly the effects of the divine operation are extended in space and time; but we really do not understand the mystery of the divine patience. We would wish to hurry things; to us, delay implies an imperfection. We know that we must wait until the time is ripe, but we do not see why God must wait. We might understand the mystery of the divine patience better if we had a better grasp of the mystery of human iniquity. We do not see what a tremendous obstacle we place to the operation of God. It is not an insuperable obstacle, but we must let Him overcome it in His own way; and His way is the way of patience. Men do not easily admit God into a world from which they have expelled Him; and we cannot say that they would admit Him more quickly if God forced His way into the world more impatiently. We have already seen that the Old Testament knows the violence of the divine impact upon the world. But it also knows that where God might force us, He prefers to persuade us. So the Old Testament finds Him in the gentle breeze rather than in the earthquake and the lightning. He is the waters of Shiloh that go softly and imperceptibly, the summer sun that invisibly and effortlessly ripens the grain. He is all these things in the Old Testament, because the Hebrews knew something about the mystery of the divine patience. They knew it because they knew something about the hard resistance which man sets up against the advances of God.

But let us accept the mystery, as we must all mysteries, and ask how the Old Testament prepared for the New. To begin with what is obvious and superficial, the Old Testament gave Jesus and His Apostles a language in which they could speak the Gospel. Only a thorough word-for-word study of the New Testament shows to what an astonishing degree its language reflects the language of the Old Testament. H. B. Swete has said that there is not a single page of the New Testament without an allusion to the Old Testament. Jesus announced the revolutionary novelty of the Gospel in a familiar language which, to some extent, disguised its radical character and made it easier to assimilate. And when we see that the religious vocabulary of the New Testament – which is our own religious vocabulary – is drawn from the Old Testament, we see that ideas as well as words are involved. The key words of the New Testament are charged with a new meaning; but if this new meaning were not a development of the meaning which the words have in the Old Testament, the words would have been unintelligible. If we look for a reason for the divine patience, we shall find it in the necessity of educating at least a portion of mankind to the point of religious understanding where it could listen to the words of Jesus with elementary intelligence.

For this reason, familiarity with the Old Testament has always been a key to the understanding of the New Testament. The full impact of the words of Jesus is not grasped unless we hear His words against the background of the history and the prophecy, the wisdom and the poetry of His own people. Even in apostolic times, this was so obvious that the Apostles took with them the Old Testament in Greek, to give to the Gentiles who knew nothing of the Jewish world. The New Testament had not yet been written; but the Old Testament was "background reading" for the Gentiles, so that they could put this strange Gospel into its proper perspective. For it would have been gibberish to them against the intellectual background of the Greek world, as St. Paul found at Athens. And even if we do not think of the Old Testament as primarily a means by which the Gospel was made more intelligible to the Gentiles, we must admit that it was the means by which the Apostles themselves acquired the concepts and the language in which they could preach the Gospel.

This is preparation on the surface; we can go beneath the surface, however, and find more profound effects of the Old Testament upon the New. Not least in importance, we think, is that feature of the Old Testament which we have emphasized many times: its affirmation of the futility of human wisdom, human power, human civilization, of the inability of man to save himself from himself. St. Paul put it into a single line when he said that the folly of God is wiser than the wisdom of men, and the weakness of God is stronger than the strength of men. We should not think that the men of the Greco-Roman world which St. Paul attacked were too much different from ourselves. After long wars, they had reached an era of general peace. They could trust public order to maintain itself, and thus they could pursue trade and commerce without fear, and exchange goods and create wealth on a scale which had never been attained in the world's history. They did not live in an age of great creative genius in literature, art, philosophy; but they were in secure possession of the great tradition of Greece, and they produced an abundance of literature, art, and philosophical thought which, if not great, was fairly competent. It was a wealthy, peaceful, literate, cultivated world, based upon the most stable government which man had ever set up. Was this a world to which a few wandering Jews could easily tell its poverty and nakedness, its spiritual destitution? Only a man steeped in the Old Testament, like St. Paul, could have written the burning lines of the first chapter of the Epistle to the Romans. Paul writes like a cultural barbarian; he has no eyes for philosophy, literature, the arts, which are the rich robes wrapped around a harlot. This great civilization was a vast human failure, as he judged it; to him and to other early Christians it was the Scarlet Woman, Babel come to life again. Through St. Paul and the Apostles, as well as directly, the Old

Testament uttered its despair of human achievements and human institutions, and forced men to consider where real and lasting security might be found.

We mentioned a third way in which the Old Testament is considered: as evidence for the truth of Christianity. For a long time this has meant the "proof text": the verse or the line in which is enunciated some proposition of the Christian faith. This use of the Old Testament has never meant very much to the laity, nor even to the clergy at large; it is a use which belongs to the theological schools and to professional theological discussions. It is a method which is still in use and still in honor; hence what we have to say about it may arouse some resentment among those who are trained in this method, and who have come to regard it as an essential part of theology. Nevertheless, we think ourselves obliged to say that an approach to literature which looks for single lines rather than larger contexts is not a proper approach to any form of literature; and there appears to be no reason why it should be proper in theology.

Here, again, we must recall what we have said earlier, basing our remarks on the words of Pius XII: it should be possible for our age to contribute something to biblical studies which past ages have not contributed. The past fifty years have been as active for the study of the Old Testament as any comparable period since the beginning of our era. Must we not admit regretfully that there has been scarcely any perceptible development in the theological use of the Old Testament as evidence for the truth of Christianity? If it be not impertinence in a simple exegete, we submit the suggestion that the theologians can well afford to re-examine their approach to the Old Testament and the methods according to which they use the Old Testament, and incorporate into their approach and their methods those discoveries of modern times which they find relevant to their purpose. We can hardly believe that theology will be poorer for such work; and we cannot believe that St. Thomas Aquinas, who wished nothing more than acquaintance with the most modern works of his day, even the works of the infidel Arab philosophers, would be slow to take advantage of the opportunities which modern biblical studies would afford him. We think he would be even more eager to do so if he lived in an age when the Protestant scholars who are grouped as "neo-orthodox" show not only a profound interest in the Old Testament, but also a remarkably creative facility in their treatment of it.

But the apologetic use of the Old Testament will hardly ever be the primary interest of its readers outside of professional circles. The Old Testament is indeed evidence for the claims of Christianity; in the preceding pages, we have tried to suggest some of the ways in which this evidence appears to us. We are aware that it is imperfect apologetics. We do not know that very many have ever been led or will be led to accept Christianity by reading the Old Testament, although we see how it can happen; we know the story of the eunuch of the queen of Ethiopia. But we would rather give those who seek instruction in the faith the New Testament and the Baltimore Catechism. One may to some extent agree with Origen that the spiritual understanding of the Old Testament is for Christian "gnostics," those who are well enough instructed in their faith to read it with profit and without danger; unlike Origen, we would not restrict this understanding to a privileged few. They will read the Old Testament not as evidence for their faith, but with a faith that seeks understanding. They expect to learn from this book a fuller meaning of the things they believe: about God, His impact on the world, and the revolutionary effect of His impact upon the world and upon their own personal life. We think that the New Testament also would be read more widely and more intelligently by the faithful if the Old Testament also were read, for the Old Testament is the first and the indispensable commentary to the New. If some might wonder in surprise whether the commentary here is not more obscure than that upon which it comments, we can only challenge them to make the effort. That the effort is great we cannot deny; those who wish to read the Bible intelligently and spiritually will have to give it the time they now give to other things. We think also that priests would present the Epistles and the Gospels to the faithful with some of the incendiary zeal of St. Paul if, like St. Paul, they were steeped in the Old Testament.

Many of the faithful, if not most of them, will know little about the Bible as a whole except what they hear from their priests; can we priests communicate to them the force of this book unless we have sensed it ourselves?

The child's voice which Augustine heard in his garden still speaks to us: "Pick it up and read it." When Augustine, moved by the incredible coincidence of this unseen voice, read the Bible, the spiritual crisis followed which altered the course of his life and the character of his personality. We need not expect anything so sensational in ourselves; but, if we can trust God who wrote the book and the experience of the ages which have used it, our faith will develop an understanding greater than we thought possible.

CONCLUSION

WE SET out to propose what we conceive to be a spiritual interpretation of the Old Testament; now we realize how ambitious this proposal was. We can say, with Job's friend Zophar: It is higher than the heavens – what can you do? It is deeper than Sheol – what can you know? We should approach the efforts of past ages to interpret the Old Testament spiritually with humility and reverence; it little becomes us to sneer at their efforts, when we behold our own stumbling and stammering attempts to explain the oracles of God. Nevertheless, we feel impelled to make the attempt; because our own generation must read the Bible in its own way. Our difficulties in understanding the Bible arise from our times, our education, our culture, and we must meet these difficulties ourselves.

We have heard, in sadness and bewilderment, many who say that they fear the Old Testament because it raises doubts in their minds. Doubts of what, we wonder? Doubts of God's existence, or His justice, or His mercy, or His love? Doubts that He is the Lord of the world which He made, or that His will is supreme in the history of human events? Doubts that man needs God desperately, and perishes without Him? Doubts of His power and will for good? Doubts that He approaches us, and can be approached by us? Doubts of His fidelity to His promises? If one doubts these things, the doubts did not come from reading the Old Testament. No, we can be honest here; the doubts which these good people mention are doubts that come from the relations of the Old Testament with theology and history and the natural sciences. Our doubters fear that their faith may become insecure if they permit themselves to consider these matters; they think it more prudent to leave the Old Testament alone.

For the reason that these doubts and fears are a curse in our generation, we have had to face some of them in the above chapters; but we do not believe that the Old Testament will be recommended to the faithful just by the discussion of these questions. We think that it is recommended and ought to be recommended because the faithful will know both God and themselves better from reading it. If this desirable result must be conditioned by the historical, scientific, theological, and biblical scholarship of the faithful, then the widespread reading of the Old Testament is an impossible dream, and the Bible must remain a closed book. But is there any worthwhile book which cannot raise doubts? If the profit to be gained by reading the book is great enough, we are willing to risk the doubts, and we do not feel obliged to resolve all the doubts personally. The Old Testament is the book of the Church, and her members ought to read it in the security of the faith which the Church has given them; the Church never intended that the word of God should be an obstacle to faith.

And the Church never intended that biblical scholarship should keep people from reading the word of God; may we biblical scholars not ask ourselves seriously whether we have closed the door of the Old Testament to the faithful? We have done this, possibly, because we have spoken so much of its difficulties, the dangers in its interpretation, the abstruse questions which its interpretation raises, the caution which is necessary in handling it; perhaps we ought to have displayed to the faithful its immense religious treasures, and told them, "Pick it up and read it." It is not surprising that people have been scared off from reading the Old Testament; we have not told them to read it in the security of their faith. It really need not make much difference to the faithful whether the Church or scholars resolve biblical questions in one way or another, or whether they resolve the questions at all. Surely we do not think that the religious values of the Old Testament depend upon the precise identification of the literary species of each verse of the Old Testament. Surely we biblical scholars do not pretend that we can give the faithful a body of biblical doctrine or a method of interpretation which will infallibly protect them from misunderstanding and error in all details, or that we foresee a time when we can do this. If we are to wait until this marvel appears, then the religious interpretation of the Bible will remain mute, as it is; and it will be a long wait.

It is essential that we secure the readers of the Bible against interpretations and conclusions which would destroy the very notion of the word of God, and this we can do; but we wonder whether the Bible is treated as the word of God when it is handled so carefully that few dare to read it. We think that the religious interpretation of the Bible will always proceed along general lines; and the general lines of Catholic biblical scholarship are sufficiently fixed to permit us to present the spiritual values of the Bible, even if many questions of detail remain uncertain. There will always be such questions of detail; there seems to be little reason for putting them in the forefront of popular presentation of the Bible.

This book is an attempt to proceed along such general lines; its success rests with those for whom it is intended. We have attempted to view the Old Testament as the beginning of a single historical process of which the New Testament is the end – which, in its turn, is another beginning. This process is the impinging of God upon human life and affairs. We want to see this process as clearly, as vividly as we can; but we look for more than vision. We want to live this process ourselves. That which God has done to the race and to the people of Israel He does to each individual person. In this sense the Old Testament is a "type" of the spiritual adventure of the soul. For the faithful, this is the "spiritual" sense of the Old Testament which is most significant. If they find the story of God and Israel strange and terrifying, they know that the story of God and themselves is no less strange and terrifying. God's mysterious ways with them, they know, are largely conditioned by the mysterious perversity of the human will; it is not my ways that are crooked, says Ezekiel in the name of the Lord, it is your ways that are crooked. The Lord must deal crookedly with us in order to reach us. No one who has ever looked into the appalling tangle of his own soul will have difficulty in understanding these words of Ezekiel. But the story of God and Israel is illumined by a mystic awareness of the divine personality who is the protagonist of the story, and lifted up by a hope which rests upon the "wholly other" goodness of that personality. Israel, once it had known God, could never despair of Him, even when He led it by strange and terrifying paths.

We think that a spirituality with a broad biblical basis will always be strong and solid. It will rest firmly upon the truths which we believe, not merely accepted by the mind, but lived and experienced in reality. For these truths are glimpses of the reality which is God, and this reality we must know and experience. Such a spirituality is not out of touch with either of the poles upon which humanity is distended, the unmixed goodness of God and the unrelieved malice of evil; spirituality is a vital awareness of these two, and of their relentless opposition. Such a spirituality will escape the danger of softness and mawkish sentimentality, which confuses imagination and knowledge, feeling and doing, velleity and achievement. It will not make things too easy, and it will not surrender because things are too hard. Such a spirituality is that of Jesus Christ and Catholic tradition.

For the Old Testament is the book of the Church, and it will always live in the Church, even when it is less generally known and read. For the life of Jesus and of the Church which is His Body is the fulfillment of the Old Testament, and the Old Testament is inseparably included in the New.

A BIBLIOGRAPHICAL NOTE

SHOULD this book fall into the hands of a professional scholar, he will at once recognize my indebtedness to all that I have ever read on the Old Testament. This indebtedness I gladly confess; but there seems to be no reason for listing, either here or in the text, the titles of books which would be neither available nor intelligible to the circle of readers to whom this book is addressed. In all honesty, however, I cannot leave unmentioned a few authors whose works have been extraordinarily helpful. I indicate Catholic writers by an asterisk (*).

For ancient Near Eastern religion and culture, I have leaned heavily on the books of Dr. W. F. Albright: *From the Stone Age to Christianity* (Baltimore: Johns Hopkins University Press, 1946); *Archaeology and the Religion of Israel* (Baltimore: Johns Hopkins University Press, 1942); *The Archaeology of Palestine* (London: Penguin Books, 1949).

For biblical theology, the *Theologie des alten Testaments* of Walther Eichrodt (Berlin: Evangelische Verlagsanstalt, 1948) has been much used, as all who work in the field would know. I should like to single out two recent French authors who have done something similar to what I have attempted, and have done it very well: *Jacques Guillet, S.J., in *Thèmes Bibliques* (Paris: Aubier, 1951) and *Dom Celestin Charlier in *La lecture chrétienne de la Bible* (Maredsous: Éditions de Maredsous, 1950).

Readers who would like to pursue the subject further will not find the story of the Old Testament told in a more graphic and lively style than it is told in *Sacred History,* by *Daniel-Rops, translated from the French by K. Madge (New York: Longmans, Green & Co., 1949). They will find both the story and the beliefs of the Old Testament set forth in the solid, if less sprightly, works of *Dr. Paul Heinisch, both translated from the German by

•William Heidt, O.S.B.: *Theology of the Old Testament* (Collegeville: Liturgical Press, 1950) and *History of the Old Testament* (Collegeville: Liturgical Press, 1952). •Frederick L. Moriarty, S.J., has prepared a splendid description of the separate books which is both brief and lucid in *Foreword to The Old Testament* (Weston, Mass.: Weston College Press, 1954). •Giuseppe Ricciotti's *History of Israel* is now available in an English translation (Milwaukee: The Bruce Publishing Co., 1955).

Quotations from the text of the Bible, where they are not my own translations (or free paraphrases) come from Smith and Goodspeed, *The Bible: An American Translation* (Chicago: University of Chicago Press). Quotations from ancient Near Eastern literature are taken from (or based upon) the translations in *Ancient Near Eastern Texts,* edited by James B. Pritchard (Princeton: Princeton University Press, 1950).

INDEX